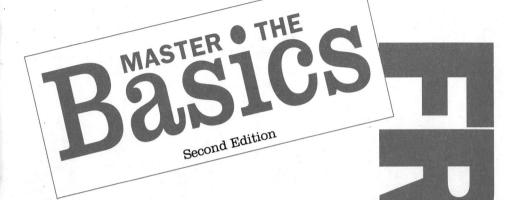

MASTER ● THE Basics

Second Edition

FRENCH

by
Christopher Kendris
B.S., M.S., Columbia University
in the City of New York
M.A., Ph.D., Northwestern University
in Evanston, Illinois

Diplômé, Faculté des Lettres, Université
de Paris et Institut de Phonétique,
Paris (en Sorbonne)

Formerly Assistant Professor
Department of French and Spanish
State University of New York
Albany, New York

BARRON'S

D0050107

*For my wife Yolanda, my two sons Alex and Ted,
my daughter-in-law Tina, and my four grandsons
Bryan, Daniel, Matthew, and Andrew*

With love

All inquiries should be addressed to:
Barron's Educational Series, Inc.
250 Wireless Boulevard
Hauppauge, New York 11788

Library of Congress Catalog Card No. 94-49345
International Standard Book No. 0-8120-9000-4

Library of Congress Cataloging-in-Publication Data

Kendris, Christopher.
 Master the basics. French / by Christopher Kendris. —2nd ed.
  p. cm.
 Includes index.
 ISBN 0-8120-9000-4
 1. French language—Textbooks for foreign speakers—English.
 2. French language—Grammar. I. Title. II. Title: French.
PC2129.E5K44 1995
448.2'421—dc20   94-49345
                                                            CIP

PRINTED IN THE UNITED STATES OF AMERICA

5678   9792   987654321

Contents

Preface to the Second Edition

This second edition contains Part Two. In this new part you will have a chance to put into practice what you studied in Part One and improve your skill in reading comprehension in a variety of short paragraphs as well as long selections.

Another new feature in this edition is the use of pictures with questions based on them. Your ability to understand what you read is tested in multiple-choice questions. You will also have considerable practice in writing French; for example, short lists of words on everyday topics to communicate your thoughts, simple guided composition for conversational expression, and word games to increase your vocabulary.

The basic vocabularies beginning on page 291 are also new. The French-English and English-French vocabularies have been revised and expanded.

These new features are offered for your enjoyment and to help you improve your knowledge of French. Answers to tests in Part Two appear on pages 201 and 211. To achieve your best, consult Part One, the end vocabularies, and the index. The verb tables and the section on definitions of basic grammatical terms with examples, beginning on pages 214 and 261 are also new features.

This book is one of a miniseries of language grammar reviews. It is designed to help you review your French grammar for instant communication and comprehension. The numerical arrangement gives you fast and easy access to what you need to know or verify.

Beginning on page 3 there is a diagnostic test that you ought to take immediately. It consists of sixty questions. Three questions are taken from each of the twenty chapters listed in the table of contents as sections §1. through §21. Take the test to find out what you know, what you don't know, and what your strengths and weaknesses are. Answers are explained at the end of the diagnostic test. There you will also find an analysis of the question numbers and the § numbers. In this way, you can refer to a particular § number where your answers were not correct and brush up where needed. The complete Review section consists of three parts: the Basics, the Parts of Speech, and Special Topics, all of which are outlined in the table of contents.

Occasionally I offer some mnemonic (memory) tips to help you remember certain aspects of French grammar and vocabulary. For example, if you cannot remember whether the French word for twenty **(vingt)** is spelled *ng* or *gn,* remember it this way:

Mnemonic tip	V I **N** G T
	T W E **N** T Y

Mnemonic devices are very useful in learning and remembering. Students learn and remember in different ways. What works for you may not work for someone else. You must think of ways to help yourself remember. If you think of a way that seems foolish, don't tell anyone; just let it work for you. One of my students in a Spanish class, for example, told me that she finally figured out a way to remember the meaning of the Spanish verb *buscar* / to look for. She said, "I'm looking for a bus or a car." How many mnemonic tips can you make up in French? Here are a few more: If someone asks you, "What are the five major Romance Languages?" are you going to say you don't know? Remember **FRIPS:**

Mnemonic tip	**F**rench
	Romanian
	Italian
	Portuguese
	Spanish

To remember that there are only four nasal vowels in French, hang on to this catchy phrase because each word contains one of the four nasal vowels:

Mnemonic tip	*un bon vin blanc* / a good white wine

If you keep pronouncing *un œuf* / an egg incorrectly, say this out loud:

Mnemonic tip	Do you want one egg? Two eggs?
	One egg is enough!
	One egg is *un œuf!*

The sound of the English word "enough" is very close to the sound of the French word *un œuf.*

There are many more mnemonic tips throughout this book. If I have omitted anything you think is important, if you spot any misprints, or if you have any suggestions for the improvement of the next edition, please write to me, care of the publisher.

Christopher Kendris
B.S., M.S., M.A., Ph.D.

How to Use This Book

To get the most out of *Master the Basics: French*, follow these steps:

Step 1 The first thing you should do is to become familiar with this book. Turn the pages and look at each page for a few seconds. When you reach the table of contents, examine it carefully. If you find something that strikes your interest, turn to that section to see exactly what is there. Do you want to know when the subjunctive should be used? Fan the pages until you come to §7.15 or go straight to the page given in the contents. I'm sure you will find §11. of special interest and value. Do not begin any studying until you have reviewed every page. It won't take more than about ten minutes.

Step 2 Now take the diagnostic test, which begins on page 3. At the end of that preliminary test, you will find the Explained Answers and a Diagnostic Analysis. Check the question numbers that you had right or wrong and, if wrong, turn to the appropriate section and study it, making certain you understand the explanations so that you can learn more about that particular element of French. If you happen to have many answers right, do not assume that you know that particular element of French thoroughly. Asking only three questions from each of the twenty sections is just to give you an idea of your strengths and weaknesses.

Step 3 The next step is to go through the entire Grammar Review, reviewing some portions and studying others in depth. The final section of Part One is Let's Review. You can do the more than two hundred items in the exercises and activities in this section either after having done the Grammar Review or as you work through the book. The questions are keyed to the numerical reference system in the Review and Answers sections. Another possibility is to do both: Try the questions corresponding to each chapter after you have studied the chapter, and then do them again for a final review after you have worked through the entire Review sections.

Step 4   Now you are ready to tackle Part Two of the book. It contains a variety of exercises for self-testing to help you improve your skills in grammar, reading comprehension, and writing by using paragraphs, long selections, simple guided composition, pictures, and word games. Answers to exercises in this part appear at the end of each section. To do your best, you must review Part One of the book and use the bilingual vocabulary lists beginning on page 291. The index provides an easy reference to any basic grammatical point that you may want to check.

Now begin with Step 1!

Abbreviations in This Book

adj.	adjective	*num.*	numeral
adv.	adverb	*obj.*	object
art.	article	*pa.*	*passé antérieur*
cond.	*conditionnel*		(past anterior)
	(conditional)	*part.*	participle
cond. p.	*conditionnel passé*	*pc.*	*passé composé*
	(conditional perfect)		(past indef.)
conj.	conjunction	*perf.*	*parfait* (perfect)
def.	definite	*pers.*	person
dem.	demonstrative	*pl.*	plural
dir.	direct	*plup.*	*plus-que-parfait*
e.g.	for example		(pluperfect or past
f.	feminine		perfect)
fam.	familiar use	*poss.*	possessive
fut.	future	*pp.*	*participe passé*
fut. ant.	*futur antérieur* (future		(past participle)
	anterior or future perfect)	*ppr.*	*participe présent*
imp.	imperative		(present participle)
impf.	imperfect	*pr.*	present
ind.	*indicatif* (indicative)	*prep.*	preposition
indef.	indefinite	*pron.*	pronoun
indir.	indirect	*ps.*	*passé simple* (past def.)
inf.	infinitive	*rel.*	relative
int.	interjection	*rv.*	reflexive verb
m.	masculine		(or pronominal verb)
n.	noun	*s.*	singular
nfpl.	plural feminine noun	*sbj.*	*subjonctif* (subjunctive)
nmpl.	plural masculine noun	*v.*	verb

FIND OUT WHAT YOU KNOW

This diagnostic test covers material presented in the Basics, the Parts of Speech, and Special Topics, all of which are included in §1.–§21. in this book. On page xi, where you find the section on how to use this book, read Step 2 again. That's what this diagnostic test is all about.

Test Yourself

Choose the correct answer by circling the letter. Do not refer to the Answer Key and Explained Answers until after you have answered all 60 questions. Time limit is 60 minutes.

THE BASICS

1. In French the vowel combination *eu* in *leur* is pronounced something like the *u* in the English word
   A. up   B. cute   C. urgent   D. you

2. In French the word *bonne* is pronounced like the English word
   A. bun   B. bone   C. bean   D. ban

3. In French the word *père*, containing the accent grave on *è*, is pronounced very much like the English word
   A. peer   B. pear   C. pour   D. pure

4. The French word for semicolon is
   A. *point*   B. *deux points*   C. *virgule*
   D. *point virgule*

5. The number of syllables in the French word *comprendre* is
   A. 2   B. 3   C. 4   D. 5

6. The four nasal vowels in French are found in the following catchy phrase
   A. *un bon vin rouge*   B. *un bon crayon blanc*
   C. *un bon fromage français*   D. *un bon vin blanc*

PARTS OF SPEECH

7. There are _____ definite articles in French and they all mean "the."
   A. two   B. three   C. four   D. five

8. When the preposition *à* is in front of the definite article *le*, it contracts to
   A. *au*   B. *aux*   C. *du*   D. *des*

9. When the preposition *de* is in front of the definite article *le*, it contracts to
   A. *au*   B. *aux*   C. *du*   D. *des*

10. A typical example of a feminine singular French noun is
    A. *logement*   B. *fromage*   C. *chapeau*
    D. *attention*

3

11. A typical example of a masculine singular French noun is
    A. *fourchette*   B. *chance*   C. *gâteau*
    D. *sucette*

12. A typical example of a French noun that is spelled the same in the singular and plural is
    A. *bras*   B. *livre*   C. *journal*   D. *feu*

13. The demonstrative adjective that precedes a masculine singular noun beginning with a vowel or silent *h* is
    A. *ce*   B. *cet*   C. *cette*   D. *ces*

14. The demonstrative adjective that precedes a feminine singular noun, whether it begins with a consonant, a vowel, or a silent *h* is
    A. *ce*   B. *cet*   C. *cette*   D. *ces*

15. The possessive adjective in front of a feminine singular noun beginning with a vowel or silent *h* (for example, *amie*) is
    A. *ma*   B. *mon*   C. *mes*   D. *m'*

Of the four choices given, select the response to each question that is sensible and grammatically correct.

16. *Avez-vous des frères?*
    A. *Oui, vous avez des frères.*   B. *Oui, j'ai frères.*
    C. *Oui, j'en ai.*   D. *Oui, il a des frères.*

17. *Est-ce que les fleurs sont sur la table?*
    A. *Oui, ils sont sur la table.*   B. *Oui, ils y sont.*
    C. *Oui, elles y sont.*   D. *Oui, la table est sur les fleurs.*

18. *Est-ce que vous lisez la lettre?*
    A. *Oui, vous lisez la lettre.*   B. *Oui, vous la lisez.*
    C. *Oui, je le lis.*   D. *Oui, je la lis.*

On the blank line write the correct form of the past participle of the verb given in parentheses.

19. *(aller)*   *Mon amie Jacqueline est* _____
    au cinéma avec Robert.

20. *(laver)*   *Marguerite s'est* _____ *avant de manger.*

21. *(partir)*   *Mes sœurs sont* _____ *pour la France hier.*

Write one adverb in French ending in *-ment* that is formed from a feminine singular adjective.

22. _____

Answer the following question in French in the affirmative; in other words, write in French, "Yes, I do like French."

23. *N'aimez-vous pas le français?* _____

Translate the following sentence into French.

24. Henry works better than Robert. _____

_____

Fill in the blank with *vers* or *envers*, whichever is appropriate.

25. *Pourquoi allez-vous* _____ *la porte?*

26. *J'ai beaucoup de respect* _____ *les vieilles personnes.*

Translate the following sentence into French.

27. Robert did that within an hour. _____

Write the French for each of the following conjunctions.

28. therefore _____ 29. unless _____ 30. whereas _____

SPECIAL TOPICS

The following sentences are scrambled. Unscramble the words and write them in the correct order.

31. *donne | me | pas | ne | les | il.* _____

32. *ne | ai | lui | le | je | donné | pas.* _____

33. *ne | pas | Yvonne | s'est | lavée.* _____

Of the four choices given, select the correct verb form and write it in the blank.

34. *J'___ l'autobus depuis vingt minutes quand il est arrivé.*
    A. *attends*   B. *ai attendu*   C. *attendrais*
    D. *attendais*

35. *Il y a vingt minutes que j'_____ l'autobus.*
    A. *attend*   B. *attends*   C. *ai attendu*
    D. *attendrais*

36. *Madame Martin est partie il y _____ une heure.*
    A. *avait*   B. *a*   C. *aurait*   D. *a eu*

Each of the following sentences is incomplete. Of the four choices given, select the one that makes a grammatically correct sentence and circle the letter of your choice.

37. *Quelle est la date aujourd'hui? C'est* _____ *octobre.*
    A. *l'un*   B. *le premier d'*   C. *l'un d'*
    D. *le premier*

38. *Je vais en France* _____ *juillet.*
    A. *au*   B. *dans*   C. *en*   D. *à*

39. *En* _____ *il neige souvent à Paris.*
    A. *été*   B. *printemps*   C. *automne*   D. *hiver*

Study the clocks and underneath each one write in French the time that is given.

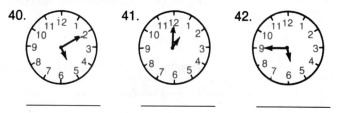

40. _____   41. _____   42. _____

Study these three drawings and underneath each one write in French a statement about the weather.

43. _____   44. _____   45. _____

Write the required number in French for the following.

46. *Comptez par dix. Dix, vingt, trente,* _____

47. *Sept fois huit font* _____

48. What number in French sounds like the English word "says"? _____

Write a French synonym for what is given.

49. *aimer mieux* _____

50. *une erreur* _____

51. *brève* _____

Write an antonym in French for what is given.

52. *absente* _____

53. *la beauté* _____

54. *perdre* _____

Write the French word and the definite article for each of the following cognates.

55. photography _____

56. memory _____

57. dictionary _____

Write the English meaning for each of the following false cognates.

58. *les actualités* _____

59. large _____

60. *le raisin* _____

Explained Answers

RIGHT   WRONG
(check one)

_____ _____ 1. C *see* §1.

_____ _____ 2. A *see* §1.

_____ _____ 3. B *see* §1.

_____ _____ 4. D *see* §2.

_____ _____ 5. B *see* §2.

_____ _____ 6. D *see* §2.

_____ _____ 7. C *see* §3.1.

_____ _____ 8. A *see* §3.1.

_____ _____ 9. C *see* §3.1.

_____ _____ 10. D *see* §4.1 and §4.2.

_____ _____ 11. C *see* §4.1 and §4.2.

_____ _____ 12. A *see* §4.1 and §4.2.

_____ _____ 13. B *see* §5.4 – 2.

_____ _____ 14. C *see* §5.4 – 2.

_____ _____ 15. B *see* §5.4 – 4.

_____ _____ 16. C *see* §6.1 – 5.

_____ _____ 17. C *see* §6.1 – 6.

_____ _____ 18. D The direct object *la lettre* is replaced by the feminine direct object pronoun, *la.* *see* §6.1 – 2.

_____ _____ 19. *allée.* You need to add *e* to the past participle *allé* to make it feminine because the verb is conjugated with *être (est)* and the subject is feminine. *see* §7.1.

_____ _____ 20. *lavée.* You need to add *e* to the past participle *lavé* to make it feminine because the reflexive pronoun *s'* is feminine and serves as the preceding direct object pronoun; it refers to the subject, *Marguerite,* which is feminine. *see* §7.1.

_____ _____ 21. *parties.* You need to add *e* to the past participle *parti* to make it feminine because the verb is conjugated with *être (sont)* and the subject, *mes sœurs,* is feminine. It is also plural, so you must also add *s* to the past participle. *see* §7.1 and §7.3 – 1.

RIGHT   WRONG
  (check one)

_____   _____   22. *seulement*. Several examples are given in **§8.1**. Review it.

_____   _____   23. *Si, j'aime le français.*   see **§8.4**.

_____   _____   24. *Henri travaille mieux que Robert.*   see **§8.3 – 3.**

_____   _____   25. *vers*   see **§9.**

_____   _____   26. *envers*   see **§9.**

_____   _____   27. *Robert a fait cela en une heure.*   see **§9.**

_____   _____   28. *donc*   see **§10.**

_____   _____   29. *à moins que*   see **§10.**

_____   _____   30. *tandis que*   see **§10.**

_____   _____   31. *Il ne me les donne pas.*   see **§11.**

_____   _____   32. *Je ne le lui ai pas donné.*   see **§11.**

_____   _____   33. *Yvonne ne s'est pas lavée.*   see **§11.**

_____   _____   34. D   You need the imperfect indicative because the verb in the other clause is in the *passé composé*.   see **§12.**

_____   _____   35. B   You need the present tense because the verb in the other clause is in the present tense (the *a* in the expression *il y a*).   see **§12.1.**

_____   _____   36. B   You need the present tense of *avoir* because *il y a* + a length of time means *ago*.   see **§12.1.**

_____   _____   37. D   see **§13.**

_____   _____   38. C   see **§13.**

_____   _____   39. D   see **§13.**

_____   _____   40. *Il est cinq heures dix.*   see **§14.**

_____   _____   41. *Il est une heure.*   see **§14.**

_____   _____   42. *Il est six heures moins le quart.*   see **§14.**

_____   _____   43. *Il pleut.*   see **§15.**

_____   _____   44. *Il neige.*   see **§15.**

_____   _____   45. *Il fait du soleil.* OR *Il fait soleil.*   see **§15.**

_____   _____   46. *quarante*   see **§16.**

_____   _____   47. *cinquante-six*   see **§16.**

_____   _____   48. *seize*   see **§16.**

RIGHT   WRONG
  (check one)

————   ————   49. *préférer* see **§17.**

————   ————   50. *une faute* see **§17.**

————   ————   51. *courte* You are given *brève* in the feminine singular form; therefore, you must write *courte,* which is also feminine singular. see **§17.**

————   ————   52. *présente* You are given *absente* in the feminine singular form; therefore, you must write *présente,* which is feminine singular. see **§18.**

————   ————   53. *la laideur* see **§18.**

————   ————   54. *trouver* see **§18.**

————   ————   55. *la photographie* see **§19.**

————   ————   56. *la mémoire* see **§19.**

————   ————   57. *le dictionnaire* see **§19.**

————   ————   58. news reports see **§20.**

————   ————   59. wide see **§20.**

————   ————   60. grape see **§20.**

Diagnostic Analysis

Section	Question Numbers	Number of Answers	
		Right	Wrong
THE BASICS			
1. Pronunciation	1, 2, 3		
2. Capitalization, Punctuation, Word Division	4, 5, 6		
THE PARTS OF SPEECH			
3. Articles	7, 8, 9		
4. Nouns	10, 11, 12		
5. Adjectives	13, 14, 15		
6. Pronouns	16, 17, 18		
7. Verbs	19, 20, 21		
8. Adverbs	22, 23, 24		
9. Prepositions	25, 26, 27		
10. Conjunctions	28, 29, 30		
SPECIAL TOPICS			
11. Word Order	31, 32, 33		
12. Idioms	34, 35, 36		
13. Dates, Days, Months, Seasons	37, 38, 39		
14. Telling Time	40, 41, 42		
15. Talking About the Weather	43, 44, 45		
16. Numbers	46, 47, 48		
17. Synonyms	49, 50, 51		
18. Antonyms	52, 53, 54		
19. Cognates	55, 56, 57		
20. Tricky Words	58, 59, 60		
TOTAL QUESTIONS:	60		

Use the following scale to see how you did.

58 to 60 right:	Excellent
55 to 57 right:	Very Good
52 to 54 right:	Average
49 to 51 right:	Below Average
Fewer than 49 right:	Unsatisfactory

PART ONE

GRAMMAR REVIEW

In the chapters that follow, a numerical decimal system has been used with the symbol § in front of it. This was done so that you may find quickly and easily the reference to a particular point in basic French grammar when you use the index. For example, if you look up the entry "adjectives" in the index, you will find the reference given as §5. Sometimes additional § reference numbers are given when the entry you consult is mentioned in other areas in the chapter §. The index also includes some key French words, for example, avoir *and* être, *with § references also given to them.*

The Basics

§1.

Guide to Pronouncing French Sounds

English words given here contain sounds that only approximate French sounds.

PURE VOWEL SOUNDS

Pronounced as in the

French word	English word
la	lolly
pas	father
été	ate
ère	egg
ici	see
hôtel	over
donne	bun
ou	too
leur	urgent
deux	pudding
tu	cute
le	ago

NASAL VOWEL SOUNDS

un	unguent
bon	song
vin	sang
blanc	dong

SEMICONSONANT SOUNDS

oui	west
huit	you eat
fille	yes, see ya later

CONSONANT SOUNDS

bonne	bun
dans	dong
fou	first, pharmacy
garçon	go
je	measure
chose	shake
café, qui	cap, kennel
le	let
mette	met
nette	net

CONSONANT SOUNDS
Pronounced as in the

French word	English word
montagne	canyon, onion, union
père	pear
rose	rose
si	see
te	lot
vous	vine
zèbre	zebra
ça	sorry

- If you can, give equal stress to all syllables in a French word; in other words, do not raise your voice on any particular syllable.
- If you can't give equal stress to all syllables in a French word, then raise your voice slightly on the last syllable.

EXAMPLES:
chapeau (shah-PO), *magazine* (mah-gah-ZEEN), *perspicacité* (per-spee-kah-see-TAY)

- Do not pronounce the last letter of a French word if it is a consonant.

EXAMPLES:
beaucoup (bo-KOO), *aéroport* (ah-air-o-POR)

Some common exceptions: *parc* (pARK), *chef* (shEFF), *avec* (ah-VEK). If you're not sure, don't pronounce the last consonant at all.

| Mnemonic tip | If you don't know which is *accent aigu* (acute) *(é)* and which is *accent grave (è)*, remember that the patient died of acute appendicitis *(é)* and ended up in the grave *(è)*.

Note: The pronunciation guide above contains French and English words as examples to illustrate sounds that are approximately like those in acceptable standard speech. It is merely a guide. If you want to improve your pronunciation of French, I would recommend Barron's *Pronounce It Perfectly in French.* The book comes with two 90-minute cassettes. You can listen to authentic French pronunciation and imitate during the pauses.

§2.

Capitalization, Punctuation Marks, and Word Division

§2.1
CAPITALIZA-
TION

Generally speaking, do not capitalize days of the week, months of the year, languages, nationalities, and religions.

dimanche, lundi, mardi, etc.; janvier, février, mars, etc.; français, espagnol, anglais, etc.; Antonio est italien, María est espagnole; Pierre est français; Jacques est catholique.

§2.2
PUNCTUATION
MARKS

The basic punctuation marks in French are:

le point / period   .
point virgule / semicolon   ;
la virgule / comma   ,
l'apostrophe (f) / apostrophe   '
deux points / colon   :
les parenthèses (f) / parentheses   ( )
les guillemets (m) / quotation marks   « »
le point d'interrogation / question mark   ?
les points de suspension / ellipses points   . . .

It is good to know how to divide a word into syllables (not only in French but also in English) because it helps you pronounce and spell the word correctly.

§2.3
WORD
DIVISION

Basic Rules

- A syllable must contain a vowel, but it may contain only one vowel and no consonant.

  é / cole (*école* / school)

- When you are dealing with single separate consonants, each consonant remains with the vowel that follows it.

  beau / coup (*beaucoup* / many, much)

- When two consonants come together, they are separated; the first remains with the preceding syllable and the second remains with the following syllable.

  im / por / tant (important)

17

But if the second of the two consonants that come together is *l* or *r*, do not separate them:

a / près (après / after); im / meu / ble (immeuble / apartment building)

- When three consonants come together, the first two remain with the preceding vowel and the third remains with the vowel that follows it.

ins / ti / tut (institut)

But if the third of the three consonants is *l* or *r*, do not separate that third consonant from the second; it remains with the second consonant.

com / pren / dre (comprendre / to understand)

Vowels

- Two vowels together are generally separated if they are strong vowels *(a, e, o)*.

a / é / ro / port (aéroport / airport)

But if you are dealing with a weak vowel *(i, u)*, it ordinarily remains in the same syllable with its neighboring vowel, especially if that other vowel is a strong vowel.

huî / tre (huître / oyster)

Nasal Vowels

- There are only four nasal vowels in French. You can remember them with the following catchy phrase:

un bon vin blanc / a good white wine

The Parts of Speech

§3.

Articles

§3.1
DEFINITE
ARTICLE

The definite article in French has four forms, and they all mean "the":

Gender	Singular	Plural
Masculine	*le, l'*	*les*
Feminine	*la, l'*	*les*

Singular	Plural
le garçon / the boy *l'arbre* (m) / the tree *la jeune fille* / the girl *l'actrice* / the actress	*les garçons* / the boys *les arbres* / the trees *les jeunes filles* / the girls *les actrices* / the actresses

Definite Article Used

WITH NOUNS

• Before each noun even when more than one noun is stated.

> *J'ai le livre et le cahier.* / I have the book and notebook.

• When you make a general statement.

> *J'aime le lait.* / I like milk.
> *J'aime l'été.* / I like summer.

• With a noun of weight or measure to express "a," "an," "per."

> *dix francs la livre* / ten francs a pound
> *vingt francs la douzaine* / twenty francs a dozen

• Before a noun indicating a profession, rank, or title followed by the name of the person.

> *Le professeur Poulin est absent aujourd'hui.* / Professor Poulin is absent today.

19

- With the name of a language.

  J'étudie le français. / I'm studying French.

  EXCEPTION: Do *not* use the definite article when the name of a language directly follows a form of the verb *parler.*

  Je parle français et russe. / I speak French and Russian.

- With the days of the week to indicate an action that is habitually repeated.

  Le samedi je vais au cinéma. / On Saturdays I go to the movies.

  But when you want to indicate a *particular* day, do not use the definite article.

  Samedi je vais au cinéma. / Saturday I am going to the movies. (understood: this Saturday)

- With parts of the body or articles of clothing if the possessor is clearly stated.

  Luigi, qui est italien, a les cheveux noirs. / Luigi, who is Italian, has black hair.

- With family names in the plural, in which case the spelling of the family name does not change.

  Nous allons chez les Durand. / We're going to the Durands.

WITH PREPOSITIONS

- When the prepositions *à* and *de* come before the definite article, it contracts as follows:

Preposition		Article		Contraction
à	+	le	>	au
	+	les	>	aux
de	+	le	>	du
	+	les	>	des

But there is *no* change with *l'* or *la.*

Je vais à l'aéroport. / I'm going to the airport.
Je vais à la bibliothèque. / I'm going to the library.
Je viens de l'aéroport. / I'm coming from the airport.
Je viens de la bibliothèque. / I'm coming from the library.

- With the preposition à (which combines to form *au* or *aux*) in front of the name of a country that is masculine.

  > *Nous allons au Canada* / We're going to Canada.
  > *Janine vient aux États-Unis.* / Janine is coming to the United
  >   States.

  With the preposition *de* (which combines to form *du* or *des*) before the name of a country that is masculine.

  > *du Portugal* / from Portugal
  > *des Etats-Unis* / from the United States

  With the preposition *de* + a common noun to indicate possession.

  > *le livre du garçon* / the boy's book
  > *les livres des garçons* / the boys' books
  > *la robe de la jeune fille* / the girl's dress
  > *les poupées des petites filles* / the little girls' dolls

  WITH CERTAIN EXPRESSIONS
- Indicating segments of the day.

  > *l'après-midi* / in the afternoon; *le matin* / in the morning;
  > *le soir* / in the evening

- Common expressions.

  > *à l'école* / to school, in school; *à la maison* / at home
  > *la semaine dernière* / last week; *l'année dernière* / last year
  > *la plupart de* / most of
  > *la plupart des jeunes filles* / most of the girls

- As a partitive in the affirmative.

  > *J'ai du café.* / I have (some) coffee.
  > *Tu as de l'argent.* / You have (some) money.
  > *Il a des amis.* / He has friends.

Definite Article Not Used

However, the definite article is *not* used when the partitive is in the negative or when the definite article is used with an adjective.

> *Je n'ai pas de café.* / I haven't any coffee.
> *Tu n'as pas d'argent.* / You haven't any money.
> *Il a de bons amis.* / He has some good friends.

Do not use the definite article:

- In direct address: *Bonjour, docteur Leduc.*
- After the preposition *en: Nous écrivons en français.* Exceptions:

  en l'air / in the air; *en l'absence de* / in the absence of
  en l'honneur de / in honor of

- After the preposition *de* in an adjective phrase: *J'aime mon livre de français.*
- With a feminine country and continents when you use *en* / at, to or *de* / of, from.

  Je vais en France, en Angleterre, en Allemagne, en Australie, en Asie, et en Amérique.
  Paul vient de France, les Armstrong viennent d'Australie et Hilda vient d'Allemagne.

- With most cities: *à Paris, à New York; de Londres, de Montréal, de Sydney.*
- With a noun in apposition: *Paul, fils du professeur Leblanc, est très aimable.*
- With titles of monarchs:

  Louis Seize (Louis XVI) / Louis the Sixteenth

- With the preposition *sans* or with the construction *ne . . . ni . . . ni . . . :*

  Je n'ai ni papier ni stylo. / I have neither paper nor pen.
  Il est parti sans argent. / He left without money.

- With certain expressions of quantity that take *de: beaucoup de, trop de, combien de, peu de, plus de, assez de*
- With the preposition *avec* when the noun after it is abstract:

  Jean-Luc parle avec enthousiasme.

§3.2 INDEFINITE ARTICLE

The forms of the indefinite article are:

Singular
J'ai **un** *frère.* / I have a brother.
J'ai **une** *sœur.* / I have a sister.
Plural
J'ai **des** *frères.* / I have brothers.
J'ai **des** *sœurs.* / I have sisters.

The indefinite article is used:

- When you want to say "a" or "an." It is also used as a numeral to mean "one":

  un livre / a book or one book
  une orange / an orange or one orange

- In front of each noun in a series:

  J'ai un cahier, un crayon et une gomme. / I have a notebook, pencil, and eraser.

- With *C'est* or *Ce sont* with or without an adjective:

  C'est un docteur. / He's a doctor.
  C'est un mauvais docteur. / He's a bad doctor.
  Ce sont des étudiants. / They are students.

The indefinite article is *not* used:

- With *cent* and *mille:*

  J'ai cent dollars. / I have a hundred dollars.
  J'ai mille dollars. / I have a thousand dollars.

- With *il est, ils sont, elle est, elles sont* + an unmodified noun of nationality, profession, or religion:

  Elle est professeur. / She is a professor.
  Il est catholique. / He is (a) Catholic.

- When you use *quel* in an exclamation:

  Quelle femme! / What a woman!
  Quel homme! / What a man!

- With negations, particularly with the verb *avoir:*

  Avez-vous un livre? Non, je n'ai pas de livre. / Have you a book? No, I don't have a book (any book).

§3.3 PARTITIVE

The partitive denotes a *part* of a whole; in other words, some. In English, we express the partitive by saying some or any in front of the noun. Use the following forms in front of the noun:

Masculine singular: *du* or *de l'*
Feminine singular: *de la* or *de l'*
Masculine or feminine plural: *des*

Simple Affirmative

> *J'ai* **du** *café.* / I have some coffee.
> *J'ai* **de la** *viande.* / I have some meat.
> *J'ai* **de** *l'eau.* / I have some water.
> *J'ai* **des** *bonbons.* / I have some candy.

Simple Negative

> *Je* **n'ai pas de** *café.* / I don't have any coffee.
> *Je* **n'ai pas de** *viande.* / I don't have any meat.
> *Je* **n'ai pas d'***eau.* / I don't have any water.
> *Je* **n'ai pas de** *bonbons.* / I don't have any candy.

With an Adjective

> *J'ai* **de jolis** *chapeaux.* / I have some pretty hats.
> *J'ai* **de jolies** *robes.* / I have some pretty dresses.

Note the following:
- When the noun is preceded by an adverb or noun of quantity or measure, use *de,* as in *J'ai beaucoup de choses.* / I have many things.
- When the noun is modified by another noun, use *de,* as in *une école de filles.*
- The partitive is not used with *sans* or *ne . . . ni . . . ni.*

  EXAMPLE:
  J'ai quitté la maison sans argent. / I left the house without any money.

- Use *quelques* and not the partitive when by "some" you mean "a few," in other words, "not many."

  EXAMPLES:
  J'ai quelques amis. / I have a few (some) friends.
  J'ai quelques bonbons. / I have a few (some) candies.

- When the negated verb is *ne . . . que* / only, the partitive consists of *de* plus the definite article.

  EXAMPLES:
  Elle ne lit que des livres. / She reads only books.
  Elle ne mange que des bonbons. / She eats only candy.

- The partitive must be repeated before each noun.

  EXAMPLE:
  Ici on vend du papier, de l'encre et des cahiers. / Here they sell paper, ink, and notebooks.

§4.

Nouns

§4.1 GENDER

A *noun* is a word that refers to a person, place, thing, or quality. Nouns are either masculine or feminine and require the article *le, la, l'*, or *les*. The gender of nouns that refer to persons or animals is obvious.

Examples

PERSONS		ANIMALS	
Masculine	**Feminine**	**Masculine**	**Feminine**
l'homme / the man	*la femme* / the woman	*le taureau* / the bull	*la vache* / the cow
le garçon / the boy	*la jeune fille* / the girl	*le coq* / the rooster	*la poule* / the hen
l'oncle / the uncle	*la tante* / the aunt	*le chat* / the cat	*la chatte* / the cat

- The gender of nouns referring to anything other than persons or animals must be learned with the noun.

Examples

Gender	Noun Endings	Examples
Masculine	-age or -âge	*l'âge* / age
		le fromage / cheese
	-ment	*le logement* / lodging
		le médicament / medicine (you take)
	-eau	*le chapeau* / hat
		le gâteau / cake
Feminine	-ance	*la circonstance* / circumstance
		la chance / chance, luck
	-ence	*l'apparence* / appearance
		la science / science
	-tion	*l'attention* / attention
		la notion / idea, notion
	-ette	*la fourchette* / fork
		la serviette / napkin
		la sucette / lollipop

25

Special Cases

	Masculine	Feminine
Some nouns have one meaning when masculine, another meaning when feminine.	*le livre* / book *le tour* / turn	*la livre* / pound *la tour* / tower
Some nouns are the same for both.	*un élève* / pupil (boy) *un enfant* / child (boy)	*une élève* / pupil (girl) *une enfant* / child (girl)
Some nouns add *-e* to the masculine to form the feminine.	*un cousin* / cousin *un ami* / friend	*une cousine* / cousin *une amie* / friend
Some nouns change the *-eur* masculine ending to *-euse* for the feminine.	*un vendeur* / salesman *un menteur* / liar	*une vendeuse* / saleswoman *une menteuse* / liar

§4.2 PLURAL OF NOUNS — THE BASICS

Add *-s* to the singular:

Singular	Plural
le livre / the book	*les livres* / the books
la maison / the house	*les maisons* / the houses
l'étudiant / the student	*les étudiants* / the students

If a noun ends in *-s, -x,* or *-z* in the singular, leave it alone:

Singular	Plural
le bras / the arm	*les bras* / the arms
la voix / the voice	*les voix* / the voices
le nez / the nose	*les nez* / the noses

If a noun ends in *-al* in the singular, change *-al* to *-aux:*

Singular
le journal / the newspaper

Plural
les journaux / the newspapers

If a noun ends in *-eu* or *-eau* in the singular, add *-x:*

Singular
le feu / the fire
le bureau / the office, the desk

Plural
les feux / the fires
les bureaux / the offices, desks

Common irregular nouns

Singular	Plural
le ciel / the sky	*les cieux* / the skies
l'œil / the eye	*les yeux* / the eyes

§5.

Adjectives

§5.1
FORMATION

Feminine Singular

- The feminine singular of an adjective is normally formed by adding -e to the masculine singular.

  EXAMPLES
  joli—jolie / pretty   *présent—présente* / present
  grand—grande / tall

- If a masculine singular adjective already ends in -e, the feminine singular is the same form.

  EXAMPLES
  aimable / kind   *énorme* / huge   *faible* / weak

- Some feminine singular forms are irregular. If a masculine singular adjective ends in -c, change it to -que for the feminine; -er to -ère; -g to gue; and -x to -se.

  EXAMPLES
  public—publique / public   *long—longue* / long
  premier—première / first   *heureux—heureuse* / happy
  actif—active / active

- Some masculine singular adjectives double the final consonant before adding -e to form the feminine.

  EXAMPLES
  ancien—ancienne / old   *cruel—cruelle* / cruel
  bas—basse / low   *gentil—gentille* / kind, nice
  bon—bonne / good

- The following feminine singular adjectives are formed from the irregular masculine singular forms:

Masculine Singular Before a Masculine Singular Noun Beginning with a Consonant	Irregular Masculine Singular Before a Masculine Singular Noun Beginning with a Vowel or Silent *H*	Feminine Singular
beau / beautiful, handsome	*bel ami*	*belle amie*
fou / crazy	*fol ami*	*folle amie*
nouveau / new	*nouvel hôtel*	*nouvelle amie*
vieux / old	*vieil ami*	*vieille amie*

28

> | Mnemonic tip | *La vieille dame a passé la veille de Noël*
> *avec son vieil ami dans un vieux cabaret.* /
> The old lady spent Christmas Eve with her
> old friend in an old cabaret.

- Some common masculine singular adjectives have irregular
  forms in the feminine singular. These do not fall into any
  particular category like those above.

  EXAMPLES
  blanc — blanche / white   *favori — favorite* /
  complet — complète / complete   favorite
  doux — douce / soft, smooth, sweet   *frais — fraîche* / fresh
  faux — fausse / false   *sec — sèche* / dry

Plural

- The plural is normally formed by adding *-s* to the masculine
  or feminine singular.

  EXAMPLES
  bon — bons; bonne — bonnes / good
  joli — jolis; jolie — jolies / pretty

- If the masculine singular already ends in *-s* or *-x*, it remains
  the same in the masculine plural.

  EXAMPLES
  gris — gris / gray   *heureux — heureux* / happy

- If a masculine singular adjective ends in *-al*, it changes to
  -aux (with some exceptions).

  EXAMPLES
  égal — égaux / equal   *principal — principaux* / principal

- If a masculine singular adjective ends in *-eau*, it changes to
  -eaux.

  EXAMPLE
  nouveau — nouveaux / new

§5.2
AGREEMENT

An adjective agrees in gender (feminine or masculine) and
number (singular or plural) with the noun or pronoun it
modifies.

EXAMPLES:
Alexandre et Théodore sont beaux et intelligents. / Alexander
  and Theodore are handsome and smart.
Yolande est belle. / Yolande is beautiful.
Janine et Monique sont belles. / Janine and Monique are
  beautiful.

Hélène et Simone sont actives. / Helene and Simone are active.
Anne est jolie. / Anne is pretty.
C'est un bel arbre. / It is a beautiful tree.
Ils sont amusants. / They are amusing.
Chaque garçon est présent. / Every boy is here (present).
Chaque jeune fille est présente. / Every girl is here (present).
Valentine est absente. / Valentine is absent.

§5.3 POSITION

- In French, most descriptive adjectives are placed after the noun; e.g., colors, nationality, religion: *une robe blanche* / a white dress, *un fromage français* / a French cheese, *une femme catholique* / a Catholic woman

  Remember: A noun indicating nationality is capitalized.

  un Américain / an American (male), *une Américaine* / an American (female), *un Français* / a French man, *une Française* / a French woman

- Here are some examples of common short adjectives that are generally placed in front of the noun:

  un autre livre / another book, *un bel arbre* / a beautiful tree, *un beau cadeau* / a beautiful gift, *un bon dîner* / a good dinner, *chaque jour* / each day, *un gros livre* / a big book, *une jeune dame* / a young lady, *une jolie maison* / a pretty house, *une petite table* / a small table, *plusieurs amis* / several friends, *un vieil homme* / an old man, *le premier rang* / the first row, *quelques bonbons* / some candy, *un tel garçon* / such a boy, *toute la journée* / all day.

- Some adjectives change in meaning, depending on whether the adjective is in front of the noun or after it. The most common are:

la semaine dernière / last week	*la dernière semaine* / the last (final) week
ma robe propre / my clean dress	*ma propre robe* / my own dress
une femme brave / a brave woman	*une brave femme* / a fine woman
le même moment / the same moment	*le moment même* / the very moment
un livre cher / an expensive book	*un cher ami* / a dear friend

§5.4
TYPES
§5.4–1
Descriptive

A descriptive adjective is a word that describes a noun or pronoun: *une belle maison* / a beautiful house, *un beau livre* / a beautiful book, *un bel arbre* / a beautiful tree, *une jolie femme* / a pretty woman.

> *Elle est grande.* / She is tall.

§5.4–2
Demonstrative

A demonstrative adjective is used to point out something or someone.

Gender	Singular	Plural
Masculine	*ce, cet* / this, that	*ces* / these, those
Feminine	*cette* / this, that	*ces* / these, those

EXAMPLES:
Ce garçon est beau. / This boy is handsome.
Cet arbre est beau. / This tree is beautiful.
Cette femme est belle. / This woman is beautiful.
Ces hommes sont beaux. / These men are handsome.
Ces livres sont beaux. / These books are beautiful.
Ces dames sont belles. / These ladies are beautiful.

If you wish to make a contrast between "this" and "that" or "these" and "those," add *-ci* this, these or *-là* that, those to the noun with a hyphen.

> *Ce garçon-ci est plus fort que ce garçon-là.* / This boy is stronger than that boy.

The form *cet* is used in front of a masculine singular noun or adjective beginning with a vowel or silent *h: cet arbre, cet homme.*
If there is more than one noun, a demonstrative adjective must be used in front of each noun: *cette dame et ce monsieur.*

§5.4–3
Interrogative

The adjective *quel* is generally regarded as interrogative because it is frequently used in a question. Its forms are *quel, quelle, quels, quelles.*

EXAMPLES:
Quel livre voulez-vous? / Which book do you want?
Quel est votre nom? / What is your name?

Quelle heure est-il? / **What time is it?**
Quelle est votre adresse? / **What is your address?**
Quels sont les mois de l'année? / **What are the months of the year?**
Quelles sont les saisons? / **What are the seasons?**

The adjective *quel* is also used in exclamations. Note that the indefinite article *un (une)* is not used in this case.

EXAMPLES

Quel garçon! / **What a boy!**
Quelle jeune fille! / **What a girl!**

§5.4 – 4 Possessive

MASCULINE	
Singular	**Plural**
mon livre / my book	*mes livres* / my books
ton stylo / your pen	*tes stylos* / your pens
son ballon / his (her, its) balloon	*ses ballons* / his (her, its) balloons
notre parapluie / our umbrella	*nos parapluies* / our umbrellas
votre sandwich / your sandwich	*vos sandwichs* / your sandwiches
leur gâteau / their cake	*leurs gâteaux* / their cakes

FEMININE	
Singular	**Plural**
ma robe / my dress	*mes robes* / my dresses
ta jaquette / your jacket	*tes jaquettes* / your jackets
sa balle / his (her, its) ball	*ses balles* / his (her, its) balls
notre maison / our house	*nos maisons* / our houses
votre voiture / your car	*vos voitures* / your cars
leur sœur / their sister	*leurs sœurs* / their sisters

• A possessive adjective agrees in gender and number with the noun it modifies.

• *Notre, votre,* and *leur* do not agree with the gender of the noun in the singular. They are all the same, whether in front of a masculine or feminine singular noun.

• Some possessive adjectives do not agree with the gender of the noun in the plural. They are all the same, whether in front of a masculine or feminine plural noun: *mes, tes, ses, nos, vos, leurs.*

- Be aware of *mon (ma), ton (ta), son (sa):* In front of a feminine singular noun beginning with a vowel or silent *h,* the masculine singular forms are used: *mon, ton, son*—not *ma, ta, sa.*

> *mon adresse* / my address
> *ton opinion* / your opinion
> *son amie* / his (or her) friend
> *mon habitude* / my habit (custom)

- Since *son, sa,* and *ses* can mean "his" or "her," you may add *à lui* or *à elle* to make the meaning clear.

> *sa maison à lui* / his house
> *sa maison à elle* / her house
> *son livre à lui* / his book
> *son livre à elle* / her book
> *ses livres à lui* / his books
> *ses livres à elle* / her books

- If there is more than one noun, a possessive adjective must be used in front of each noun: *ma mère et mon père, mon livre et mon cahier.*

Possessive Adjectives with Parts of the Body and Clothing

- When using the verb *avoir,* the definite article is normally used with parts of the body, **not** the possessive adjective.

  Henri a les mains sales. / Henry has dirty hands.
  Simone a les cheveux roux. / Simone has red hair.

- When using a reflexive verb, the definite article is normally used, **not** the possessive adjective.

  Paulette s'est lavé les cheveux. / Paulette washed her hair.

- The *definite article* is used instead of the possessive adjective when referring to parts of the body or clothing if it is clear who the possessor is.

  Henri tient le livre dans la main. / Henry is holding the book in his hand.

§5.4–5
Comparative and Superlative

Comparative

Of the same degree: *aussi . . . que* / as . . .as
Of a lesser degree: *moins . . . que* / less . . . than
Of a higher degree: *plus . . . que* / more . . . than

> *Janine est aussi grande que Monique.* / Janine is as tall as Monique.
> *Monique est moins intelligente que Janine.* / Monique is less intelligent than Janine.
> *Janine est plus jolie que Monique.* / Janine is prettier than Monique.

- *Aussi . . . que* becomes *si . . . que* in a negative sentence.

> *Robert n'est pas si grand que Joseph.* / Robert is not as tall as Joseph.

The comparative forms of the adjective "bad" are *mauvais, pire, le pire.*

> *Ce crayon est mauvais.* / This pencil is bad.
> *Ce crayon est pire que l'autre.* / This pencil is worse than the other.
> *Ce crayon est le pire.* / This pencil is the worst.

- *Plus que* / more than becomes *plus de* + a number.

> **EXAMPLES**
> *Il a plus de cinquante ans.* / He is more than fifty years old.
> *Je lui ai donné plus de cent dollars.* / I gave him (her) more than a hundred dollars.

Superlative

- The superlative is formed by placing the appropriate definite article *(le, la, les)* in front of the comparative:

> *Marie est la plus jolie jeune fille de la classe.* / Mary is the prettiest girl in the class.

- If the adjective normally follows the noun, the definite article must be used twice—in front of the noun and in front of the superlative:

> *Monsieur Hibou fut le président le plus sage de la nation.* / Mr. Hibou was the wisest president of the nation.

- After a superlative, the preposition *de* (not *dans*) is normally used to express "in":

> *Pierre est le plus beau garçon de la classe.* / Peter is the most handsome boy in the class.

- If more than one comparative or superlative is expressed, each is repeated:

> *Marie est la plus intelligente et la plus sérieuse de l'école.* / Mary is the most intelligent and most serious in the school.

Une devinette (a riddle) using a superlative:

> *Quelle est la chose la plus sale de la maison?* / What is the dirtiest thing in the house?
>
> *un balai* / a broom

Irregular Comparative and Superlative Adjectives

Adjective (m)	Comparative	Superlative
bon / good	*meilleur* / better	*le meilleur* / (the) best
mauvais / bad	*plus mauvais* / *pire* } worse	*le plus mauvais* / *le pire* } (the) worst
petit / small	*plus petit* / smaller (in size)	*le plus petit* / (the) smallest
	moindre / less (in importance)	*le moindre* / (the) least

§5.4 – 6
Meilleur and *Mieux*

Meilleur is an adjective and must agree in gender and number with the noun or pronoun it modifies.

EXAMPLE
Cette pomme est bonne, cette pomme-là est meilleure que celle-ci et celle-là est la meilleure. / This apple is good, that apple is better than this one, and that one is the best.

Mieux is an adverb and does not change in form.

EXAMPLE
Marie chante bien, Anne chante mieux que Marie et Claire chante le mieux. / Mary sings well, Anne sings better than Mary, and Claire sings the best.

> | Mnemonic tip | The adverb *bien* / (well) and the adverb *mieux* / (better) both contain *ie*.

§5.4 – 7
Adjectives Used in an Adverbial Sense

An adjective used as an adverb does not normally change in form.

Cette rose sent bon. / This rose smells good.
Ces bonbons coûtent cher. / These candies are expensive.

§6.

Pronouns

§6.1
TYPES

§6.1–1
Subject
Pronouns

The subject pronouns are:

Person	Singular	Plural
1st	*je (j')* / I	*nous* / we
2d	*tu* / you (familiar)	*vous* / you (singular polite or plural)
	il / he, it	
3d	*elle* / she, it	*ils* / they *(m.)*
	on / one	*elles* / they *(f.)*

- Note that *je* becomes *j'* before a vowel or a silent *h:*

  j'aime / I love; *j'hésite* / I hesitate.

- Remember that *vous* is not always plural; it is also the polite form of the second person; *tu* is the familiar form. You can use the *tu* form with members of the family and close friends, but always use the *vous* form with strangers and with people you do not know well.

The direct object pronouns are:

§6.1–2
Direct Object
Pronouns

Person	Singular	Plural
1st	*me (m')* / me	*nous* / us
2d	*te (t')* / you (familiar)	*vous* / you (singular polite or plural)
3d	⎰ *le (l')* / him, it ⎱ (person or thing) ⎰ *la (l')* / her, it ⎱	*les* / them (persons or things)

- A direct object pronoun takes the place of a direct object noun.

- A direct object noun ordinarily comes after the verb, but a direct object pronoun is ordinarily placed *in front* of the verb or infinitive.

36

EXAMPLES

J'ai les lettres. / I have the letters. →*Je les ai.* / I have them.
Je connais Luigi. / I know Luigi. →*Je le connais.* / I know him.

> | Mnemonic tip | *Je lis la leçon.* / I'm reading the lesson.
> Drop the noun *leçon;* what remains is *la,* the
> feminine singular definite article. It now
> becomes the direct object pronoun. Place it in
> front of the verb: *Je la lis.* / I'm reading it.

- *Me, te, le,* and *la* become *m', t', l'* when directly followed by a verb that starts with a vowel or silent *h.*

§6.1–3
Indirect Object Pronouns

The indirect object pronouns are:

Person	Singular		Plural	
1st	*me (m')*	to me	*nous*	to us
2d	*te (t')*	to you (familiar)	*vous*	to you (singular polite or plural)
3d	*lui*	to him, to her	*leur*	to them

- An indirect object pronoun takes the place of an indirect object noun.

- An indirect object pronoun is ordinarily placed *in front* of the verb.

  EXAMPLES

  Je parle à Janine. / I'm talking to Janine. →*Je lui parle.* / I'm talking to her.
  Je parle à Luigi et à mon ami. / I'm talking to Luigi and my friend. →*Je leur parle.* / I'm talking to them.

§6.1–4
Double Object Pronouns

To get a picture of what the word order is when you have more than one object pronoun (direct and indirect) in a sentence, see Word Order of Elements in French Sentences, §11.

§6.1–5
En

- The pronoun *en* takes the place of the partitive and serves as a direct object. It can refer to persons or things.

  EXAMPLES

  Avez-vous des frères? / Do you have any brothers?
  Oui, j'en ai. / Yes, I have (some).

Avez-vous de l'argent? / Have you any money?
Oui, j'en ai. / Yes, I have (some). *Non, je n'en ai pas.* / No, I don't have any.

- The past participle of a compound verb does not agree with the preceding direct object *en*.

    Avez-vous écrit des lettres? / Did you write any letters?
    Oui, j'en ai écrit trois. / Yes, I wrote three (of them).

- When using a reflexive verb, use *en* to take the place of the preposition *de* + a thing.

    Est-ce que vous vous souvenez de l'adresse? / Do you remember the address?
    Oui, je m'en souviens. / Yes, I remember it.

    Est-ce que vous prenez des hors-d'œuvre? / Are you helping yourself to the hors d'œuvre?
    Oui, merci, j'en prends. / Yes, thank you, I'm helping myself to some.

    Do not use *en* to take the place of the preposition *de* + a person. Use a disjunctive pronoun (see §6.1–7).

    Est-ce que vous vous souvenez de cette dame? / Do you remember this lady?
    Oui, je me souviens d'elle. / Yes, I remember her.

- Use *en* to take the place of *de* + noun and retain the word of quantity.

    Avez-vous beaucoup d'amis? / Do you have many friends?
    Oui, j'en ai beaucoup. / Yes, I have many (of them).

    Madame Paquet a-t-elle mis trop de sel dans le ragoût? / Did Mrs. Paquet put too much salt in the stew?
    Oui, elle en a mis trop dans le ragoût. / Yes, she put too much (of it) in the stew.

- Use *en* to take the place of the preposition *de* + the place to mean "from there."

    Est-ce que vous venez de l'école? / Are you coming from school?
    Oui, j'en viens. / Yes, I'm coming from there.
    Non, je n'en viens pas. / No, I am not coming from there.

§6.1–6
Y

Use *y* as a pronoun to serve as an object replacing a prepositional phrase beginning with *à, dans, sur,* or *chez* that refers to things, places, or ideas.

Est-ce que vous pensez à l'examen? / **Are you thinking of the exam?**
Oui, j'y pense. / **Yes, I'm (thinking of it).**

Je réponds à la lettre. / **I'm answering the letter.**
J'y réponds. / **I'm answering it.**

Est-ce que les fleurs sont sur la table? / **Are the flowers on the table?**
Oui, elles y sont. / **Yes, they are (there).**

Est-ce que vous allez chez Pierre? / **Are you going to Pierre's?**
Oui, j'y vais. / **Yes, I'm going (there).**

§6.1–7 Disjunctive Pronouns

Person	Singular		Plural	
1st	*moi*	me, I	*nous*	us, we
2nd	*toi*	you (familiar)	*vous*	you (formal singular or plural)
3rd	*soi*	oneself	*eux*	them, they (m.)
	lui	him, he	*elles*	them, they (f.)
	elle	her, she		

> **Mnemonic tip**

Je vais chez moi. / **I'm going to my house.**
Tu vas chez toi. / **You're going to your house.**
Il va chez lui. / **He's going to his house.**
Elle va chez elle. / **She's going to her house.**
On va chez soi. / **One is going to one's own house.**

Nous allons chez nous. / **We're going to our house.**
Vous allez chez vous. / **You're going to your house.**
Ils vont chez eux. / **They're going to their house.**
Elles vont chez elles. / **They're going to their house.**

A disjunctive pronoun is used:

● as object of a preposition.

Elle parle avec moi. / **She is talking with me.**
Je pense toujours à toi. / **I always think of you.**

● in a compound subject or object.

Elle et lui sont amoureux. / **He and she are in love.**
Je vous connais—toi et lui. / **I know you—you and him.**

- for emphasis.

  Moi, je parle bien; lui, il ne parle pas bien. / I speak well; he does not speak well.

- to indicate possession with *à* if the verb is *être* and if the subject is a noun, personal pronoun, or demonstrative pronoun.

  Ce livre est à moi. / This book is mine.
  Je suis à toi. / I am yours.

- with *c'est*.

  Qui est à la porte?—C'est moi. / Who is at the door? It is I.
  C'est toi? Oui, c'est moi. / Is it you? Yes, it is I.

- with *ce sont* in a statement but not usually in a question.

  Est-ce que ce sont eux?—Oui, ce sont eux. / Is it they?—Yes, it's they.

- with *même* and *mêmes*.

  Est-ce Pierre?—Oui, c'est lui-même. / Is it Peter? Yes, it's he himself.
  Vont-ils les manger eux-mêmes? / Are they going to eat them themselves?

- when no verb is stated.

  Qui est à l'appareil? Moi. / Who is on the phone? I (am).
  Qui a brisé le vase? Eux. / Who broke the vase? They (did).

See also Order of Elements in French Sentences, §11.

§6.1–8 Demonstrative Pronouns

The demonstrative pronouns are:

	Singular	**Plural**
Masculine	*celui* / the one	*ceux* / the ones
Feminine	*celle* / the one	*celles* / the ones

EXAMPLES

J'ai mangé mon gâteau et celui de Pierre. / I ate my cake and Peter's.
Il aime beaucoup ma voiture et celle de Jacques. / He likes my car very much and Jack's.

J'ai mangé mes petits pois et ceux de David. / I ate my peas and David's.

J'aime tes jupes et celles de Jeanne. / I like your skirts and Joan's.

J'ai deux éclairs; est-ce que tu préfères celui-ci ou celui-là? / I have two eclairs; do you prefer this one or that one?

J'ai deux pommes; est-ce que tu préfères celle-ci ou celle-là? / I have two apples; do you prefer this one or that one?

Une devinette / a riddle

J'ai un chapeau, mais je n'ai pas de tête. Ne trouvez-vous pas que c'est bête? / I have a hat, but I don't have a head. Don't you think it's stupid?

un champignon / a mushroom

---

ce (c'), ceci, cela, ça

These are demonstrative pronouns but they are invariable; that is, they do not change in gender and number. They refer to things that are not identified by name and may refer to an idea or a statement mentioned.

EXAMPLES

C'est vrai. / It's true.

Ceci est vrai. / This is true. *Ceci est faux.* / This is false.

Cela est vrai. / That is true. *Cela est faux.* / That is false.

Ça m'intéresse beaucoup. / That interests me very much.

Qu'est-ce que c'est que cela?   *Qu'est-ce que c'est que ça?* / What's that?

Note that *cela* shortens to *ça.*

§6.1–9 Indefinite Pronouns

aucun (aucune) / not any, not one, none

un autre (une autre) / another, another one

nous autres Français / we French (people)

nous autres Américains / we American (people)

certains (certaines) / certain ones

chacun (chacune) / each one

nul (nulle) / not one, not any, none

n'importe qui, n'importe quel / anyone

n'importe quoi / anything

on / people, one, they, you, we

On dit qu'il va pleuvoir. / They say that it's going to rain.

personne / no one, nobody

plusieurs / several

> *J'en ai plusieurs.* / I have several (of them).

quelque chose / something
quelqu'un (quelqu'une) / someone, somebody
quelques-uns (quelques-unes) / some, a few
quiconque / whoever, whosoever
soi / oneself

> *On est chez soi dans cet hôtel.* / People feel at home in this hotel.

tout / all, everything

> *Tout est bien qui finit bien.* / All is well that ends well.

§6.1–10 Interrogative Pronouns

Referring to Persons

- As subject of a verb:

  > *Qui est à l'appareil?* / Who is on the phone?
  > *Qui est-ce qui est à l'appareil?* / Who is on the phone?
  > *Lequel des deux garçons arrive?* / Which (one) of the two boys is arriving?
  > *Laquelle des deux jeunes filles est ici?* / Which (one) of the two girls is here?

- As direct object of a verb:

  > *Qui aimez-vous?* / Whom do you love?
  > *Qui est-ce que vous aimez?* / Whom do you love?
  > *Lequel de ces deux garçons aimez-vous?* / Which (one) of these two boys do you love?
  > *Laquelle de ces deux jeunes filles aimez-vous?* / Which (one) of these two girls do you love?

- As object of a preposition:

  > *Avec qui allez-vous au cinĕma?* / With whom are you going to the movies?
  > *A qui parlez-vous au téléphone?* / To whom are you talking on the telephone?

Note that when the interrogative pronouns *lequel (laquelle),
lesquels (lesquelles)* are objects of the prepositions *à* or *de,*
their forms are:

Singular	**Plural**
auquel (à laquelle)	*auxquels (auxquelles)*
duquel (de laquelle)	*desquels (desquelles)*

Auquel de ces deux garçons parlez-vous? / To which (one) of these two boys are you talking?

A laquelle de ces deux jeunes filles parlez-vous? / To which (one) of these two girls are you talking?

Auxquels de ces hommes parlez-vous? / To which (ones) of these men do you talk?

Auxquelles de ces femmes parlez-vous? / To which (ones) of these women are you talking?

Duquel de ces deux garçons parlez-vous? / About which (one) of these two boys are you talking?

Referring to Things

● As subject of a verb:

Qu'est-ce qui est arrivé? / What arrived? OR What happened?

Qu'est-ce qui s'est passé? / What happened?

Une devinette avec qu'est-ce qui

Qu'est-ce qui vous appartient et dont les autres se servent souvent? / What belongs to you that others use often?

votre nom / your name

Laquelle de ces deux voitures marche bien? / Which (one) of these two cars runs well?

Lesquels de tous ces trains sont modernes? / Which (ones) of all these trains are modern?

● As direct object of a verb:

Que faites-vous? / What are you doing?

Qu'a-t-elle? / What does she have? OR What's the matter with her?

Qu'est-ce que vous faites? / What are you doing?

Laquelle de ces voitures préférez-vous? / Which (one) of these cars do you prefer?

● As object of a preposition:

Avec quoi écrivez-vous? / With what are you writing?

A quoi pensez-vous? / Of what are you thinkng? OR What are you thinking of?

§6.1–11
Possessive
Pronouns

MASCULINE			
Singular		**Plural**	
le mien	mine	*les miens*	mine
le tien	yours (familiar)	*les tiens*	yours (familiar)
le sien	his, hers, its	*les siens*	his, hers, its
le nôtre	ours	*les nôtres*	ours
le vôtre	yours	*les vôtres*	yours
le leur	theirs	*les leurs*	theirs
FEMININE			
Singular		**Plural**	
la mienne	mine	*les miennes*	mine
la tienne	yours (familiar)	*les tiennes*	yours (familiar)
la sienne	his, hers, its	*les siennes*	his, hers, its
la nôtre	ours	*les nôtres*	ours
la vôtre	yours	*les vôtres*	yours
la leur	theirs	*les leurs*	theirs

- A possessive pronoun takes the place of a possessive adjective + noun.

  mon livre / my book; *le mien* / mine.

- A possessive pronoun agrees in gender and number with what it is replacing.

  son livre / his (her) book; *le sien* / his (hers).

- When the definite articles *le* and *les* are preceded by the prepositions *à* and *de,* they combine as follows: *au mien, aux miens, du mien, des miens.*

  Paul me parle de ses parents et je lui parle des miens. / Paul is talking to me about his parents and I am talking to him about mine.
  Je préfère ma voiture à la tienne. / I prefer my car to yours.

- Possessive pronouns are used with *être* to emphasize a distinction.

  Ce livre-ci est le mien et celui-là est le tien. / This book is mine and that one is yours.

- If no distinction is made as to who owns what, use *être* + *à* + disjunctive pronoun.

  Ce livre est à lui. / This book is his.

- Instead of using the possessive pronouns in French, we say "one of my friends," "one of my books," etc.

  un de mes amis / a friend of mine; *un de mes livres* / a book of mine

  une de ses amies / a girlfriend of his (hers)
  un de nos amis / a friend of ours

§6.1–12 Reflexive Pronouns

- The reflexive pronouns, which are used with reflexive verbs, are *me, te, se, nous,* and *vous.*

- The corresponding English pronouns are: myself, yourself, herself, himself, oneself, itself, ourselves, yourselves, themselves.

- To form the present tense of a reflexive verb in a simple affirmative sentence, put the reflexive pronoun in front of the verb.

  Je me lave. / I wash myself.

- A reflexive verb expresses an action that turns back upon the subject.

  Jacqueline se lave tous les jours. / Jacqueline washes herself every day.

  You must be careful to use the appropriate reflexive pronoun—the one that matches the subject pronoun. You already know the subject pronouns, but here they are again, beside the reflexive pronouns.

Person	Singular	Plural
1st	*je me lave*	*nous nous lavons*
2d	*tu te laves*	*vous vous lavez*
3d	*il se lave* *elle se lave* *on se lave*	*ils se lavent* *elles se lavent*

  To get a picture of what the word order is when you have more than one pronoun of any kind in a sentence, see Word Order of Elements in French Sentences (§11.).

§6.1–13 Relative Pronouns

A *relative pronoun* is a word that refers to an antecedent. An *antecedent* is something that comes before something; it can be a word, a phrase, a clause that is replaced by a pronoun or some other substitute. For example, in the sentence "Is it Mary who did that?" "who" is the relative pronoun and "Mary" is the antecedent. Another example: "It seems to me that you are wrong, which is what I had suspected right along." The relative pronoun is "which" and the antecedent is the clause, "that you are wrong."

Some common relative pronouns are:

- *dont* / of whom, of which, whose, whom, which

    Voici le livre dont j'ai besoin. / Here is the book (that) I need.
    Monsieur Béry, dont le fils est avocat, est maintenant en France. / Mr. Béry, whose son is a lawyer, is now in France.

- *ce dont* / what, of which, that of which

    Je ne trouve pas ce dont j'ai besoin. / I don't find what I need.
    Ce dont vous parlez est absurde. / What you are talking about is absurd.

- *ce que (ce qu')* / what, that which

    Comprenez-vous ce que je vous dis? / Do you understand what I am telling you?
    Comprenez-vous ce qu'elle vous dit? / Do you understand what she is saying to you?
    Je comprends ce que vous dites et je comprends ce qu'elle dit. / I understand what you are saying and I understand what she is saying.

- *ce qui* / what, that which

    Ce qui est vrai est vrai. / What is true is true.
    Je ne sais pas ce qui s'est passé. / I don't know what happened.

    Note that *ce qui* is a subject.

- *lequel* (in all its forms) / which

    As a relative pronoun, *lequel* (in its various forms) is used as object of a preposition referring to things.

    Donnez-moi un autre morceau de papier sur lequel je peux écrire mon adresse. / Give me another piece of paper on which I can write my address.

- *où* / where, in which, on which

   Aimez-vous la salle à manger où nous mangeons? / **Do you like the dining room where we eat?**
   Je vais ouvrir le tiroir où j'ai mis l'argent. / **I am going to open the drawer where I put the money.**

- *que* or *qu'* / whom, which, that

   Le garçon que vous voyez là-bas est mon meilleur ami. / **The boy whom you see over there is my best friend.**
   La composition qu'elle a écrite est excellente. / **The composition (that) she wrote is excellent.**

- *qui* / who, whom, which, that

   Connais-tu la jeune fille qui parle avec mon frère? / **Do you know the girl who is talking with my brother?**
   Avez-vous une bicyclette qui marche bien? / **Do you have a bicycle that (which) runs well?**

§6.1–14
C'est + adjective + *à* + infinitive

C'EST + ADJECTIVE + *À* + INFINITIVE

C'est difficile à faire. / **It is difficult to do.**

Use this construction when what is being referred to *has already been mentioned.*

EXAMPLES
Le devoir pour demain est difficile, n'est-ce pas? / **The homework for tomorrow is difficult, isn't it?**
Oui, c'est difficile à faire. / **Yes, it [the homework] is difficult to do.**

J'aimerais faire une blouse. / **I would like to make a blouse.**
C'est facile à faire! Je vais vous montrer. / **It's easy to do! I'll show you.**

Il est + adjective + *de* + infinitive

IL EST + ADJECTIVE + *DE* + INFINITIVE

Il est impossible de lire ce gros livre en une heure. / **It is impossible to read this thick book within one hour.**

Use this construction when the thing that is impossible, or difficult, or easy (or any adjective) to do is mentioned in the same sentence at the same time.

§6.1 – 15
Neuter
Pronoun *le*

The word *le* is the masculine singular definite article. It is also the masculine singular direct object. *Le* is used as a neuter pronoun and functions as a direct object referring to an adjective, a phrase, a clause, or a complete statement. It is generally not translated into English, except to mean "it" or "so."

> *Janine est jolie, mais Henriette ne l'est pas.* / Janine is pretty, but Henrietta isn't.
> *Moi, je crois qu'ils vont gagner le match, et vous? Je le crois aussi.* / I think they are going to win the game, and you? I think so too.

To get a picture of what the word order is when you have more than one pronoun of any kind in a sentence, see Word Order of Elements in French Sentences, §11.

§7.

Verbs

SUBJECT AND VERB
A subject and its corresponding verb form must agree in *person* (first, second, or third) and number (singular or plural).

EXAMPLE:
Je vais au cinéma. / I'm going to the movies.

SUBJECT AND REFLEXIVE PRONOUN OF A REFLEXIVE VERB
A subject and reflexive pronoun must agree in person and number.

EXAMPLE
Je me lave tous les matins. / I wash myself every morning.

SUBJECT AND PAST PARTICIPLE OF AN *ÊTRE* VERB
The past participle of an *être* verb agrees with the subject in gender and number.

Elle est allée au cinéma. / She went to the movies. OR She has gone to the movies.
Elles sont allées au cinéma. / They went to the movies. OR They have gone to the movies.

PRECEDING REFLEXIVE PRONOUN AND PAST PARTICIPLE OF A REFLEXIVE VERB

Elle s'est lavée. / She washed herself.
Elles se sont lavées. / They washed themselves.

However, there is *no* agreement made with the past participle of a reflexive verb if the reflexive pronoun serves as an indirect object pronoun. In the following example, *se (s')* is the indirect object; *les mains* the direct object.

Elle s'est lavé les mains. / She washed her hands.
Elles se sont lavé les mains. / They washed their hands.

Note this:

Elles se sont regardées. / They looked at each other.

49

Here, the reflexive pronoun *se* serves as the direct object. How do you know? There is no other obvious direct object mentioned, so what they looked at was *se* (each other); of course, you have to look at the subject to see what the gender and number is of the reflexive pronoun *se* in the sentence you are dealing with. The action of the verb is reciprocal.

Remember that the verb *regarder* in French means "to look at" in English; the preposition "at" is not expressed with *à* in French; it is included in the verb—that is why we are dealing with the reflexive pronoun as a direct object here, not an indirect object pronoun.

This same sentence, *Elles se sont regardées,* might also mean: "They looked at themselves." The principle of agreement is still the same. If you mean to say "They looked at each other," in order to avoid two meanings, add *l'une et l'autre.* If more than two persons, add *les unes les autres.*

And note:

Elles se sont parlé au téléphone. / They talked to each other on the telephone.

Here, the reflexive pronoun *se* is the indirect object because they spoke to each other; *parler à* is what you are dealing with here. And remember that no agreement is made on a past participle with an indirect object. The action of the verb is reciprocal.

PAST PARTICIPLE OF AN *AVOIR* VERB WITH A PRECEDING DIRECT OBJECT

EXAMPLES
Je l'ai vue au concert. / I saw her at the concert.

- There is agreement on the past participle *(vue)* because the preceding direct object is *la (l').* Agreement is made in gender and number.

Aimez-vous les fleurs que je vous ai données? / Do you like the flowers (that) I gave you?

- There is agreement on the past participle *(données)* of this *avoir* verb because there is a preceding direct object, *les fleurs;* the relative pronoun *que* refers to *les fleurs.* Since this direct object noun precedes the verb, the past participle must agree in gender and number. A preceding direct object, therefore, can be a pronoun or noun.

Quels films avez-vous vus? / What films did you see?

- There is agreement on the past participle *(vus)* of this *avoir* verb because the preceding direct object, *films,* is a masculine plural noun.

Avez-vous mangé les pâtisseries? / Did you eat the pastries?
Oui, je les ai mangées. / Yes, I ate them.

- In the response to this question, there is agreement on the past participle *(mangées)* of this *avoir* verb because the preceding direct object, *les,* refers to *les pâtisseries,* a feminine plural noun.

J'en ai mangé assez. / I ate enough (of them).

- There is no agreement on the past participle *(mangé)* of this *avoir* verb because the preceding direct object is, in this sentence, the pronoun *en.* We do not normally make an agreement with *en,* whether it precedes or follows. This is an exception.

§7.2
PAST
PARTICIPLE

REGULAR FORMATION

Infinitive	Type Ending	Drop	Add	Past Participle
donner	*-er*	*-er*	*é*	*donné*
finir	*-Ir*	*-ir*	*i*	*fini*
vendre	*-re*	*-re*	*u*	*vendu*

COMMON IRREGULAR PAST PARTICIPLES

Infinitive	Past Participle
apprendre	appris
asseoir	assis
avoir	eu
boire	bu
comprendre	compris
conduire	conduit
connaître	connu
construire	construit
courir	couru
couvrir	couvert
craindre	craint
croire	cru
devenir	devenu
devoir	dû
dire	dit
écrire	écrit
être	été
faire	fait
falloir	fallu
lire	lu
mettre	mis
mourir	mort
naître	né
offrir	offert
ouvrir	ouvert
paraître	paru
permettre	permis
plaire	plu
pleuvoir	plu
pouvoir	pu
prendre	pris
promettre	promis
recevoir	reçu
revenir	revenu
rire	ri
savoir	su
suivre	suivi
taire	tu
tenir	tenu
valoir	valu
venir	venu
vivre	vécu
voir	vu
vouloir	voulu

§7.3 TYPES

§7.3–1 Auxiliary Verbs *avoir* and *être*

The auxiliary (helping) verbs *avoir* and *être* are used in any of the seven simple tenses + the past participle of the main verb you are using to form any of the compound tenses. You must be careful to choose the proper helping verb with the main verb. Some verbs take *avoir* and some take *être* to form the compound tenses.

- Most French verbs are conjugated with *avoir* to form a compound tense.
- All reflexive verbs, such as *se laver,* are conjugated with *être.*

The following is a list of common nonreflexive verbs that are conjugated with *être.*

1. *aller* to go *Elle est allée au cinéma.*
2. *arriver* to arrive *Elle est arrivée.*
3. **descendre* to go down, come down *Elle est descendue vite. /* She came down quickly. BUT: **Elle a descendu la valise. /* She brought down the suitcase.
4. *devenir* to become *Elle est devenue folle.*
5. *entrer* to enter, go in, come in *Elle est entrée.*
6. **monter* to go up, come up *Elle est montée lentement. /* She went up slowly. BUT: **Elle a monté l'escalier. /* She went up the stairs.
7. *mourir* to die *Elle est morte.*
8. *naître* to be born *Elle est née le premier octobre.*
9. *partir* to leave *Elle est partie.*
10. **passer* to go by, pass by *Elle est passée par chez moi. /* She came by my house.

BUT: **Elle m'a passé le sel. /* She passed me the salt. AND: **Elle a passé un examen. /* She took an exam.

11. **rentrer* to go in again; to return (home) *Elle est rentrée tôt. /* She returned home early. BUT: **Elle a rentré le chat dans la maison. /* She brought (took) the cat into the house.
12. *rester* to remain, stay *Elle est restée chez elle.*
13. *retourner* to return, go back *Elle est retournée*
14. *revenir* to come back *Elle est revenue.*
15. **sortir* to go out *Elle est sortie hier soir. /* She went out last night. BUT: **Elle a sorti son mouchoir. /* She took out her handkerchief.
16. *tomber* to fall *Elle est tombée.*
17. *venir* to come *Elle est venue.*

* Some of these verbs, as noted above, are conjugated with *avoir* if the verb is used in a transitive sense and has a direct object.

§7.3–2
Transitive
Verbs

A transitive verb is a verb that takes a direct object. It is transitive because the action passes over and directly affects something or someone in some way.

> *Je vois mon ami.* / I see my friend. → *Je le vois.* / I see him.
> *Je ferme la fenêtre.* / I am closing the window. → *Je la ferme.* / I'm closing it.

When the direct object of the verb is a pronoun, it is usually placed in front of the verb. The only time it is placed after the verb is in the affirmative imperative. To get an idea of the position of direct object pronouns, see Word Order of Elements in French Sentences, §11.

§7.3–3
Intransitive
Verbs

An intransitive verb is a verb that does not take a direct object. Such a verb is called intransitive because the action does not pass over and directly affect anyone or anything.

> *La maîtresse parle.* / The teacher is talking.
> *Elle est partie tôt.* / She left early.
> *Elles sont descendues vite.* / They came down quickly.
> *Nous sommes montées lentement.* / We went up slowly.

An intransitive verb takes an indirect object.

> *La maîtresse parle aux élèves.* / The teacher is talking to the students.

Here the indirect object noun is *élèves* because it is preceded by *aux* / to the.

> *La maîtresse leur parle.* / The teacher is talking to them.

Here the indirect object is the pronoun *leur,* meaning "to them."

§7.4
PRESENT
PARTICIPLE

Regular Formation

The present participle is regularly formed in the following way: Take the *nous* form of the present indicative tense of the verb you have in mind, drop the first person plural ending *-ons,* and add *-ant.* That ending is equivalent to *-ing* in English.

Infinitive	**Present Tense 1st Person Plural**	**Drop -ons**	**add -ant**	**Present Participle**
finir / to finish	*nous finissons*	*finiss*	*ant*	*finissant*
manger / to eat	*nous mangeons*	*mange*	*ant*	*mangeant*
vendre / to sell	*nous vendons*	*vend*	*ant*	*vendant*
faire / to do; make	*nous faisons*	*fais*	*ant*	*faisant*
dire / to say; tell	*nous disons*	*dis*	*ant*	*disant*

Common Irregular Present Participles

Infinitive	Present Participle
avoir to have *être* to be *savoir* to know	*ayant* *étant* *sachant*

| Mnemonic tip | If you're not sure which is a present participle and which is a past participle in French, associate the n in present with the *n* in the French ending -*ant* of a present participle. |

En + Present Participle

The present participle in French is used primarily with the preposition *en,* meaning "on," "upon," "in," "while," "by."

> *en chantant* / while singing
> *en finissant* / upon finishing
> *en vendant* / by selling
> *en mangeant* / upon eating, while eating
> *en voyageant* / by traveling
> *en ayant* / on having
> *en étant* / on being, upon being
> *en sachant* / upon knowing

The present participle is sometimes used as an adjective.

> *un enfant amusant* / an amusing child (boy)
> *une enfant amusante* / an amusing child (girl)

§7.5 VERBS AND PREPOSITIONS

Verb + à + Noun or Pronoun

- *assister à quelque chose (à un assemblage, à une réunion, à un spectacle, etc.)* / to attend or be present at (a gathering, a meeting, a theatrical presentation, etc.)

  Allez-vous assister à la conférence du professeur Godard? / Are you going to attend (be present at) Professor Godard's lecture? —*Oui, je vais y assister.* / Yes, I am going to attend it.

- *demander à quelqu'un* / to ask someone

  Demandez à la dame où s'arrête l'autobus. / Ask the lady where the bus stops.

- *désobéir à quelqu'un* / to disobey someone

  Ce chien ne désobéit jamais à son maître. / This dog never disobeys his master.
  Il ne lui désobéit jamais. / He never disobeys him.

- *être à quelqu'un* / to belong to someone

  Ce livre est à Victor. / This book belongs to Victor.

- *faire attention à quelqu'un ou à quelque chose* / to pay attention to someone or to something

  Faites attention au professeur. / Pay attention to the professor.

- *s'intéresser à quelqu'un ou à quelque chose* / to be interested in someone or something

  Je m'intéresse aux sports. / I am interested in sports.

- *jouer à* / to play (a game or sport)

  Il aime bien jouer à la balle. / He likes to play ball.
  Elle aime bien jouer au tennis. / She likes to play tennis.

- *obéir à quelqu'un* / to obey someone

  Une personne honorable obéit à ses parents. / An honorable person obeys his (her) parents.

- *participer à quelque chose* / to participate in something

  Je participe aux sports. / I participate in sports.

- *penser à quelqu'un ou à quelque chose* / to think of (about) someone or something

  Je pense à mes amis. / I am thinking of my friends.
  Je pense à eux. / I am thinking of them.
  Je pense à mon travail. / I am thinking about my work.
  J'y pense. / I am thinking about it.

- *répondre à quelqu'un ou à quelque chose* / to answer someone or something

    J'ai répondu au professeur. / I answered the teacher.
    Je lui ai répondu. / I answered him.
    J'ai répondu à la lettre. / I answered the letter.
    J'y ai répondu. / I answered it.

- *ressembler à quelqu'un* / to resemble someone

    Il ressemble beaucoup à sa mère. / He resembles his mother a lot.

- *réussir à quelque chose* / to succeed in something
  réussir à un examen / to pass an examination

    Il a réussi à l'examen. / He passed the exam.

- *téléphoner à quelqu'un* / to telephone someone

    Marie a téléphoné à Paul. / Marie telephoned Paul.
    Elle lui a téléphoné. / She telephoned him.

Verb + *à* + Infinitive

- *aider à* / to help

    Roger aide son petit frère à faire son devoir de mathématiques.
    Roger is helping his little brother to do his math homework.

- *s'amuser à* / to amuse oneself, enjoy, have fun

    Il y a des élèves qui s'amusent à mettre le professeur en colère. / There are pupils who enjoy making the teacher angry.

- *apprendre à* / to learn

    J'apprends à lire. / I am learning to read.

- *s'attendre à* / to expect

    Je m'attendais à trouver une salle de classe vide. / I was expecting to find an empty classroom.

- *avoir à* / to have to, to be obliged to (do something)

    J'ai mes devoirs à faire ce soir. / I have to do my homework tonight.

- *commencer à* / to begin

    il commence à pleuvoir. / It is beginning to rain.

- *continuer à* / to continue

    Je continue à étudier le français. / I am continuing to study French.

- *décider quelqu'un à* / to persuade someone

  J'ai décidé mon père à me prêter quelques francs. / I persuaded my father to lend me a few francs.

- *se décider à* / to make up one's mind

  Il s'est décidé à l'épouser. / He made up his mind to marry her.

- *demander à* / to ask, request

  Elle demande à parler. / She asks to speak.

- *encourager à* / to encourage

  Je l'ai encouragé à suivre un cours de français. / I encouraged him to take a course in French.

- *enseigner à* / to teach

  Je vous enseigne à lire en français. / I am teaching you to read in French.

- *s'habituer à* / to get used (to)

  Je m'habitue à parler français couramment. / I am getting used to speaking French fluently.

- *hésiter à* / to hesitate

  J'hésite à répondre à sa lettre. / I hesitate to reply to her (his) letter.

- *inviter à* / to invite

  Monsieur et Madame Boivin ont invité les Béry à dîner chez eux. / Mr. and Mrs. Boivin invited the Bérys to have dinner at their house.

- *se mettre à* / to begin

  L'enfant se met à rire. / The child is beginning to laugh.

- *parvenir à* / to succeed

  Elle est parvenue à être docteur. / She succeeded in becoming a doctor.

- *se plaire à* / to take pleasure in

  Il se plaît à taquiner ses amis. / He takes pleasure in teasing his friends.

- *recommencer à* / to begin again

  Il recommence à pleuvoir. / It is beginning to rain again.

- *réussir à* / to succeed in

  Henri a réussi à me convaincre. / Henry succeeded in convincing me.

- *songer à* / to dream; to think

  Elle songe à trouver un millionnaire. / She is dreaming of finding a millionaire.

- *tenir à* / to insist, be anxious

  Je tiens absolument à voir mon enfant immédiatement. / I am very anxious to see my child immediately.

Verb + *de* + Noun

- *s'agir de* / to be a question of, a matter of

  Il s'agit de l'amour. / It is a matter of love.

- *s'approcher de* / to approach

  La dame s'approche de la porte et elle l'ouvre. / The lady approaches the door and opens it.

- *changer de* / to change

  Je dois changer de train à Paris. / I have to change trains in Paris.

- *se douter de* / to suspect

  Je me doute de ses opinions. / I suspect his (her) opinions.

- *féliciter de* / to congratulate on

  Je vous félicite de vos progrès. / I congratulate you on your progress.

- *jouer de* / to play (a musical instrument)

  Je sais jouer du piano. / I know how to play the piano.

- *manquer de* / to lack

  Cette personne manque de politesse. / This person lacks courtesy.

- *se méfier de* / to distrust, to mistrust, to beware of

  Je me méfie des personnes que je ne connais pas. / I distrust persons whom I do not know.

- *se moquer de* / to make fun of

  Les enfants aiment se moquer d'un singe. / Children like to make fun of a monkey.

- *s'occuper de* / to be busy with

> *Madame Boulanger s'occupe de son mari infirme.* / Mrs. Boulanger is busy with her disabled husband.
> *Je m'occupe de mes affaires.* / I mind my own business.
> *Occupez-vous de vos affaires!* / Mind your own business!

- *partir de* / to leave

> *Il est parti de la maison à huit heures.* / He left the house at eight o'clock.

- *se plaindre de* / to complain about

> *Il se plaint toujours de son travail.* / He always complains about his work.

- *remercier de* / to thank

> *Je vous remercie de votre bonté.* / I thank you for your kindness.

(Use *remercier de* + an abstract noun or infinitive; *remercier pour* + a concrete object; e.g., *Je vous remercie pour le cadeau.* / I thank you for the present.)

- *se rendre compte de* / to realize, to be aware of

> *Je me rends compte de la condition de cette personne.* / I am aware of the condition of this person.

- *se servir de* / to employ, use, make use of

> *Je me sers d'un stylo quand j'écris une lettre.* / I use a pen when I write a letter.

- *se souvenir de* / to remember

> *Oui, je me souviens de Gervaise.* / Yes, I remember Gervaise.
> *Je me souviens de lui.* / I remember him.
> *Je me souviens d'elle.* / I remember her.
> *Je me souviens de l'été passé.* / I remember last summer.
> *Je m'en souviens.* / I remember it.

- *tenir de* / to take after (to resemble)

> *Julie tient de sa mère.* / Julie takes after her mother.

Verb + *de* + Infinitive

- *s'agir de* / to be a question of, a matter of

> *Il s'agit de faire les devoirs tous les jours.* / It is a matter of doing the homework every day.

- *avoir peur de* / to be afraid of

  Le petit garçon a peur de traverser la rue seul. / The little boy is afraid of crossing the street alone.

- *cesser de* / to stop, cease

  Il a cessé de pleuvoir. / It has stopped raining.

- *craindre de* / to be afraid of, fear

  La petite fille craint de traverser la rue seule. / The little girl is afraid of crossing the street alone.

- *décider de* / to decide

  J'ai décidé de partir tout de suite. / I decided to leave immediately.

- *demander de* / to ask, request

  Je vous demande de parler. / I am asking you to speak.

  [Note that here the subjects are different: *I* am asking *you* to speak; but when the subjects are the same, use *demander à: Elle demande à parler.* / She is asking to speak.]

- *se dépêcher de* / to hurry

  Je me suis dépêché de venir chez vous pour vous dire quelque chose. / I hurried to come to your place in order to tell you something.

- *empêcher de* / to keep from, prevent

  Je vous empêche de sortir. / I prevent you from going out.

- *essayer de* / to try

  J'essaye d'ouvrir la porte mais je ne peux pas. / I'm trying to open the door but I can't.

- *féliciter de* / to congratulate

  On m'a félicité d'avoir gagné le prix. / I was congratulated on having won the prize.

- *finir de* / to finish

  J'ai fini de travailler sur cette composition. / I have finished working on this composition.

- *se hâter de* / to hurry

  Je me hâte de venir chez toi. / I am hurrying to come to your house.

- *offrir de* / to offer

  > *J'ai offert d'écrire une lettre pour elle.* / I offered to write a letter for her.

- *oublier de* / to forget

  > *J'ai oublié de vous donner la monnaie.* / I forgot to give you the change.

- *persuader de* / to persuade

  > *J'ai persuadé mon père de me prêter quelques francs.* / I persuaded my father to lend me a few francs.

- *prendre garde de* / to take care not to

  > *Prenez garde de tomber.* / Be careful not to fall.

- *prier de* / to beg

  > *Je vous prie d'arrêter.* / I beg you to stop.

- *promettre de* / to promise

  > *J'ai promis de venir chez toi à huit heures.* / I promised to come to your place at eight o'clock.

- *refuser de* / to refuse

  > *Je refuse de le croire.* / I refuse to believe it.

- *regretter de* / to regret, be sorry

  > *Je regrette d'être obligé de vous dire cela.* / I am sorry to be obliged to tell you that.

- *remercier de* / to thank

  > *Je vous remercie d'être venu si vite.* / I thank you for coming (having come) so quickly. (Use *remercier de* + infinitive or + abstract noun. Use *remercier pour* + concrete object.)

- *se souvenir de* / to remember

  > *Tu vois? Je me suis souvenu de venir chez toi.* / You see? I remembered to come to your house.

- *tâcher de* / to try

  > *Tâche de finir tes devoirs avant de sortir.* / Try to finish your homework before going out.

- *venir de* / to have just (done something)

  > *Je viens de manger.* / I have just eaten. (I just ate.)

Verb + *à* + Noun + *de* + Infinitive

The model to follow is: *J'ai conseillé à Robert de suivre un cours de français.* / I advised Robert to take a course in French.

- *conseiller à* / to advise

  J'ai conseillé à Jeanne de se marier. / I advised Joan to get married.

- *défendre à* / to forbid

  Mon père défend à mon frère de fumer. / My father forbids my brother to smoke.

- *demander à* / to ask, request

  J'ai demandé à Marie de venir. / I asked Mary to come.

- *dire à* / to say, to tell

  J'ai dit à Charles de venir. / I told Charles to come.

- *interdire à* / to forbid

  Mon père interdit à mon frère de fumer. / My father forbids my brother to smoke.

- *permettre à* / to permit

  J'ai permis à l'étudiant de partir quelques minutes avant la fin de la classe. / I permitted the student to leave a few minutes before the end of class.

- *promettre à* / to promise

  J'ai promis à mon ami d'arriver à l'heure. / I promised my friend to arrive on time.

- *téléphoner à* / to telephone

  J'ai téléphoné à Marcel de venir me voir. / I phoned Marcel to come to see me.

Verb + Other Prepositions

- *commencer par* + infinitive / to begin by + present participle

  La présidente a commencé par discuter des problèmes de la société. / The president began by discussing problems in society.

- *s'entendre avec quelqu'un* / to get along with someone

  Jean s'entend avec Christophe. / John gets along with Christopher.

- *entrer dans* + noun / to enter, go in

   Elle est entrée dans le restaurant. / She went into the restaurant.

- *insister pour* + infinitive / to insist on, upon

   J'insiste pour obtenir tous mes droits. / I insist on obtaining all my rights.

- *se marier avec quelqu'un* / to marry someone

   Elle va se marier avec lui. / She is going to marry him.

- *se mettre en colère* / to become angry, upset

   Monsieur Leduc se met en colère facilement. / Mr. Leduc gets angry easily.

- *se mettre en route* / to start out, set out

   Ils se sont mis en route dès l'aube. / They started out at dawn.

- *remercier pour* + a concrete noun / to thank for

   Je vous remercie pour le joli cadeau. / I thank you for the pretty present. (Remember to use *remercier de* + an abstract noun or + infinitive: *Je vous remercie de votre bonté.* / I thank you for your kindness. *Je vous remercie d'être venue si vite.* / I thank you for coming so quickly.)

Verb + no preposition + Infinitive

The following verbs take *no* preposition and are followed directly by the infinitive.

- *adorer* / to adore, love

   Madame Morin adore mettre tous ses bijoux avant de sortir. / Mrs. Morin loves to put on all her jewelry before going out.

- *aimer* / to like

   J'aime lire. / I like to read.

- *aimer mieux* / to prefer

   J'aime mieux rester ici. / I prefer to stay here.

- *aller* / to go

   Je vais faire mes devoirs. / I am going to do my homework.

- *compter* / to intend

   Je compte aller en France l'été prochain. / I intend to go to France next summer.

- *croire* / to believe

  Il croit être innocent. / He believes he is innocent.

- *désirer* / to desire, wish

  Je désire prendre une tasse de café. / I wish to have a cup of coffee.

- *devoir* / to have to, ought to

  Je dois faire mes devoirs avant de sortir. / I have to do my homework before going out.

- *écouter* / to listen to

  J'écoute chanter les enfants. / I am listening to the children singing.

- *entendre* / to hear

  J'entends chanter les enfants. / I hear the children singing.

- *espérer* / to hope

  J'espère aller en France. / I hope to go to France.

- *faire* / to cause; to make; to have something done by someone

  Le professeur fait travailler les élèves dans la salle de classe. / The teacher has the pupils work in the classroom.

- *falloir* / to be necessary

  Il faut être honnête. / One must be honest.

- *laisser* / to let, allow

  Je vous laisse partir. / I am letting you go.

- *paraître* / to appear, seem

  Elle paraît être capable. / She appears to be capable.

- *penser* / to think, plan, intend

  Je pense aller à Paris. / I intend to go to Paris.

- *pouvoir* / to be able, can

  Je peux marcher mieux maintenant. / I can walk better now.

- *préférer* / to prefer

  Je préfère manger maintenant. / I prefer to eat now.

- *regarder* / to look at

  Je regarde voler les oiseaux. / I am looking at the birds flying.

- *savoir* / to know, know how

    Je sais nager. / I know how to swim.

- *valoir mieux* / to be better

    Il vaut mieux être honnête. / It is better to be honest.

- *vouloir* / to want

    Je veux venir chez vous. / I want to come to your house.

Verbs That Do Not Require a Preposition

- *attendre* / to wait for

    J'attends l'autobus depuis vingt minutes. / I have been waiting for the bus for twenty minutes.

- *chercher* / to look for

    Je cherche mon livre. / I'm looking for my book.

- *demander* / to ask for

    Je demande une réponse. / I am asking for a reply.

- *écouter* / to listen to

    J'écoute la musique. / I am listening to the music.
    J'écoute le professeur. / I am listening to the teacher.

- *envoyer chercher* / to send for

    J'ai envoyé chercher le docteur. / I sent for the doctor.

- *essayer* / to try on

    Elle a essayé une jolie robe. / She tried on a pretty dress.

- *mettre* / to put on

    Elle a mis la robe rouge. / She put on the red dress.

- *payer* / to pay for

    J'ai payé le dîner. / I paid for the dinner.

- *pleurer* / to cry about, cry over

    Elle pleure la perte de son petit chien. / She is crying over the loss of her little dog.

- *regarder* / to look at

    Je regarde le ciel. / I am looking at the sky.

§7.6 COMPLETE CONJUGATION OF AN *AVOIR* VERB

Present participle: *parlant* / talking, speaking; Past participle: *parlé* / talked, spoken; Infinitive *parler* / to talk, to speak

Present indicative

je parle, tu parles, il (elle, on) parle; nous parlons, vous parlez, ils (elles) parlent

I talk, you talk, he (she, it, one) talks; we talk, you talk, they talk

OR

I do talk, etc.

OR

I am talking, etc.

Imperfect indicative

je parlais, tu parlais, il (elle, on) parlait; nous parlions, vous parliez, ils (elles) parlaient

I was talking, you were talking, he (she, it, one) was talking; we were talking, you were talking, they were talking

OR

I used to talk, etc.

OR

I talked, etc.

Past definite

je parlai, tu parlas, il (elle, on) parla; nous parlâmes, vous parlâtes, ils (elles) parlèrent

I talked, you talked, he (she, it, one) talked; we talked, you talked, they talked

OR

I did talk, etc.

Future

je parlerai, tu parleras, il (elle, on) parlera; nous parlerons, vous parlerez, ils (elles) parleront

I shall talk, you will talk, he (she, it, one) will talk; we shall talk, you will talk, they will talk

Conditional present

je parlerais, tu parlerais, il (elle, on) parlerait; nous parlerions, vous parleriez, ils (elles) parleraient

I would talk, you would talk, he (she, it, one) would talk; we would talk, you would talk, they would talk

Present subjunctive	*que je parle, que tu parles, qu'il (qu'elle, qu'on) parle; que nous parlions, que vous parliez, qu'ils (qu'elles) parlent*

that I may talk, that you may talk, that he (she, it, one) may talk; that we may talk, that you may talk, that they may talk

Imperfect subjunctive	*que je parlasse, que tu parlasses, qu'il (qu'elle, qu'on) parlât; que nous parlassions, que vous parlassiez, qu'ils (qu'elles) parlassent*

that I might talk, that you might talk, that he (she, it, one) might talk; that we might talk, that you might talk, that they might talk

Past indefinite	*j'ai parlé, tu as parlé, il (elle, on) a parlé; nous avons parlé, vous avez parlé, ils (elles) ont parlé*

I talked, you talked, he (she, it, one) talked; we talked, you talked, they talked

OR

I have talked, you have talked, he (she, it, one) has talked; we have talked, you have talked, they have talked

OR

I did talk, you did talk, he (she, it, one) did talk; we did talk, you did talk, they did talk

Pluperfect indicative	*j'avais parlé, tu avais parlé, il (elle, on) avait parlé; nous avions parlé, vous aviez parlé, ils (elles) avaient parlé*

I had talked, you had talked, he (she, it, one) had talked; we had talked, you had talked, they had talked

Past anterior	*j'eus parlé, tu eus parlé, il (elle, on) eut parlé; nous eûmes parlé, vous eûtes parlé, ils (elles) eurent parlé*

I had talked, you had talked, he (she, it, one) had talked; we had talked, you had talked, they had talked

Future perfect	*j'aurai parlé, tu auras parlé, il (elle, on) aura parlé; nous aurons parlé, vous aurez parlé, ils (elles) auront parlé*
	I shall have talked, you will have talked, he (she, it, one) will have talked; we shall have talked, you will have talked, they will have talked

Conditional perfect	*j'aurais parlé, tu aurais parlé, il (elle, on) aurait parlé; nous aurions parlé, vous auriez parlé, ils (elles) auraient parlé*
	I would have talked, you would have talked, he (she, it, one) would have talked; we would have talked, you would have talked, they would have talked

Past subjunctive	*que j'aie parlé, que tu aies parlé, qu'il (qu'elle, qu'on) ait parlé; que nous ayons parlé, que vous ayez parlé, qu'ils (qu'elles) aient parlé*
	that I may have talked, that you may have talked, that he (she, it, one) may have talked; that we may have talked, that you may have talked, that they may have talked

Pluperfect subjunctive	*que j'eusse parlé, que tu eusses parlé, qu'il (qu'elle, qu'on) eût parlé; que nous eussions parlé, que vous eussiez parlé, qu'ils (qu'elles) eussent parlé*
	that I might have talked, that you might have talked, that he (she, it, one) might have talked; that we might have talked, that you might have talked, that they might have talked

Imperative	*parle, parlons, parlez*
	talk, let's talk, talk

§7.7 COMPLETE CONJUGA-TION OF AN *ÊTRE* VERB

Present participle: *venant* / coming; Past participle; *venu* / come; Infinitive: *venir* / to come

Present indicative	*je viens, tu viens, il (elle, on) vient; nous venons, vous venez, ils (elles) viennent*

I come, you come, he (she, it, one) comes; we come, you come, they come

OR

I do come, etc.

OR

I am coming, etc.

Imperfect indicative	*je venais, tu venais, il (elle, on) venait; nous venions, vous veniez, ils (elles) venaient*

I was coming, you were coming, he (she, it, one) was coming; we were coming, you were coming, they were coming

OR

I used to come, etc.

OR

I came, etc.

Past definite	*je vins, tu vins, il (elle, on) vint; nous vînmes, vous vîntes, ils (elles) vinrent*

I came, you came, he (she, it, one) came; we came, you came, they came

OR

I did come, etc.

Future	*je viendrai, tu viendras, il (elle, on) viendra; nous viendrons, vous viendrez, ils (elles) viendront*

I shall come, you will come, he (she, it, one) will come; we shall come, you will come, they will come

Conditional present	*je viendrais, tu viendrais, il (elle, on) viendrait; nous viendrions, vous viendriez, ils (elles) viendraient*

I would come, you would come, he (she, it, one) would come; we would come, you would come, they would come

Present subjunctive	*que je vienne, que tu viennes, qu'il (qu'elle, qu'on) vienne; que nous venions, que vous veniez, qu'ils (qu'elles) viennent*

that I may come, that you may come, that he (she, it, one) may come; that we may come, that you may come, that they may come

Imperfect subjunctive	*que je vinsse, que tu vinsses, qu'il (qu'elle, qu'on) vînt; que nous vinssions, que vous vinssiez, qu'ils (qu'elles) vinssent*

that I might come, that you might come, that he (she, it, one) might come; that we might come, that you might come; that they might come

Past indefinite	*je suis venu(e), tu es venu(e), il (on) est venu, elle est venue; nous sommes venu(e)s, vous êtes venu(e)(s), ils sont venus, elles sont venues*

I came, you came, he (she, it, one) came; we came, you came, they came
OR

I have come, etc.
OR

I did come, etc.

Pluperfect indicative	*j'étais venu(e), tu étais venu(e), il, on était venu, elle était venue; nous étions venu(e)s, vous étiez venu(e)(s), ils étaient venus, elles étaient venues*

I had come, you had come, he (she, it, one) had come; we had come, you had come, they had come

Past anterior	*je fus venu(e), tu fus venu(e), il (on) fut venu, elle fut venue; nous fûmes venu(e)s, vous fûtes venu(e)(s), ils furent venus, elles furent venues*

I had come, you had come, he (she, it, one) had come; we had come, you had come, they had come

Future perfect	*je serai venu(e), tu seras venu(e), il (on) sera venu, elle sera venue; nous serons venu(e)s, vous serez venu(e)(s), ils seront venus, elles seront venues*
	I shall have come, you will have come, he (she, it, one) will have come; we shall have come, you will have come, they will have come
Conditional perfect	*je serais venu(e), tu serais venu(e), il (on) serait venu, elle serait venue; nous serions venu(e)s, vous seriez venu(e)(s), ils seraient venus, elles seraient venues*
	I would have come, you would have come, he (she, it, one) would have come; we would have come, you would have come, they would have come
Past subjunctive	*que je sois venu(e), que tu sois venu(e), qu'il (on) soit venu, qu'elle soit venue; que nous soyons venu(e)s, que vous soyez venu(e)(s), qu'ils soient venus, qu'elles soient venues*
	that I may have come, that you may have come, that he (she, it, one) may have come; that we may have come, that you may have come, that they may have come
Pluperfect subjunctive	*que je fusse venu(e), que tu fusses venu(e), qu'il (qu'on) fût venu, qu'elle fût venue; que nous fussions venu(e)s, que vous fussiez venu(e)(s), qu'ils fussent venus, qu'elles fussent venues*
	that I might have come, that you might have come, that he (she, it, one) might have come; that we might have come, that you might have come, that they might have come
Imperative	*viens, venons, venez*
	come, let's come, come

§7.8
TENSES AND MOODS
§7.8 – 1
Present Indicative Tense

The *present indicative* is the most frequently used tense in French and English. It indicates:

- An action or a state of being at the present time.

  Je vais à l'école maintenant. / I am going to school now.
  Je pense; donc, je suis. / I think; therefore, I am.

- Habitual action.

  Je vais à la bibliothèque tous les jours. / I go to the library every day.

- A general truth, something that is permanently true.

  Deux et deux font quatre. / Two and two are four.
  Voir c'est croire. / Seeing is believing.

- Vividness when talking or writing about past events.

  Marie-Antoinette est condamnée à mort. Elle monte dans la charrette qui est en route pour la guillotine. / Marie-Antoinette is condemned to die. She gets into the cart and is on her way to the guillotine.

- A near future.

  Il arrive demain. / He arrives tomorrow.

- An action or state of being that occurred in the past and continues up to the present. In English, this tense is the present perfect, which is formed with the present tense of "to have" plus the past participle of the verb you are using.

  Je suis ici depuis dix minutes. / I have been here for ten minutes. (I am still here at present.)

This tense is regularly formed as follows:

- Drop the *-er* ending of an infinitive like *parler,* and add *-e, -es, -e; -ons, -ez, -ent.*

  You then get:
  je parle, tu parles, il (elle, on) parle; nous parlons, vous parlez, ils (elles) parlent

- Drop the -*ir* ending of an infinitive like *finir,* and add
  -*is, -is, -it; -issons, -issez, -issent.*

  You then get:
  *je finis, tu finis, il (elle, on) finit; nous finissons, vous finissez,
  ils (ells) finissent*

- Drop the -*re* ending of an infinitive like *vendre,* and add
  -*s, -s, —; -ons, -ez, -ent.*

  You then get:
  *je vends, tu vends, il (elle, on) vend; nous vendons, vous
  vendez, ils (elles) vendent*

  For the present tense of *avoir* and *être,* see §7.19.

§7.8 – 2
Imperfect
Indicative
Tense

The *imperfect indicative* is a past tense. It is used to indicate:

- An action that was going on in the past at the same time as
  another action.

  Il lisait pendant que j'écrivais. / He was reading while I was
  writing.

- An action that was going on in the past when another
  action occurred.

  Il lisait quand je suis entré. / He was reading when I came in.

- An action that was performed habitually in the past.

  Nous allions à la plage tous les jours. / We used to go to the
  beach every day.

- A description of a mental or physical condition in the past.

  (mental) *Il était triste quand je l'ai vu.* / He was sad when I
  saw him.
  (physical) *Quand ma mère était jeune, elle était belle.* / When
  my mother was young, she was beautiful.

- An action or state of being that occurred in the past and
  lasted for a certain length of time prior to another past action.

  J'attendais l'autobus depuis dix minutes quand il est arrivé. / I
  had been waiting for the bus for ten minutes when it arrived.

This tense is regularly formed as follows:
    For -*er*, -*ir*, and -*re* verbs, take the "*nous*" form in the
present indicative tense of the verb you have in mind, drop
the first person plural ending *(-ons),* and add the endings
-*ais, -ais, -ait; -ions, -iez, -aient.*

| Mnemonic tip | The vowel *i* is in each of the six endings and *i* is the first letter of the *imperfect* tense. |

For the imperfect indicative of *avoir* and *être*, see §7.19.

§7.8 – 3
Past Simple Tense

This past tense expresses an action that took place at some definite time. It is not ordinarily used in conversational French or in informal writing. It is a literary tense — used in formal writing, such as history and literature.

The past simple tense is regularly formed as follows:
For all -*er* verbs, drop the -*er* of the infinitive and add -*ai*, -*as*, -*a*; -*âmes*, -*âtes*, -*èrent*.
For regular -*ir* and -*re* verbs, drop the ending of the infinitive and add the endings -*is*, *is*, -*it*; -*îmes*, -*îtes*, -*irent*.

Il alla en Afrique. / He went to Africa.
Il voyagea en Amérique. / He traveled to America.
Elle fut heureuse. / She was happy.
Elle eut un grand bonheur. / She had great happiness.

For the past definite of *avoir* and *être*, see §7.19.

§7.8 – 4
Future Tense

In French and English the *future* tense is used to express an action or a state of being which will take place at some time in the future.

J'irai en France l'été prochain. / I will go to France next summer.
J'y penserai. / I will think about it.
Je partirai dès qu'il arrivera. / I will leave as soon as he arrives.
Je te dirai tout quand tu seras ici. / I will tell you all when you are here.

If the action of the verb you are using is not past or present and if future time is implied, the future tense is used when the clause begins with the following conjunctions: *aussitôt que* / as soon as, *dès que* / as soon as, *quand* / when, *lorsque* / when, and *tant que* / as long as.

This tense is regularly formed as follows:
Add the following endings to the whole infinitive: -*ai*, -*as*, -*a*, -*ons*, -*ez*, -*ont*. For -*re* verbs you must drop the *e* in -*re* before you add the future endings.

For the future of *avoir* and *être*, see §7.19.

§7.8 – 5
Conditional Present Tense

The conditional tense is used in French and English to express:

- An action that you would do if something else were possible.

  Je ferais le travail si j'en avais le temps. / I would do the work if I had the time.

- A conditional desire.

  J'aimerais du thé. / I would like some tea.
  Je voudrais du café. / I would like some coffee.

- An obligation or duty.

  Je devrais étudier pour l'examen. / I should study for the examination.

The conditional has two tenses, the present and the past.

The present conditional is regularly formed as follows:
   Add the following endings to the whole infinitive: *-ais, -ais, -ait; -ions, -iez, -aient.* For *-re* verbs you must drop the e in *-re* before you add the conditional endings. Note that these endings are the same ones you use to form regularly the imperfect indicative. For the conditional of *avoir* and *être*, see §7.19.

§7.8 – 6
Present Subjunctive Tense

The subjunctive mood is used in French much more than in English. It is used in the following ways:

- After a verb that expresses some kind of insistence, preference, or suggestion.

  Nous insistons que vous soyez ici à l'heure. / We insist that you be here on time.
  Je préfère qu'il fasse le travail maintenant. / I prefer that he do the work now.
  Le juge exige qu'il soit puni. / The judge demands that he be punished.

- After a verb that expresses doubt, fear, joy, sorrow, or some other emotion.

  Sylvie doute qu'il vienne. / Sylvia doubts that he is coming.
  Je suis heureux qu'il vienne. / I'm happy that he is coming.
  Je regrette qu'il soit malade. / I'm sorry that he is sick.

- After certain conjunctions.

> *Elle partira à moins qu'il ne vienne.* / She will leave unless he comes.
> *Je resterai jusqu'à ce qu'il vienne.* / I will stay until he comes.
> *Quoiqu'elle soit belle, il ne l'aime pas.* / Although she is beautiful, he does not love her.
> *Le professeur l'explique pour qu'elle comprenne.* / The teacher is explaining it so that she may understand.

- After certain impersonal expressions that show a need, a doubt, a possibility or an impossibility.

> *Il est urgent qu'il vienne.* / It is urgent that he come.
> *Il vaut mieux qu'il vienne.* / It is better that he come.
> *Il est possible qu'il vienne.* / It is better that he will come.
> *Il est douteux qu'il vienne.* / It is doubtful that he will come.

The present subjunctive is regularly formed by dropping the *-ant* ending of the present participle of the verb you are using and adding the endings *-e, -es, -e; -ions, -iez, -ent.*

For the present subjunctive of *avoir* and *être*, see §7.19. See also subjunctive, §7.15.

§7.8–7 Imperfect Subjunctive Tense

The *imperfect subjunctive* is used in the same ways as the present subjunctive, that is, after certain verbs, conjunctions, and impersonal expressions. The main difference between these two is the time of the action. If present, use the present subjunctive. If the action is related to the past, the imperfect subjunctive is used, provided that the action was not completed.

> *Je voulais qu'il vînt.* / I wanted him to come. (action not completed; he did not come while I wanted him to come)

Note: The subjunctive of *venir* is used because *vouloir* requires the subjunctive *after* it. In conversational French and informal writing, the imperfect subjunctive is avoided. Use, instead, the present subjunctive.

> *Je voulais qu'il vienne.* / I wanted him to come.
> *Je le lui expliquais pour qu'elle le comprît.* / I was explaining it to her so that she might understand it. (action not completed; the understanding was not completed at the time of the explaining)

Note: The subjunctive of *comprendre* is used because the conjunction *pour que* requires the subjunctive *after* it. Again, avoid using the imperfect subjunctive in conversation and informal writing. Use, instead, the present subjunctive: *Je le lui expliquais pour qu'elle le comprenne.*

The imperfect subjunctive is regularly formed by dropping the endings of the *passé simple* of the verb you are using and adding the following endings:

-er verbs: *-asse, -asses, -ât; -assions, -assiez, -assent*
-ir verbs: *-isse, -isses, -ît; -issions, -issiez, -issent*
-re verbs: *-usse, -usses, -ût; -ussions, -ussiez, -ussent*

For the imperfect subjunctive of *avoir* and *être*, see §7.19. See also subjunctive, §7.15.

§7.8–8
Past Indefinite Tense

This past tense expresses an action that took place at no definite time. It is used in conversational French, correspondence, and other informal writing. The past indefinite is used more and more in literature these days and is taking the place of the past definite. It is a compound tense because it is formed with the present indicative of *avoir* or *être* (depending on which of these two auxiliaries is required to form a compound tense) plus the past participle. See §7.3 for the distinction made between verbs conjugated with *avoir* or *être*.

Il est allé à l'école. / He went to school; He did go to school; He has gone to school.
J'ai mangé dans ce restaurant de nombreuses fois. / I have eaten in this restaurant many times.
J'ai parlé au garçon. / I spoke to the boy; I have spoken to the boy; I did speak to the boy.

§7.8–9
Pluperfect Tense

In French and English this tense (also called the *past perfect*) is used to express an action that happened in the past before another past action. Since it is used in relation to another past action, the other past action is expressed in either the past indefinite or the imperfect indicative in French. The pluperfect is used in formal writing and literature as well as in conversational French and informal writing. It is a compound tense because it is formed with the imperfect indicative of *avoir* or *être* (depending on which of these two auxiliaries is required to form a compound tense) plus the past participle. See §7.3 for the distinction made between verbs conjugated with *avoir* or *être*.

Je me suis rappelé que j'avais oublié de le lui dire. / I remembered that I had forgotten to tell him.

Note: It would be incorrect to say: I remembered that I forgot to tell him. The point here is that first I forgot; then I remembered. Both actions are in the past. The action that occurred in the past *before* the other past action is in the pluperfect. And in this example it is "I had forgotten" *(j'avais oublié).*

J'avais étudié la leçon que le professeur a expliquée. / I had studied the lesson that the teacher explained.

Note: First I studied the lesson; then the teacher explained it. Both actions are in the past. The action that occurred in the past before the other past action is in the pluperfect. And in this example it is "I had studied" *(j'avais étudié).*

J'étais fatigué ce matin parce que je n'avais pas dormi. / I was tired this morning because I had not slept.

§7.8–10
Past Anterior Tense

This tense is similar to the pluperfect indicative. The main difference is that in French it is a literary tense; that is, it is used in formal writing such as history and literature. More and more French writers today use the pluperfect indicative instead of the past anterior. The past anterior is a compound tense and is formed with the *passé simple* of *avoir* or *être* (depending on which of these two auxiliaries is required to form a compound tense) plus the past participle. It is ordinarily introduced by conjunctions of time: *après que, aussitôt que, dès que, lorsque, quand.*

Quand il eut tout mangé, il partit. / When he had eaten everything, he left.

§7.8–11
Future Perfect Tense

In French and English this tense (also called the *future anterior*) is used to express an action that will happen in the future *before* another future action. Since it is used in relation to another future action, the other future action is expressed in the simple future in French. It is used in conversation and informal writing as well as in formal writing and in literature. It is a compound tense because it is formed with the future of *avoir* or *être* (depending on which of these two auxiliaries is required to form a compound tense) plus the past participle of the verb you are using. In English, it is formed by using "will have" plus the past participle of the verb you are using.

Elle arrivera demain et j'aurai fini le travail. / She will arrive tomorrow and I will have finished the work.

Note: First I will finish the work; then she will arrive. The action that will occur in the future *before* the other future action is in the future anterior.

Quand elle arrivera demain, j'aurai fini le travail. / When she arrives tomorrow, I will have finished the work.

Note: The idea of future time here is the same as in the preceding example. In English, the present tense is used ("When she arrives . . .") to express a near future. In French, the future is used *(Quand elle arrivera . . .)* because *quand* precedes and the action will take place in the future.

§7.8–12 Conditional Perfect Tense

This is used in French and English to express an action that you would have done if something else had been possible; that is, you would have done something on condition that something else had been possible. It is a compound tense because it is formed with the conditional of *avoir* or *être* plus the past participle of the verb you are using. In English, it is formed by using "would have" plus the past participle.

J'aurais fait le travail si j'avais étudié. / I would have done the work if I had studied.
J'aurais fait le travail si j'en avais eu le temps. / I would have done the work if I had had the time.

§7.8–13 Past Subjunctive Tense

This tense is used to express an action that took place in the past in relation to the present. It is like the past indefinite, except that the auxiliary verb (*avoir* or *être*) is in the present subjunctive. The subjunctive is used because what precedes is a certain verb, conjunction, or impersonal expression. The past subjunctive is also used in relation to a future time when another action will be completed. In French this tense is used in formal writing and in literature as well as in conversation and informal writing. It is a compound tense because it is formed with the present subjunctive of *avoir* or *être* as the auxiliary plus the past participle of the verb you are using.

A past action in relation to the present:
Il est possible qu'elle soit partie. / It is possible that she has left.
Je doute qu'il ait fait cela. / I doubt that he did that.

An action that will take place in the future:
Je désire que vous soyez rentré avant dix heures. / I want you to be back before ten o'clock.

§7.8 – 14
Pluperfect
Subjunctive
Tense

This tense (also called the *past perfect*) is used for the same reasons as the imperfect subjunctive — that is, after certain verbs, conjunctions, and impersonal expressions. The main difference between the imperfect and the pluperfect subjunctive is the time of the action in the past. If the action was not completed, the imperfect subjunctive is used; if the action was completed, the pluperfect is used. In French, it is used only in formal writing and literature.

Il était possible qu'elle fût partie. / It was possible that she might have left.

NOTE: Avoid this tense in French. Use the past subjunctive instead: *Il était possible qu'elle soit partie.*

§7.8 – 15
Imperative
Mood

The *imperative* mood is used in French and English to express a command or request. It is also used to express an indirect request made in the third person. In both languages it is formed by dropping the subject and using the present tense. There are a few exceptions in both languages when the present subjunctive is used.

Sortez! / Get out!   *Asseyez-vous!* / Sit down!
Entrez! / Come in!   *Levez-vous!* / Get up!
Soyez à l'heure! / Be on time! (subjunctive used)
Dieu le veuille! / May God grant it! (subjunctive used)
Qu'ils mangent du gâteau! / Let them eat cake! (subjunctive used)

You must drop the final *s* in the second person singular of an *-er* verb. This is done in the affirmative and negative, as in: *Mange!* / Eat! *Ne mange pas!* / Don't eat! However, when the pronouns *y* and *en* are linked to it, the *s* is retained in all regular *-er* verbs and in the verb *aller*. The reason for this is that it makes it easier to link the two elements by pronouncing the *s* as a *z*.

Donnes-en! / Give some!
Manges-en! / Eat some!
Vas-y! / Go there!

§7.9 PASSIVE VOICE

When verbs are used in the active voice, which is almost all the time, the subject performs the action. When the *passive* voice is used, the subject of the sentence is not the performer; the action falls on the subject. The agent (the performer) is sometimes expressed, sometimes not, as is done in English. The passive voice, therefore, is composed of the verb in the passive, which is any tense of *être* + the past participle of the verb you are using to indicate the action performed upon the subject. Since *être* is the verb used in the passive voice, the past participle of your other verb must agree with the subject in gender and number.

Jacqueline a été reçue à l'université. / Jacqueline has been accepted at the university.
Ce livre est écrit par un auteur célèbre. / This book is written by a famous author.
Cette composition a été écrite par un jeune élève. / This composition was written by a young student.

There are certain rules you must remember about the passive voice:

• Usually the preposition *de* is used instead of *par* with such verbs as *aimer, admirer, accompagner, apprécier, voir.*

Jacqueline est aimée de tout le monde. / Jacqueline is liked (loved) by everyone.

BUT

Nous avons été suivis par un chien perdu. / We were followed by a lost dog.

• Avoid the passive voice if the thought can be expressed in the active voice with the indefinite pronoun *on* as the subject.

On vend de bonnes choses dans ce magasin. / Good things are sold in this store.
On parle français ici. / French is spoken here.

- You must avoid using the passive voice with a reflexive verb. Always use a reflexive verb with an active subject.

  Elle s'appelle Jeanne. / She is called Joan.
  Comment se prononce ce mot? / How is this word pronounced?

§7.10 SI CLAUSE: A SUMMARY

When the Verb in the *SI* clause is in the:	The Verb in the Main or Result Clause is:
present indicative	present indicative, future, or imperative
imperfect indicative	conditional
pluperfect indicative	conditional perfect

- By *si* we mean "if." Sometimes *si* can mean "whether" and in that case, this summary does not apply because there are no restrictions about the tenses. The sequence of tenses with a *si-* clause is the same in English with an "if" clause.

  Si elle arrive, je pars. / If she arrives, I'm leaving.
  Si elle arrive, je partirai. / If she arrives, I will leave.
  Si elle arrive, partez! / If she arrives, leave!
  Si Paul étudiait, il aurait de meilleures notes. / If Paul studied, he would have better grades.
  Si Georges avait étudié, il aurait eu de bonnes notes. / If George had studied, he would have had good grades.

§7.11 SPECIAL USES OF COMMON VERBS

DEVOIR / TO OWE; OUGHT TO

- Present

  Je dois étudier. / I have to study; I must study; I am supposed to study.
  Il doit être fou! / He must be crazy! He's probably crazy!
  Mon père doit avoir cinquante ans. / My father must be 50 years old.

- Imperfect

  Je devais étudier. / I had to study; I was supposed to study.
  Quand j'étais à l'école, je devais toujours étudier. / When I was in school, I always had to study.
  Ma mère devait avoir cinquante ans quand elle est morte. / My mother was probably 50 years old when she died.

- Future

  Je devrai étudier. **/** I will have to study.
  Nous devrons faire le travail ce soir. **/** We will have to do the
  work this evening.

- Conditional

  Je devrais étudier. **/** I ought to study. / I should study.
  Vous devriez étudier davantage. **/** You ought to study more;
  You should study more.

- Past indefinite

  Je ne suis pas allé(e) au cinéma parce que j'ai dû étudier. **/** I
  did not go to the movies because I had to study.
  *J'ai dû prendre l'autobus parce qu'il n'y avait pas de train à
  cette heure-là.* **/** I had to take the bus because there was no
  train at that hour.
  Robert n'est pas ici. **/** Robert is not here.
  Il a dû partir. **/** He must have left; He has probably left; He had
  to leave.

- Conditional perfect

  J'aurais dû étudier! **/** I should have studied!
  Vous auriez dû me dire la vérité. **/** You should have told me the
  truth.

- With a direct or an indirect object there is still another meaning.

  Je dois de l'argent. **/** I owe some money.
  Je le lui dois. **/** I owe it to him (to her).

POUVOIR **/ TO BE ABLE TO, CAN**

- Present

  Je ne peux pas sortir aujourd'hui parce que je suis malade. **/** I
  cannot (am unable to) go out today because I am sick.
  Est-ce que je peux entrer? Puis-je entrer? **/** May I come in?
  Madame Marin peut être malade. **/** Mrs. Marin may be sick.

  This use of *pouvoir* suggests possibility.

  Je n'en peux plus. **/** I can't go on any longer.

  This use suggests physical exhaustion.

Il se peut. / It is possible.

This use as a reflexive verb suggests possibility.

Cela ne se peut pas. / That can't be done.

This use as a reflexive verb suggests impossibility.

- Conditional

    Pourriez-vous me prêter dix francs? / Could you lend me ten francs?

- Conditional perfect

    Auriez-vous pu venir chez moi? / Could you have come to my place?
    Ils auraient pu rater le train. / They might have missed the train.

VOULOIR / TO WANT

- Present

    Je veux aller en France. / I want to go to France.
    Je veux bien sortir avec vous ce soir. / I am willing to go out with you this evening.
    Voulez-vous bien vous asseoir? / Would you be good enough to sit down?
    Que veut dire ce mot? / What does this word mean?
    Que voulez-vous dire? / What do you mean?
    Qu'est-ce que cela veut dire? / What does that mean?

- Conditional

    Je voudrais un café crème, s'il vous plaît. / I would like coffee with cream, please.

- Imperative

    Veuillez vous asseoir. / Kindly sit down.
    Veuillez accepter mes meilleurs sentiments. / Please accept my best regards.

SAVOIR / TO KNOW (a fact)

- Present

    Je sais la réponse. / I know the answer.
    Je sais lire en français. / I know how to read in French.

- Conditional

> *Sauriez-vous où est le docteur?* / Would you know where the doctor is?
> *Je ne saurais penser à tout!* / I can't think of everything!

- Imperative

> *Sachons-le bien!* / Let's be well aware of it!
> *Sachez que votre père vient de mourir.* / Be informed that your father has just died.

SAVOIR AND CONNAÎTRE

The main difference between the meaning of these two verbs in the sense of "to know" is that *connaître* means merely to be acquainted with; for example, to be acquainted with a person, a city, a neighborhood, a country, the title of a book, the works of an author.

> *Savez-vous la réponse?* / Do you know the answer?
> *Savez-vous quelle heure il est?* / Do you know what time it is?
> *Connaissez-vous cette dame?* / Do you know this lady?
> *Connaissez-vous Paris?* / Do you know Paris?
> *Connaissez-vous ce livre?* / Do you know this book?

ENTENDRE AND COMPRENDRE

The main difference between the meaning of these two verbs is that *entendre* means "to hear" and *comprendre* "to understand." Sometimes *entendre* can mean "to understand" or "to mean."

> *Entendez-vous la musique?* / Do you hear the music?
> *Comprenez-vous la leçon?* / Do you understand the lesson?
> *"M'entends-tu?!" dit la mère à l'enfant. "Ne fais pas cela!"* / "Do you understand me?!" says the mother to the child. "Don't do that!"
> *Je ne comprends pas le docteur Fu Manchu parce qu'il ne parle que chinois.* / I do not understand Dr. Fu Manchu because he speaks only Chinese.
> *Qu'entendez-vous par là?* / What do you mean by that? What are you insinuating by that remark?
> *Je vous entends, mais je ne vous comprends pas; expliquez-vous, s'il vous plaît.* / I hear you, but I don't understand you; explain yourself, please.

QUITTER, PARTIR, SORTIR, AND LAISSER

These four verbs all mean "to leave," but note the differences in their uses:

- Use *quitter* when you state a direct object noun or pronoun that could be a person or a place.

  J'ai quitté mes amis devant le théâtre. / I left my friends in front of the theater.
  J'ai quitté la maison à six heures du matin. / I left the house at six in the morning.

- Use *partir* when there is no direct object noun or pronoun.

  Elle est partie tout de suite. / She left immediately.

  However, if you use the preposition *de* after *partir,* you may add a direct object, but it would be object of the preposition *de,* not of the verb *partir.*

  Elle est partie de la maison à six heures du matin. / She left (from) the house at six in the morning.

- Use *sortir,* in the sense of "to go out." With no direct object:

  Elle est sortie il y a une heure. / She went out an hour ago.

  However, if you use the preposition *de* after *sortir,* you may add a direct object, but it would be object of the preposition *de,* not of the verb *sortir.*

  Elle est sortie de la maison il y a une heure. / She left (went out of) the house an hour ago.

  Note that *sortir* can also be conjugated with *avoir* to form a compound tense, but then the meaning changes because it can take a direct object.

  Elle a sorti son mouchoir pour se moucher. / She took out her handkerchief to wipe her nose.
  Elle a sorti son mouchoir pour moucher son enfant. / She took out her handkerchief to wipe her child's nose.

- Use *laisser* when you leave behind something that is not stationary; in other words, something movable, for example, books and articles of clothing.

  J'ai laissé mes livres sur la table dans la cuisine. / I left my books on the table in the kitchen.
  J'ai laissé mon imperméable à la maison. / I left my raincoat at home.

Note that *laisser* also has the meaning "to let, allow a person to do something":

> *J'ai laissé mon ami partir.* / I let (allowed) my friend to leave.

| Mnemonic tip | *Partir* / to leave, go away contains an *a* and so does "away." *Sortir* / to go out contains an *o* and so does "out." |

FALLOIR

- Falloir is an impersonal verb, which means that it is used only in the third person singular (*il* form) in all the tenses; its primary meaning is "to be necessary."

  > *Il faut étudier pour avoir de bonnes notes.* / It is necessary to study in order to have good grades.
  > *Faut-il le faire tout de suite?* / Is it necessary to do it at once?
  > *Oui, il le faut.* / Yes, it is (understood: necessary to do it).

The use of the neuter direct object *le* is needed to show emphasis and to complete the thought.

> *Il faut être honnête.* / It is necessary to be honest.

In the negative:

> *Il ne faut pas être malhonnête.* / One must not be dishonest.

Note that *il faut* in the negative means "one must not."

> *Il ne faut pas fumer à l'école.* / One must not smoke in school.

§7.12 OTHER VERBS WITH SPECIAL MEANINGS

arriver / to happen   *Qu'est-ce qui est arrivé?* / What happened?

avoir / to have something the matter   *Qu'est-ce que vous avez?* / What's the matter with you?

entendre dire que / to hear it said that, hear that   *J'entends dire que Robert s'est marié.* / I hear that Robert got married.

entendre parler de / to hear of, about   *J'ai entendu parler d'un grand changement dans l'administration.* / I've heard about a big change in the administration.

envoyer chercher / to send for   *Je vais envoyer chercher le médecin.* / I'm going to send for the doctor.

être à quelqu'un / to belong to someone   *Ce livre est à moi.* / This book belongs to me.

faillir + *infinitive*   to almost do something   *Le bébé a failli tomber.* / The baby almost fell.

mettre / to put on   *Gisèle a mis sa plus jolie robe.* / Gisèle put on her prettiest dress.

mettre la table / to set the table

profiter de / to take advantage of

rendre visite à / to pay a visit to

venir à / to happen to   *Si nous venons à nous rencontrer, nous pourrons prendre une tasse de café.* / If we happen to meet each other, we can have a cup of coffee.

venir de + *infinitive* / to have just done something   *Joseph vient de partir.* / Joseph has just left; *Barbara venait de partir quand Françoise est arrivée.* / Barbara had just left when Françoise arrived.

§7.13 INFINITIVES

- In English, an *infinitive* contains the preposition "to" in front of it: "to give," "to finish," "to sell." In French an infinitive has a certain ending. There are three major types of infinitives in French: those that end in *-er (donner);* those that end in *-ir (finir);* and those that end in *-re (vendre).*

- Make an infinitive negative in French by placing *ne pas* in front of it.

  Je vous dis de ne pas sortir. / I am telling you not to go out.

- The infinitive is often used after a verb of perception to express an action that is in progress.

  J'entends quelqu'un chanter. / I hear somebody singing.
  Je vois venir les enfants. / I see the children coming.

  Some common verbs of perception are: *apercevoir* / to perceive, *écouter* / to listen to, *entendre* / to hear, *re-garder* / to look at, *sentir* / to feel, *voir* / to see.

- There are certain French verbs that take either the preposition à or *de* + infinitive.

  Il commence à pleuvoir. / It is beginning to rain.
  Il a cessé de pleuvoir. / It has stopped raining.

- *Avant de* and *sans* + infinitive

  > *Sylvie a mangé avant de sortir.* / Sylvia ate before going out.
  > *André est parti sans dire un mot.* / Andrew left without saying a word.

- Use of infinitive instead of a verb form

  Generally speaking, an infinitive is used instead of a verb form if the subject in a sentence is the same for the actions expressed.

  > *Je veux faire le travail.* / I want to do the work.

  BUT if there are two different subjects, you must use a new clause and a new verb form.

  > *Je veux que vous fassiez le travail.* / I want you to do the work.
  > *Je préfère me coucher tôt.* / I prefer to go to bed early.

  BUT

  > *Je préfère que vous vous couchiez tôt.* / I prefer that you go to bed early.

- Past infinitive

  In French the past infinitive is expressed by using the infinitive form of *avoir* or *être* + the past participle of the main verb being used.

  > *Après avoir quitté la maison, Monsieur et Madame Dubé sont allés au cinéma.* / After leaving the house, Mr. and Mrs. Dubé went to the movies.
  > *Après être arrivée, Jeanne a téléphoné à sa mère.* / After arriving, Jeanne telephoned her mother.

§7.14 CAUSATIVE (CAUSAL) FAIRE

The construction *faire* + infinitive means to have something done by someone. The causative *faire* can be in any tense, but it must be followed by an infinitive.

Examples with nouns and pronouns as direct and indirect objects:

> *Madame Smith fait travailler ses élèves dans la classe de français.* / Mrs. Smith makes her students work in French class.

In this example, the direct object is the noun *élèves* and it is placed right after the infinitive.

> *Madame Smith les fait travailler dans la classe de français.* /
> Mrs. Smith makes them work (has them work) in French class.

In this example, the direct object is the pronoun *les*, referring to *les élèves.* It is placed in front of the verb form of
faire, where it logically belongs.

> *Madame Smith fait lire la phrase.* / Mrs.Smith is having the
> sentence read. OR Mrs. Smith has the sentence read.

In this example, the direct object is the noun *phrase* and it
is placed right after the infinitive, as in the first example.

> *Madame Smith la fait lire.* / Mrs. Smith is having it read.

In this example, the direct object is the pronoun *la,* referring
to *la phrase.* It is placed in front of the verb form of *faire,*
where it logically belongs. This is like the second example,
but here the direct object is a thing. In the other two
examples, the direct object is a person.

§7.15
SUBJUNCTIVE

The subjunctive is not a tense, but a *mood,* or mode.
Usually when we speak in French or English, we use the
indicative mood but the subjunctive mood in French must be
used in specific cases. They are:

After Certain Conjunctions

When the following conjunctions introduce a new clause,
the verb in that new clause is usually in the subjunctive mood.

> *à condition que* / on condition that
> *à moins que* / unless
> *afin que* / in order that, so that
> *attendre que* / to wait until
> *au cas que; en cas que* / in case
> *bien que* / although
> *de crainte que* / for fear that
> *de peur que* / for fear that
> *de sorte que* / so that
> *en attendant que* / until
> *jusqu'à ce que* / until
> *malgré que* / although
> *pour que* / in order that
> *pourvu que* / provided that
> *quoique* / although

Je vous explique pour que vous compreniez. / I am explaining
to you so that you will understand.
Attendez que je finisse mon dîner / Wait until I finish my dinner.
Au cas que nous soyons d'accord . . . / In case we are in
agreement . . .
En cas qu'il vienne, soyez prêts. / In case he comes, be ready.

After Indefinite Expressions

> *où que* / wherever
> *quel que* / whatever
> *qui que* / whoever
> *quoi que* / whatever, no matter what

After an Indefinite Antecedent

The subjunctive is needed after an indefinite antecedent
because the person or thing desired may possibly not exist;
or, if it does exist, you may never find it.

Je cherche une personne qui soit honnête. / I am looking for a
person who is honest.
Je cherche un appartement qui ne soit pas trop cher. / I am
looking for an apartment that is not too expensive.
*Connaissez-vous quelqu'un qui puisse réparer mon téléviseur
une fois pour toutes?* / Do you know someone who can repair
my TV set once and for all?
Y a-t-il un élève qui comprenne le subjonctif? / Is there a
student who understands the subjunctive?

After a Superlative Expressing an Opinion

> The most common superlatives expressing an opinion
> are: *le seul (la seule)* / the only, *le premier (la pre-
> mière)* / the first, *le dernier (la dernière)* / the last, *le
> plus petit (la plus petite)* / the smallest, *le plus grand
> (la plus grande)* / the biggest

*A mon avis, Marie est la seule étudiante qui comprenne le
subjonctif.* / In my opinion, Mary is the only student who
understands the subjunctive.
*Selon mon opinion, Henriette est l'élève la plus jolie que j'aie
jamais vue.* / According to my opinion, Henrietta is the prettiest
pupil I have ever seen.

After *que*, Meaning "Let" or "May"

The subjunctive is required after *que* to express a wish, an order, or a command in the third person singular or plural.

Qu'il parte! / Let him leave!
Que Dieu nous pardonne! / May God forgive us!
Qu'ils s'en aillent! / Let them go away!

After Certain Impersonal Expressions

c'est dommage que / it's a pity that
il est bizarre que / it is odd that
il est bon que / it is good that
il est douteux que / it is doubtful that
il est essentiel que / it is essential that
il est étonnant que / it is astonishing that
il est étrange que / it is strange that
il est heureux que / it is fortunate that
il est honteux que / it is a shame that
il est important que / it is important that
il est impossible que / it is impossible that
il est nécessaire que / it is necessary that
il est possible que / it is possible that
il est regrettable que / it is regrettable that
il est temps que / it is time that
il est urgent que / it is urgent that
il faut que / it is necessary that
il se peut que / it may be that
il semble que / it seems that
il vaut mieux que / it is better that

After Certain Verbs Expressing Doubt, Emotion, or Wishing

aimer que / to like that
aimer mieux que / to prefer that
s'attendre à ce que / to expect that
avoir peur que / to be afraid that
craindre que / to fear that
défendre que / to forbid that

désirer que / to desire that
douter que / to doubt that
empêcher que / to prevent that
s'étonner que / to be astonished that
être bien aise que / to be pleased that
être content que / to be glad that
être désolé que / to be distressed that
être étonné que / to be astonished that
être heureux que / to be happy that
être joyeux que / to be joyful that
être ravi que / to be delighted that
être triste que / to be sad that
exiger que / to demand that
se fâcher que / to be angry that
insister que / to insist that
ordonner que / to order that
préférer que / to prefer that
regretter que / to regret that
souhaiter que / to wish that
tenir à ce que / to insist upon
vouloir que / to want

EXAMPLES

J'aimerais que vous restiez ici. / I would like you to stay here.
J'aime mieux que vous restiez ici. / I prefer that you stay here.
Nous nous attendons à ce qu'elle vienne immédiatement. / We expect her to come immediately.
Ta mère est contente que tu sois heureux. / Your mother is glad that you are happy.

After Verbs of Believing and Thinking

Such verbs are *croire, penser, trouver* (meaning "to think, to have an impression"), and *espérer* when used in the negative or interrogative.

Je ne pense pas qu'il soit coupable. / I don't think that he is guilty.
Croyez-vous qu'il dise la vérité? / Do you believe he is telling the truth?
Trouvez-vous qu'il y ait beaucoup de crimes dans la société d'aujourd'hui? / Do you find (think) that there are many crimes in today's society?

§7.16 SUMMARY OF TENSES AND MOODS

The 7 simple tenses	The 7 compound tenses
Present indicative	Past indefinite *(passé composé)*
Imperfect indicative	Pluperfect indicative
Past definite	Past anterior
Future	Future perfect
Conditional present	Conditional perfect
Present subjunctive	Past subjunctive
Imperfect subjunctive	Pluperfect subjunctive
Imperative or Command	

§7.17 SPELLING IRREGULAR-ITIES OF SOME COMMON VERBS

The verbs conjugated here all undergo certain spelling changes in the tenses indicated.*

The subject pronouns have been omitted in order to eliminate repetition and to emphasize the verb forms. They are:

	Singular	**Plural**
1st	*je (j')*	*nous*
2d	*tu*	*vous*
3d	*il, elle, on*	*ils, elles*

PRESENT INDICATIVE

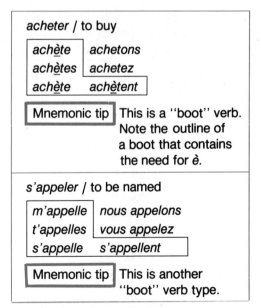

acheter / to buy

achète	achetons
achètes	achetez
achète	achètent

| Mnemonic tip | This is a "boot" verb. Note the outline of a boot that contains the need for è. |

s'appeler / to be named

m'appelle	nous appelons
t'appelles	vous appelez
s'appelle	s'appellent

| Mnemonic tip | This is another "boot" verb type. |

For additional verb conjugations, see *501 French Verbs* by Christopher Kendris, © 1995, Fourth Edition by Barron's Educational Series, Inc.

apprendre / to learn

apprends	*apprenons*
apprends	*apprenez*
apprend	*apprennent*

boire / to drink

bois	*buvons*
bois	*buvez*
boit	*boivent*

Mnemonic tip This too is a "boot" verb. Note the *"s, s, t"* pattern in the singular.

commencer / to begin, start

commence	*commençons*
commences	*commencez*
commence	*commencent*

comprendre / to understand (like *prendre;* add *com* at the beginning of *prendre*)

conduire / to drive; to lead

conduis	*conduisons*
conduis	*conduisez*
conduit	*conduisent*

connaître / to know, to be acquainted with

connais	*connaissons*
connais	*connaissez*
connaît	*connaissent*

courir / to run

cours	*courons*
cours	*courez*
court	*courent*

croire / to believe

crois	*croyons*
crois	*croyez*
croit	*croient*

devenir / to become

deviens	devenons
deviens	devenez
devient	deviennent

devoir / to owe; to have to

dois	devons
dois	devez
doit	doivent

dire / to say; to tell

dis	disons
dis	dites
dit	disent

dormir / to sleep

dors	dormons
dors	dormez
dort	dorment

écrire / to write

écris	écrivons
écris	écrivez
écrit	écrivent

envoyer / to send

envoie	envoyons
envoies	envoyez
envoie	envoient

espérer / to hope

espère	espérons
espères	espérez
espère	espèrent

falloir / to be necessary
il faut

se lever / to get up

me lève	nous levons
te lèves	vous levez
se lève	se lèvent

lire / to read

lis	*lisons*
lis	*lisez*
lit	*lisent*

manger / to eat

mange	*mangeons*
manges	*mangez*
mange	*mangent*

mettre / to place, put; to put on

mets	*mettons*
mets	*mettez*
met	*mettent*

mourir / to die

meurs	*mourons*
meurs	*mourez*
meurt	*meurent*

nager / to swim

nage	*nageons*
nages	*nagez*
nage	*nagent*

naître / to be born

nais	*naissons*
nais	*naissez*
naît	*naissent*

offrir / to offer

offre	*offrons*
offres	*offrez*
offre	*offrent*

ouvrir / to open

ouvre	*ouvrons*
ouvres	*ouvrez*
ouvre	*ouvrent*

partir / to leave

pars	*partons*
pars	*partez*
part	*partent*

pleuvoir | to rain

il pleut

---

pouvoir | to be able, can

peu<u>x</u> OR pui<u>s</u>	pouvons
peu<u>x</u>	pouvez
peu<u>t</u>	peuven<u>t</u>

---

préférer | to prefer

préf<u>è</u>re	préférons
préf<u>è</u>res	préférez
préf<u>è</u>re	préf<u>è</u>rent

---

prendre | to take

prends	prenons
prends	prenez
prend	prennent

---

protéger | to protect

prot<u>è</u>ge	protégeons
prot<u>è</u>ges	protégez
prot<u>è</u>ge	prot<u>è</u>gent

---

recevoir | to receive

reçoi<u>s</u>	recevons
reçoi<u>s</u>	recevez
reçoi<u>t</u>	reçoiven<u>t</u>

---

revenir | to return, come back (like *venir;* add *re-* at the beginning of *venir*)

---

rire | to laugh

ris	rions
ris	riez
rit	rient

---

savoir | to know (a fact)

sais	savons
sais	savez
sait	savent

servir / to serve

sers	*servons*
sers	*servez*
sert	*servent*

sortir / to go out; to leave

sors	*sortons*
sors	*sortez*
sort	*sortent*

tenir / to hold

tiens	*tenons*
tiens	*tenez*
tient	*tiennent*

venir / to come

viens	*venons*
viens	*venez*
vient	*viennent*

vivre / to live

vis	*vivons*
vis	*vivez*
vit	*vivent*

voir / to see

vois	*voyons*
vois	*voyez*
voit	*voient*

vouloir / to want

veux	*voulons*
veux	*voulez*
veut	*veulent*

voyager / to travel

voyage	*voyageons*
voyages	*voyagez*
voyage	*voyagent*

IMPERFECT INDICATIVE

---

apprendre / to learn

apprenais   apprenions
apprenais   appreniez
apprenait   apprenaient

---

boire / to drink

bu̱vais   bu̱vions
bu̱vais   bu̱viez
bu̱vait   bu̱vaient

---

commencer / to begin, to start

commençais   commencions
commençais   commenciez
commençait   commençaient

---

comprendre / to understand (like *prendre;* add *com* at the beginning of *prendre*)

---

conduire / to drive; to lead

condui̱sais   condui̱sions
condui̱sais   condui̱siez
condui̱sait   condui̱saient

---

connaître / to know, be acquainted with

connaissais   connaissions
connaissais   connaissiez
connaissait   connaissaient

---

courir / to run

courais   courions
courais   couriez
courait   couraient

---

croire / to believe

croy̱ais   croy̱ions
croy̱ais   croy̱iez
croy̱ait   croy̱aient

---

devenir / to become

devenais   devenions
devenais   deveniez
devenait   devenaient

---

devoir / to owe; to have to

devais	devions
devais	deviez
devait	devaient

---

dire / to say; to tell

disais	disions
disais	disiez
disait	disaient

---

dormir / to sleep

dormais	dormions
dormais	dormiez
dormais	dormaient

écrire / to write

écrivais	écrivions
écrivais	écriviez
écrivait	écrivaient

---

falloir / to be necessary

il fallait

---

lire / to read

lisais	lisions
lisais	lisiez
lisait	lisaient

---

manger / to eat

mangeais	mangions
mangeais	mangiez
mangeait	mangeaient

---

mourir / to die

mourais	mourions
mourais	mouriez
mourait	mouraient

---

nager / to swim

nageais	nagions
nageais	nagiez
nageait	nageaient

naître / to be born

naissais	*naissions*
naissais	*naissiez*
naissait	*naissaient*

offrir / to offer

offrais	*offrions*
offrais	*offriez*
offrait	*offraient*

ouvrir / to open

ouvrais	*ouvrions*
ouvrais	*ouvriez*
ouvrait	*ouvraient*

partir / to leave

partais	*partions*
partais	*partiez*
partait	*partaient*

pleuvoir / to rain

il pleuvait

prendre / to take

prenais	*prenions*
prenais	*preniez*
prenait	*prenaient*

protéger / to protect

protégeais	*protégions*
protégeais	*protégiez*
protégeait	*protégeaient*

revenir / to return, to come back
(like *venir;* add *re* at the beginning of *venir*)

rire / to laugh

riais	*riions*
riais	*riiez*
riait	*riaient*

savoir / to know (a fact)	
savais	savions
savais	saviez
savait	savaient

servir / to serve	
servais	servions
servais	serviez
servait	servaient

sortir / to go out; to leave	
sortais	sortions
sortais	sortiez
sortait	sortaient

tenir / to hold	
tenais	tenions
tenais	teniez
tenait	tenaient

venir / to come	
venais	venions
venais	veniez
venait	venaient

vivre / to live	
vivais	vivions
vivais	viviez
vivait	vivaient

voir / to see	
voyais	voyions
voyais	voyiez
voyait	voyaient

vouloir / to want	
voulais	voulions
voulais	vouliez
voulait	voulaient

voyager / to travel	
voyageais	voyagions
voyageais	voyagiez
voyageait	voyageaient

§7.18 BASIC NEGATIONS OF VERBS

The common negations of verbs are *ne* + verb + any of the following:

aucun, aucune / no, not one, not any

> *Je n'ai aucun livre.* / I have no book.
> *Robert n'a aucune amie.* / Robert has no girlfriend.

guère / hardly, scarcely

> *Paul ne parle guère.* / Paul hardly (scarcely) talks.

jamais / never

> *Jean n'étudie jamais.* / John never studies.

ni . . . ni / neither . . . nor

> *Je n'ai ni argent ni billet.* / I have neither money nor tickets.

nul, nulle / no, not any

> *Je n'en ai nul besoin.* / I have no need of it.
> *Je ne vais nulle part.* / I'm not going anywhere.

pas / not

> *Je n'ai pas de papier.* / I haven't any paper.

pas du tout / not at all

> *Je ne comprends pas du tout.* / I do not understand at all.

personne / nobody, no one, not anybody

> *Je ne vois personne.* / I don't see anybody. I see no one.

plus / any longer, no more, not any more

> *Mon père ne travaille plus.* / My father doesn't work any more.

point / not at all

> *Cet enfant n'a point d'argent.* / This child has no money at all.

que / only, but only

> *Je n'ai que deux francs.* / I have (but) only two francs.

rien / nothing

> *Je n'ai rien sur moi.* / I have nothing on me.

Note that all these negations require *ne* in front of the main verb. Also note that *aucun, aucune, nul, nulle, personne, rien* can be used as subjects and you still need to use *ne* in front of the verb.

> *Personne n'entend le bruit.* / Nobody hears the noise.
> *Rien n'est jamais parfait.* / Nothing is ever perfect.

Une devinette / a riddle

J'ai des yeux mais je n'ai pas de paupières et je vis dans l'eau. Qui suis-je? / I have eyes but I don't have eyelids and I live in the water. Who am I?

un poisson

---

§7.19 FOUR CONJUGATED VERBS

The following verbs—*aller, avoir, être,* and *faire*—have been fully conjugated in all their tenses because they are so frequently used.

aller / to go
Present participle: *allant*   Past participle: *allé(e)(s)*

THE SEVEN SIMPLE TENSES		THE SEVEN COMPOUND TENSES	
Singular	**Plural**	**Singular**	**Plural**
Present indicative		Past indefinite	
vais	*allons*	*suis allé(e)*	*sommes allé(e)s*
vas	*allez*	*es allé(e)*	*êtes allé(e)(s)*
va	*vont*	*est allé(e)*	*sont allé(e)s*
Imperfect indicative		Pluperfect OR Past perfect indicative	
allais	*allions*	*étais allé(e)*	*étions allé(e)s*
allais	*alliez*	*étais allé(e)*	*étiez allé(e)(s)*
allait	*allaient*	*était allé(e)*	*étaient allé(e)s*
Past definite		Past anterior	
allai	*allâmes*	*fus allé(e)*	*fûmes allé(e)s*
allas	*allâtes*	*fus allé(e)*	*fûtes allé(e)(s)*
alla	*allèrent*	*fut allé(e)*	*furent allé(e)s*
Future		Future perfect OR Future anterior	
irai	*irons*	*serai allé(e)*	*serons allé(e)s*
iras	*irez*	*seras allé(e)*	*serez allé(e)(s)*
ira	*iront*	*sera allé(e)*	*seront allé(e)s*
Conditional		Conditional perfect	
irais	*irions*	*serais allé(e)*	*serions allé(e)s*
irais	*iriez*	*serais allé(e)*	*seriez allé(e)(s)*
irait	*iraient*	*serait allé(e)*	*seraient allé(e)s*
Present subjunctive		Past subjunctive	
aille	*allions*	*sois allé(e)*	*soyons allé(e)s*
ailles	*alliez*	*sois allé(e)*	*soyez allé(e)(s)*
aille	*aillent*	*soit allé(e)*	*soient allé(e)s*
Imperfect subjunctive		Pluperfect OR Past perfect subjunctive	
allasse	*allassions*	*fusse allé(e)*	*fussions allé(e)s*
allasses	*allassiez*	*fusses allé(e)*	*fussiez allé(e)(s)*
allât	*allassent*	*fût allé(e)*	*fussent allé(e)s*

Imperative OR Command
va
allons
allez

Common idiomatic expressions using this verb:

Comment allez-vous? / Je vais bien (mal) (mieux).

aller à la pêche / to go fishing
aller à la rencontre de quelqu'un / to go to meet someone
aller à pied / to walk, to go on foot
aller au fond des choses / to get to the bottom of things
Ça va? / Is everything OK? *Oui, ça va!* / Yes, everything's OK.

For more idioms using *aller*, see §12.2.

| Mnemonic tip | *Un ver vert va vers un verre vert.* |

A green worm is going toward a green glass.

The words *ver, vers, vert, verre* are all pronounced the same as *ver* in the English word "very."

avoir / to have
Present participle: *ayant*   Past participle: *eu*

THE SEVEN SIMPLE TENSES		THE SEVEN COMPOUND TENSES	
Singular	**Plural**	**Singular**	**Plural**
Present indicative		*Past indefinite*	
ai	avons	ai eu	avons eu
as	avez	as eu	avez eu
a	ont	a eu	ont eu
Imperfect indicative		*Pluperfect* OR *Past perfect indicative*	
avais	avions	avais eu	avions eu
avais	aviez	avais eu	aviez eu
avait	avaient	avait eu	avaient eu
Past definite		*Past anterior*	
eus	eûmes	eus eu	eûmes eu
eus	eûtes	eus eu	eûtes eu
eut	eurent	eut eu	eurent eu
Future		*Future perfect* OR *Future anterior*	
aurai	aurons	aurai eu	aurons eu
auras	aurez	auras eu	aurez eu
aura	auront	aura eu	auront eu
Conditional		*Conditional perfect*	
aurais	aurions	aurais eu	aurions eu
aurais	auriez	aurais eu	auriez eu
aurait	auraient	aurait eu	auraient eu
Present subjunctive		*Past subjunctive*	
aie	ayons	aie eu	ayons eu
aies	ayez	aies eu	ayez eu
ait	aient	ait eu	aient eu
Imperfect subjunctive		*Pluperfect* OR *Past perfect subjunctive*	
eusse	eussions	eusse eu	eussions eu
eusses	eussiez	eusses eu	eussiez eu
eût	eussent	eût eu	eussent eu

Imperative OR *Command*
aie
ayons
ayez

Common idiomatic expressions using this verb:

avoir . . . ans / to be . . . years old
avoir à + infinitive / to have to, to be obliged to + inf.
avoir besoin de / to need, to have need of
avoir chaud / to be (feel) warm (persons)
avoir froid / to be (feel) cold (persons)
avoir sommeil / to be (feel) sleepy

avoir quelque chose à faire / to have something to do
avoir de la chance / to be lucky
avoir faim / to be hungry
avoir soif / to be thirsty
avoir honte / to be (feel) ashamed

For more idioms using *avoir*, see §12.2.

être / to be

Present participle: *étant*   Past participle: *été*

THE SEVEN SIMPLE TENSES		THE SEVEN COMPOUND TENSES	
Singular	**Plural**	**Singular**	**Plural**
Present indicative		*Past indefinite*	
suis	*sommes*	*ai été*	*avons été*
es	*êtes*	*as été*	*avez été*
est	*sont*	*a été*	*ont été*
Imperfect indicative		*Pluperfect* OR *Past perfect indicative*	
étais	*étions*	*avais été*	*avions été*
étais	*étiez*	*avais été*	*aviez été*
était	*étaient*	*avait été*	*avaient été*
Past definite		*Past anterior*	
fus	*fûmes*	*eus été*	*eûmes été*
fus	*fûtes*	*eus été*	*eûtes été*
fut	*furent*	*eut été*	*eurent été*
Future		*Future perfect* OR *Future anterior*	
serai	*serons*	*aurai été*	*aurons été*
seras	*serez*	*auras été*	*aurez été*
sera	*seront*	*aura été*	*auront été*
Conditional		*Conditional perfect*	
serais	*serions*	*aurais été*	*aurions été*
serais	*seriez*	*aurais été*	*auriez été*
serait	*seraient*	*aurait été*	*auraient été*
Present subjunctive		*Past subjunctive*	
sois	*soyons*	*aie été*	*ayons été*
sois	*soyez*	*aies été*	*ayez été*
soit	*soient*	*ait été*	*aient été*
Imperfect subjunctive		*Pluperfect* OR *Past perfect subjunctive*	
fusse	*fussions*	*eusse été*	*eussions été*
fusses	*fussiez*	*eusses été*	*eussiez été*
fût	*fussent*	*eût été*	*eussent été*

Imperative OR *Command*

sois

soyons

soyez

Common idiomatic expressions using this verb:

être en train de + infinitive / to be in the act of + present participle, to be in the process of, to be busy + present participle: *Mon père est en train d'écrire une lettre à mes grands-parents.* / My father is writing a letter to my grandparents.

être à l'heure / to be on time   *Je suis à vous.* / I am at your service.
être à temps / to be in time   *Je suis d'avis que . . .* / I am of the opinion that . . .
être pressé(e) / to be in a hurry   *être au courant de* / to be informed about

For more idioms using *être*, see §12.2.

faire / to do, to make
Present participle: *faisant*   Past participle: *fait*

THE SEVEN SIMPLE TENSES		THE SEVEN COMPOUND TENSES	
Singular	**Plural**	**Singular**	**Plural**
Present indicative		Past indefinite	
fais	faisons	ai fait	avons fait
fais	faites	as fait	avez fait
fait	font	a fait	ont fait
Imperfect indicative		Pluperfect OR Past perfect indicative	
faisais	faisions	avais fait	avions fait
faisais	faisiez	avais fait	aviez fait
faisait	faisaient	avait fait	avaient fait
Past definite		Past anterior	
fis	fîmes	eus fait	eûmes fait
fis	fîtes	eus fait	eûtes fait
fit	firent	eut fait	eurent fait
Future		Future perfect OR Future anterior	
ferai	ferons	aurai fait	aurons fait
feras	ferez	auras fait	aurez fait
fera	feront	aura fait	auront fait
Conditional		Conditional perfect	
ferais	ferions	aurais fait	aurions fait
ferais	feriez	aurais fait	auriez fait
ferait	feraient	aurait fait	auraient fait
Present subjunctive		Past subjunctive	
fasse	fassions	aie fait	ayons fait
fasses	fassiez	aies fait	ayez fait
fasse	fassent	ait fait	aient fait
Imperfect subjunctive		Pluperfect OR Past perfect subjunctive	
fisse	fissions	eusse fait	eussions fait
fisses	fissiez	eusses fait	eussiez fait
fît	fissent	eût fait	eussent fait

Imperative OR Command
fais
faisons
faites

Common idiomatic expressions using this verb:

faire beau / to be beautiful weather
faire chaud / to be warm weather
faire froid / to be cold weather
faire de l'autostop / to hitchhike
faire attention à quelqu'un ou à quelque chose / to pay attention to someone or something

For more idioms using *faire*, see §12.2.

§8.

Adverbs

DEFINITION An *adverb* is a word that modifies a verb, an adjective, or another adverb.

§8.1
FORMATION

Many French adverbs are not formed from another word, for example: *bien, mal, vite, combien, comment, pourquoi, où.*

There are many other adverbs that are formed from another word. The usual way is to add the suffix *-ment* to the masculine singular form of an adjective whose last letter is a vowel; for example: *probable, probablement; poli, poliment; vrai, vraiment.*

The suffix *-ment* is added to the feminine singular form if the masculine singular ends in a consonant; for example: *affreux, affreuse, affreusement; seul, seule, seulement; amer, amère, amèrement; franc, franche, franchement.*

The ending *-ment* is equivalent to the English ending "-ly": *lent, lente, lentement* / slow, slowly.

Some adjectives that end in *-ant* or *-ent* become adverbs by changing *-ant* to *-amment* and *-ent* to *-emment: innocent, innocemment; constant, constamment; récent, récemment.*

Some adverbs take *é* instead of *e* before adding *-ment: profond, profondément; confus, confusément; précis, précisément.*

The adjective *gentil* becomes *gentiment* as an adverb and *bref* becomes *brièvement.*

§8.2
POSITION

1. *David aime beaucoup les chocolats.*
2. *Paulette a parlé distinctement.*
3. *Julie a bien parlé.*

- In French, an adverb ordinarily follows the simple verb it modifies, as in the first model sentence above.
- If a verb is compound, as in the *past indefinite* (sentence 2), the adverb generally follows the past participle if it is a long adverb. The adverb *distinctement* is long. Some exceptions: *certainement, complètement,* and *probablement* are usually placed between the helping verb and the past participle: *Elle est probablement partie. Il a complètement fini le travail.*

111

- If a verb is compound, as in the *past indefinite* (sentence 3), short common adverbs (like *beaucoup, bien, déjà, encore, mal, mieux, souvent, toujours*) ordinarily precede the past participle; in other words, they may be placed between the helping verb and the past participle.
- For emphasis, an adverb may be placed at the beginning of a sentence: *Malheureusement, Suzanne est déjà partie.*

§8.3 TYPES

§8.3–1 Interrogative Adverbs

Some common interrogative adverbs are *comment, combien, pourquoi, quand, où*.

EXAMPLES
Comment allez-vous? Combien coûte ce livre? Pourquoi partez-vous? Quand arriverez-vous? Où allez-vous?

§8.3–2 Adverbs of Quantity

Some adverbial expressions of quantity are *beaucoup de, assez de, peu de, trop de, plus de*. With these, no article is used: *peu de sucre, beaucoup de travail, assez de temps, trop de lait, combien d'argent*.

§8.3–3 Comparative and Superlative Adverbs

Adverb	Comparative	Superlative
vite / quickly	*plus vite (que) /* more quickly (than) faster (than)	*le plus vite /* (the) most quickly, (the) fastest
	moins vite (que) / less quickly (than)	*le moins vite /* (the) least quickly
	aussi vite (que) / as quickly (as), as fast (as)	

EXAMPLES
Arlette parle plus vite que Marie-France. / Arlette speaks faster than Marie-France.
Madame Legrange parle moins vite que Madame Duval. / Madame Legrange speaks less quickly than Madame Duval.
Monsieur Bernard parle aussi vite que Monsieur Claude. / Monsieur Bernard speaks as fast as Monsieur Claude.

Madame Durocher parle le plus vite tandis que Madame Milot parle le moins vite. / Madame Durocher speaks the fastest whereas Madame Milot speaks the least fast (the slowest).
Aussi . . . que becomes *si . . . que* in a negative sentence.

EXAMPLE
Justin ne parle pas si vite que Justine. / Justin does not talk as fast as Justine.

Irregular Comparative and Superlative Adverbs

Adverb	Comparative	Superlative
bien / well	*mieux* / better	*le mieux* / best, the best
beaucoup / much	*plus* / more	*le plus* / most, the most
mal / badly	{ *plus mal* / worse *pis* / worse	{ *le plus mal* / worst, the worst *le moins bien* / the worst *le pis* / worst, the worst
peu / little	*moins* / less	*le moins* / least, the least

EXAMPLES
Pierre travaille bien, Henri travaille mieux que Robert et Georges travaille le mieux.
Marie étudie beaucoup, Paulette étudie plus que Marie, et Henriette étudie le plus.

§8.4
OUI AND *SI*

Ordinarily, *oui* is used to mean "yes." However, *si* can also be used to mean "yes" in response to a question in the negative.

EXAMPLES
Aimez-vous le français? —Oui, j'aime le français.
N'aimez-vous pas le français? —Si, j'aime le français.

| Mnemonic tip | *Une scie* (pronounced like the English "see") is a carpenter's "saw."

§9.

Prepositions — Special Uses

§9.1

Dans and *en* + a length of time

These two prepositions mean "in," but each is used in a different sense.

Dans + a length of time indicates that something will happen *at the end* of that length of time.

> *Le docteur va venir dans une demi-heure.* / The doctor will come in a half-hour (i.e., at the end of a half-hour).

Dans and a duration of time can be at the beginning of the sentence or at the end of it and future time is ordinarily implied.

En + a length of time indicates that something happened or will happen at any time *within* that length of time.

EXAMPLES
Robert a fait cela en une heure. / Robert did that in (within) an (one) hour.
Robert fera cela en une heure. / Robert will do that in (within) an (one) hour.

BUT

Robert fera cela dans une heure. / Robert will do that in (at the end of) an (one) hour.

§9.2

Envers and *vers*

Envers is used in a figurative sense in the meaning of "with regard to" someone, "with respect to" someone, "for" someone, or "for" something.

EXAMPLES
Je montre beaucoup de respect envers les vieilles personnes. / I show a lot of respect toward old persons.
Je ne montre aucun respect envers un criminel. / I show no respect toward a criminal.

Vers also means "toward," but is used in the physical sense (in the direction of) as well as in the figurative sense.

EXAMPLES

Pourquoi allez-vous vers la porte? / **Why are you going toward the door?**

Je vais partir vers trois heures. / **I am going to leave toward (around) three o'clock.**

§9.3   *Pendant* and *pour*

IN THE PRESENT TENSE

Combien de temps étudiez-vous chaque soir? / **How long do you study every evening?**

J'étudie une heure chaque soir. / **I study one hour each night. OR** *J'étudie pendant une heure chaque soir.* / **I study for one hour each night.**

IN THE PAST INDEFINITE

Combien de temps êtes-vous resté(e) à Paris? / **How long did you stay in Paris?**

Je suis resté(e) à Paris deux semaines. / **I stayed in Paris two weeks. OR** *Je suis resté(e) à Paris pendant deux semaines.* / **I stayed in Paris for two weeks.**

IN THE FUTURE

Combien de temps resterez-vous à Paris? / **How long will you stay in Paris?**

J'y resterai pendant deux semaines. / **I will stay there for two weeks. OR** *J'y resterai deux semaines.* / **I will stay there two weeks.**

§10.

Conjunctions

DEFINITION

A conjunction is a word that connects words, phrases, clauses, or sentences, such as *et* / and, *mais* / but, *ou* / or, *parce que* / because. The following is a list of the most common conjunctions.

Basic Conjunctions:

à moins que / unless
afin que / in order that, so that
aussitôt que / as soon as
avant que ' before
bien que / although
car / for
comme / as, since
de crainte que / for fear that
de peur que / for fear that
de sorte que / so that, in such a way that
depuis que / since
dès que / as soon as
donc / therefore, consequently
en même temps que at the same time as

et / and
jusqu'à ce que / until
lorsque / when, at the time when
maintenant que / now that
mais / but
ou / or
parce que / because
pendant le temps que / while
pendant que / while
pour que / in order that
pourvu que / provided that
puisque / since
quand / when
que / that
quoi que / whatever, no matter what
quoique / although
si / if
tandis que / while, whereas

| Mnemonic tip | Pronounce the final <u>c</u> in <u>donc</u> as a *k* when it means *c*onsequently (therefore). *Je pense; donc, je suis,* I think; therefore, I am. |

116

Special Topics

§11.

Order of Elements in French Sentences

Negative Constructions

Some common negative constructions are *ne* + verb + any of the following:

aucun (aucune) / no, not one, not any

> *Je n'ai aucun livre.* / I have no book.
> *Robert n'a aucune amie.* / Robert has no girlfriend.

guère / hardly, scarcely

> *Paul ne parle guère.* / Paul hardly (scarcely) talks.

jamais / never

> *Jean n'étudie jamais.* / John never studies.

ni . . . ni / neither . . . nor

> *Je n'ai ni argent ni billets.* / I have neither money nor tickets.

nul (nulle) / no, not any

> *Je n'en ai nul besoin.* / I have no need of it.
> *Je ne vais nulle part.* / I'm not going anywhere.

pas / not

> *Je n'ai pas de papier.* / I haven't any paper.

pas du tout / not at all

> *Je ne comprends pas du tout.* / I do not understand at all.

personne / nobody, no one, not anybody

> *Je ne vois personne.* / I don't see anybody. I see no one.

plus / any longer, no more, not anymore

> *Mon père ne travaille plus.* / My father doesn't work anymore.

point / not at all

> *Cet enfant n'a point d'argent.* / This child has no money at all.

que / only, but only

> *Je n'ai que deux francs.* / I have (but) only two francs.

rien / nothing

> *Je n'ai rien sur moi.* / I have nothing on me.

Remember that all these negations require *ne* in front of the main verb. Also note that *aucun (aucune)*, *nul (nulle)*, *personne*, and *rien* can be used as subjects, but you still need to use *ne* in front of the verb.

EXAMPLES

Personne n'est ici. / Nobody is here.
Rien n'est dans ce tiroir. / Nothing is in this drawer.

Une devinette
J'ai des yeux mais je n'ai pas de paupières et je vis dans l'eau. Qui suis-je? / I have eyes, but I don't have eyelids and I live in the water. Who am I?

> *un poisson* / a fish

Declarative Sentence with a Verb in a Simple Tense (e.g., present)

$$\textbf{SUBJECT} \rightarrow \textbf{\textit{ne (n')}} + \begin{Bmatrix} me\ (m') \\ te\ (t') \\ se\ (s') \\ nous \\ vous \end{Bmatrix} \text{ OR } \begin{Bmatrix} le \\ la \\ l' \\ les \end{Bmatrix} \text{ AND/OR } \begin{Bmatrix} lui \\ leur \end{Bmatrix}$$

OR *y* + *en* + **VERB** → *pas*

EXAMPLES

Il ne me les donne pas. / He is not giving them to me.
Je ne le leur donne pas. / I am not giving it to them.
Il n'y en a pas. / There aren't any of them.

Declarative Sentence with a Verb in a Compound Tense (e.g., *passé composé*)

$$\text{SUBJECT} \rightarrow \textbf{ne (n')} + \begin{Bmatrix} me\ (m') \\ te\ (t') \\ se\ (s') \\ nous \\ vous \end{Bmatrix} \text{OR} \begin{Bmatrix} le \\ la \\ l' \\ les \end{Bmatrix} \text{AND/OR} \begin{Bmatrix} lui \\ leur \end{Bmatrix}$$

OR *y* + *en* + **VERB** → *pas* + past participle
(auxiliary verb
avoir or *être* in
a simple tense)

EXAMPLES

Yvonne ne s'est pas lavée. / Yvonne did not wash herself.
Il ne m'en a pas envoyé. / He did not send any of them to me.
Je ne le lui ai pas donné. / I did not give it to him (to her).
Nous ne vous les avons pas données. / We have not given
  them to you.
Ils ne s'en sont pas allés. / They did not go away.

Affirmative Imperative Sentence

$$\textbf{VERB} + \begin{Bmatrix} le \\ la \\ l' \\ les \end{Bmatrix} \text{OR} \begin{Bmatrix} moi\ (m') \\ toi\ (t') \\ nous \\ vous \end{Bmatrix} \text{AND/OR} \begin{Bmatrix} lui \\ leur \end{Bmatrix} \text{OR } y + en$$

EXAMPLES

Donnez-les-leur. / Give them to them.
Assieds-toi. / Sit down.
Allez-vous-en! / Go away!
Apportez-le-moi! / Bring it to me!
Donnez-m'en! / Give me some!
Allez-y! / Go to it! Go there!

Negative Imperative Sentence

$$\mathbf{Ne\ (N')} + \begin{Bmatrix} me\ (m') \\ te\ (t') \\ nous \\ vous \end{Bmatrix} \text{OR} \begin{Bmatrix} le \\ la \\ l' \\ les \end{Bmatrix} \text{OR} \begin{Bmatrix} lui \\ leur \end{Bmatrix} \text{OR } y + en + \mathbf{VERB} \rightarrow \mathbf{pas}$$

EXAMPLES
Ne l'y mettez pas. / Do not put it in it. Do not put it there.
Ne les leur donnez pas. / Do not give them to them.
Ne t'assieds pas! / Don't sit down!
Ne vous en allez pas! / Don't go away!

| Mnemonic tip | Object pronouns fall in the right order if you alphabetize them!

The order is always the same, whether before or after a verb or before an infinitive.

§12.

Idioms

Depuis

- With the present indicative tense
  When an action of some sort began in the past and is still going on in the present, use the present tense with *depuis* + the length of time.

  Je travaille dans ce bureau depuis trois ans. / I have been working in this office for three years.

  > Use *depuis combien de temps* + the present indicative of the verb to ask how long one has been + verb:
  > *Depuis combien de temps travaillez-vous dans ce bureau?* / How long have you been working in this office? *Je travaille dans ce bureau depuis un an.* / I have been working in this office for one year.

- With the imperfect indicative tense
  When an action of some sort began in the past and continued up to another point in the past that you are telling about, use the imperfect indicative tense with depuis + the length of time:

  J'attendais l'autobus depuis vingt minutes quand il est arrivé. / I had been waiting for the bus for twenty minutes when it arrived.

- In a question
  Depuis combien de temps

  Depuis combien de temps attendez-vous l'autobus? / How long have you been waiting for the bus?
  J'attends l'autobus depuis vingt minutes. / I have been waiting for the bus for twenty minutes.

  Note: When you use *depuis combien de temps* in a question, you expect the other person to tell you how long, how much time — how many minutes, how many hours, how many days, weeks, months, years, etc.

121

- *Depuis quand*

  Depuis quand habitez-vous cet appartement? / **Since when have you been living in this apartment?**
  J'habite cet appartement depuis le premier septembre. / **I have been living in this apartment since September first.**

  Note: When you use *depuis quand* in your question, you expect the other person to tell you since what particular point in time in the past — a particular day, date, month; in other words, since *when,* not *how long.*

  Depuis quand êtes-vous malade? / **Since when have you been sick?**
  Je suis malade depuis samedi. / **I have been sick since Saturday.**
  Depuis quand habitiez-vous l'appartement quand vous avez déménagé? / **Since when had you been living in the apartment when you moved?**
  J'habitais l'appartement depuis le cinq avril dernier quand j'ai déménagé. / **I had been living in the apartment since last April fifth, when I moved.**

Il y a + Length of Time + *que; voici* + Length of Time + *que; voilà* + Length of Time + *que*

- **In Questions and Answers**

  Depuis combien de temps attendez-vous l'autobus? / **How long have you been waiting for the bus?**
  J'attends l'autobus depuis vingt minutes. / **I have been waiting for the bus for twenty minutes.**
  Voici vingt minutes que je l'attends. / **I have been waiting for it for twenty minutes.**
  Voilà vingt minutes que je l'attends. / **I have been waiting for it for twenty minutes.**

  Note: When you use these expressions, you generally use them at the beginning of your answer + the verb.
  When you use the *depuis* construction, the verb comes first: *J'attends l'autobus depuis vingt minutes.*

- *Il y a* + length of time
  Il y a + length of time means "ago." Do not use *que* in this construction as in the above examples because the meaning is entirely different.

  Madame Martin est partie il y a une heure. / **Mrs. Martin left an hour ago.**
  L'autobus est arrivé il y a vingt minutes. / **The bus arrived twenty minutes ago.**

- *Il y a* and *Il y avait*

   Il y a alone means "there is" or "there are" when you are merely making a statement.

   > *Il y a vingt élèves dans cette classe.* / There are twenty students in this class.
   > *Il y a une mouche dans la soupe.* / There is a fly in the soup.

   Il y avait alone means "there was" or "there were" when you are merely making a statement.

   > *Il y avait vingt élèves dans cette classe.* / There were (used to be) twenty students in this class.
   > *Il y avait deux mouches dans la soupe.* / There were two flies in the soup.

Voici and *Voilà*

These two expressions are used to point out someone or something.

> *Voici un taxi!* / Here's a taxi!
> *Voilà un taxi là-bas!* / There's a taxi over there!
> *Voici ma carte d'identité et voilà mon passeport.* / Here's my ID card and there's my passport.
> *Voici mon père et voilà ma mère.* / Here's my father and there's my mother.

§12.2 BASIC EX-PRESSIONS

With *à*

à bicyclette / by bicycle, on a bicycle	*à haute voix* / aloud, out loud, in a loud voice
à bientôt / so long, see you soon	*à jamais* / forever
à cause de / on account of, because of	*à l'école* / at (in, to) school
à cette heure / at this time, at the present moment	*à l'étranger* / abroad, overseas
à cheval / on horseback	*à l'heure* / on time
à côté de / beside, next to	*à l'instant* / instantly
à demain / until tomorrow, see you tomorrow	*à l'occasion* / on the occasion
à droite / at (on, to) the right	*à la campagne* / at (in, to) the country(side)
à gauche / at (on, to) the left	*à la fin* / at last, finally
	à la fois / at the same time
	à la main / in one's hand, by hand
	à la maison / at home

à la mode / fashionable, in style, in fashion
à la radio / on the radio
à la recherche de / in search of
à la télé / on TV
à mon avis / in my opinion
à part / aside
à partir de / beginning with
à peine / hardly, scarcely
à peu près / approximately, about, nearly
à pied / on foot
à plus tard / see you later
à présent / now, at present
à propos / by the way
à propos de / about, with reference to, concerning
à quelle heure? / at what time?

à qui est ce livre? / whose is this book?
à quoi bon? / what's the use?
à son gré / to one's liking
à temps / in time
à tour de rôle / in turn
à tout à l'heure / see you in a little while
à tout prix / at any cost
à travers / across, through
à tue-tête / at the top of one's voice, as loud as possible
à vélo / on a bike
à voix basse / in a low voice, softly
à volonté / at will, willingly
à vrai dire / to tell the truth
à vue d'œil / visibly

With *au*

au bas de / at the bottom of
au besoin / if need be, if necessary
au bout de / at the end of, at the tip of
au contraire / on the contrary
au début / at (in) the beginning
au-dessous de / below, beneath
au-dessus de / above, over
au fond de / in the bottom of
au haut de / at the top of
au lieu de / instead of

au milieu de / in the middle of
au moins / at least
au pied de / at the foot of
au printemps / in the spring
au revoir / goodbye
au sous-sol / in the basement
au sujet de / about, concerning
au téléphone / on the telephone
café au lait / coffee with milk
rosbif au jus / roast beef with gravy

With *aux*

aux dépens / at the expense	*rire aux éclats* / to roar with laughter
aux pommes frites / with French fries	*sauter aux yeux* / to be evident, self-evident

With *aller*

aller / to feel (health): *Comment allez-vous?*	*aller à la rencontre de quelqu'un* / to go to meet someone
aller à / to be becoming, fit, suit: *Cette robe lui va bien.* / This dress suits her fine. *Sa barbe ne lui va pas.* / His beard does not look good on him.	*aller à pied* / to walk, go on foot
	aller au fond des choses / to get to the bottom of things
aller à la chasse / to go hunting	*aller chercher* / to go get
aller à la pêche / to go fishing	*allons donc!* / nonsense! come on, now!

With *avoir*

avoir . . . ans / to be . . . years old: *Quel âge — avez-vous?* / J'ai dix-sept ans.	*avoir besoin de* / to need, to have need of
avoir à + infinitive / to have to	*avoir bonne mine* / to look well
avoir affaire à quelqu'un / to deal with someone	*avoir chaud* / to be (feel) warm (persons)
avoir beau + infinitive / to be useless + infinitive, to do something in vain: *Vous avez beau parler; je ne vous écoute pas.* / You are talking in vain; I am not listening to you.	*avoir congé* / to have a day off, a holiday
	avoir de la chance / to be lucky
	avoir de quoi + infinitive / to have the material, means, enough + infinitive: *As-tu de quoi manger?* / Have you something (enough) to eat?

avoir des nouvelles / to receive news

avoir du savoir-faire / to have tact

avoir du savoir-vivre / to have good manners

avoir envie de + infinitive / to have a desire to

avoir faim / to be (feel) hungry

avoir froid / to be (feel) cold (persons)

avoir hâte / to be in a hurry

avoir honte / to be ashamed, to feel ashamed

avoir l'air + adjective / to seem, to look + adjective: *Vous avez l'air malade.* / You look sick.

avoir l'air de + infinitive / to appear + infinitive: *Vous avez l'air d'être malade.* / You appear to be sick.

avoir l'habitude de + infinitive / to be accustomed to, to be in the habit of: *J'ai l'habitude de faire mes devoirs avant le dîner.* / I'm in the habit of doing my homework before dinner.

avoir l'idée de + infinitive / to have a notion + infinitive

avoir l'intention de + infinitive / to intend + infinitive

avoir la bonté de + infinitive / to have the kindness

avoir la langue bien pendue / to have the gift of gab

avoir la parole / to have the floor (to speak)

avoir le cœur gros / to be heartbroken

avoir le temps de + infinitive / to have (the) time + infinitive

avoir lieu / to take place

avoir mal / to feel sick

avoir mal à + (place where it hurts) / to have a pain or ache in . . . : *J'ai mal à la jambe.* / My leg hurts. *J'ai mal au dos.* / My back hurts. *J'ai mal au cou.* / I have a pain in the neck.

avoir mauvaise mine / to look ill, not to look well

avoir peine à + infinitive / to have difficulty in + present participle

avoir peur de / to be afraid of

avoir pitié de / to take pity on

avoir raison / to be right (persons)

avoir soif / to be thirsty

avoir sommeil / to be sleepy

avoir son mot à dire / to have one's way

avoir tort / to be wrong (persons)

avoir une faim de loup / to be starving

With *bas*

au bas de / at the bottom of	*parler tout bas* / to speak very softly
en bas / downstairs, below	*de haut en bas* / from top to bottom
là-bas / over there	
A bas les devoirs! / Down with homework!	

With *bien*

bien des / many: *Roger a bien des amis.* / Roger has many friends.	*être bien aise* / to be very glad, happy
bien entendu / of course	*tant bien que mal* / rather badly, so-so
dire du bien de / to speak well of	

With *bon*

à quoi bon? / what's the use?	*de bon appétit* / with good appetite, heartily
bon gré, mal gré / willing or not, willy nilly	*de bon cœur* / gladly, willingly
bon marché / cheap, at a low price	*savoir bon gré à quelqu'un* / to be thankful, grateful to someone
bon pour quelqu'un / good to someone	

With *ça*

çà et là / here and there	*Ça va?* / Is everything okay?
Ça m'est égal. / It makes no difference to me.	*C'est comme ça!* / That's how it is!
comme ci, comme ça / so-so	*Pas de ça!* / None of that!

With *cela*

Cela est égal. / It's all the same. It doesn't matter. It makes no difference.

Cela m'est égal. / It doesn't matter to me. It's all the same to me.

Cela n'importe. / That doesn't matter.

Cela ne fait rien. / That makes no difference.

Cela ne sert à rien. / That serves no purpose.

Cela ne vous regarde pas. / That's none of your business.

malgré cela / in spite of that

malgré tout cela / in spite of all that

Qu'est-ce que cela veut dire? / What does that mean?

With *ce, c'est, est-ce*

c'est-à-dire / that is, that is to say

C'est aujourd'hui lundi. / Today is Monday.

C'est dommage. / It's a pity. It's too bad.

C'est entendu. / It's understood. It's agreed. All right. OK.

C'est épatant! / It's wonderful!

C'est trop fort! / That's just too much!

n'est-ce pas? / isn't that so? isn't it?, etc.

Qu'est-ce que c'est? / What is it?

Quel jour est-ce aujourd'hui? / What day is it today? C'est lundi. / It's Monday.

Qu'est-ce qui s'est passé? / What happened?

With *d'*

comme d'habitude / as usual

d'abord / at first

d'accord / okay, agreed

d'ailleurs / besides, moreover

d'aujourd'hui en huit / a week from today

d'avance / in advance, beforehand

d'habitude / ordinarily, usually, generally

d'ici longtemps / for a long time to come

d'ordinaire / ordinarily, usually, generally

changer d'avis / to
change one's opinion,
one's mind

tout d'un coup / all of a
sudden

With *de*

au haut de / at the top of
autour de / around

changer de train / to
change trains: *changer
de vêtements* / to
change clothes
combien de / how much,
how many

de bon appétit / with
good appetite, heartily
de bon cœur / gladly,
willingly
de bonne heure / early
de cette façon / in this way
de jour en jour / from day
to day
de l'autre côté de / on the
other side of
de la part de / on behalf
of, from
de nouveau / again
de parti pris / on purpose,
deliberately
de plus / furthermore
de plus en plus / more
and more
*de quelle cou-
leur . . . ?* / what
color . . . ?
de quoi + infinitive /
something, enough +
infinitive: *de quoi
écrire* / something to
write with; *de quoi
manger* / something or
enough to eat; *de quoi
vivre* / something or
enough to live on

de rien / you're welcome,
don't mention it
de rigueur / required,
obligatory
de son mieux / one's best
de suite / one after
another, in succession
de temps en temps / from
time to time, occasion-
ally
de toutes ses forces /
with all one's might,
strenuously
du côté de / in the
direction of, toward
éclater de rire / to burst
out laughing
en face de / opposite
entendre parler de / to
hear about
être de retour / to be back
être en train de / to be in
the act of, in the
process of
être temps de + infinitive /
to be time + infinitive
faire semblant de +
infinitive / to pretend +
infinitive
*féliciter quelqu'un de
quelque chose* / to
congratulate someone
for something
Il n'y a pas de quoi! /
You're welcome!
jamais de la vie! / never
in one's life! never! out
of the question!

jouer de / to play (a musical instrument)

manquer de + infinitive / to fail to, to almost do something: *Victor a manqué de se noyer.* / Victor almost drowned.

mettre de côté / to lay aside, to save

pas de mal! / no harm!

près de / near

quelque chose de + adjective / something + adjective: *J'ai bu quelque chose de bon!* / I drank something good!

Quoi de neuf? / What's new?

Rien de neuf! / Nothing's new!

tout de même / all the same

tout de suite / immediately, at once

venir de + infinitive / to have just done something; *Je viens de manger.* / I have just eaten.

With *du*

dire du bien de quelqu'un / to speak well of someone

dire du mal de quelqu'un / to speak ill of someone

donner du chagrin à quelqu'un / to give someone grief

du côté de / in the direction of, toward

du matin au soir / from morning until night

du moins / at least

du reste / besides, in addition, furthermore

montrer du doigt / to point out, to show, to indicate by pointing

pas du tout / not at all

With *en*

de jour en jour / from day to day

de temps en temps / from time to time

en anglais, en français, etc. / in English, in French, etc.

en arrière / backwards, to the rear, behind

en automne, en hiver, en été / in the fall, in winter, in summer

en automobile / by car

en avion / by plane

en avoir plein le dos / to be sick and tired of something

en bas / downstairs, below

en bateau / by boat

en bois, en pierre, en + a material / made of wood, of stone, etc.

en chemin de fer / by train

en dessous (de) / underneath

en dessus (de) / above, on top, over

en effet / in fact, indeed, yes, indeed

en face de / opposite

en famille / as a family

en haut / upstairs, above

en huit jours / in a week

en même temps / at the same time

en panne / mechanical breakdown

en plein air / in the open air, outdoors

en retard / late, not on time

en tout cas / in any case, at any rate

en toute hâte / with all possible speed, haste

en ville / downtown, in (at, to) town

En voilà assez! / Enough of that!

en voiture / by car: *en voiture!* / all aboard!

être en train de + infinitive / to be in the act of + present participle, to be in the process of, to be busy + present participle

Je vous en prie. / I beg you. You're welcome.

mettre en pièces / to tear to pieces, to break into pieces

voir tout en rose / to see the bright side of things, to be optimistic

With *être*

être à l'heure / to be on time

être à quelqu'un / to belong to someone: *Ce livre est à moi.* / This book belongs to me.

être au courant de / to be informed about

être bien / to be comfortable

être d'accord avec / to agree with

être de retour / to be back

être en retard / to be late, not to be on time

être en train de + infinitive / to be in the act of, to be in the process of, to be busy + present participle

être en vacances / to be on vacation

être enrhumé / to have a cold, be sick with a cold

être pressé(e) / to be in a hurry

Quelle heure est-il? /What time is it? *Il est une heure.* / It is one o'clock. *Il est deux heures.* / It is two o'clock

With *faire*

Cela ne fait rien. / That doesn't matter.

Comment se fait-il? / How come?

faire à sa tête / to have one's way

faire attention (à) / to pay attention (to)

faire beau / to be pleasant, nice weather

faire bon accueil / to welcome

faire chaud / to be warm (weather)

faire de l'autostop / to hitchhike

faire de son mieux / to do one's best

faire des châteaux en Espagne / to build castles in the air

faire des emplettes; faire des courses; faire du shopping / to do or to go shopping

faire des progrès / to make progress

faire du bien à quelqu'un / to do good for someone

faire du vélo / to ride a bike

faire exprès / to do on purpose

faire face à / to oppose

faire froid / to be cold (weather)

faire jour / to be daylight

faire la bête / to act like a fool

faire la connaissance de quelqu'un / to make the acquaintance of someone, meet someone for the first time

faire la cuisine / to do the cooking

faire la grasse matinée / to sleep late in the morning

faire la lessive / to do the laundry

faire (une) la malle / to pack (a) the trunk

faire la queue / to line up, to get in line, to stand in line

faire la vaisselle / to do (wash) the dishes

faire le ménage / to do housework

faire les bagages / to pack the baggage, luggage

faire les valises / to pack the suitcases, valises

faire mal à quelqu'un / to hurt, to harm someone

faire nuit / to be night(time)

faire peur à quelqu'un / to frighten someone

faire plaisir à quelqu'un / to please someone

faire sa toilette / to wash and dress oneself

faire ses adieux / to say goodbye

faire son possible / to do one's best

faire suivre le courrier / to forward mail

faire un tour / to go for a stroll

faire un voyage / to take a trip

faire une partie de / to play a game of

faire une promenade / to take a walk

faire une visite / to pay a visit

faire venir quelqu'un / to have someone come: *Il a fait venir le docteur.* / He had the doctor come.

faire venir l'eau à la bouche / to make one's mouth water

Faites comme chez vous! / Make yourself at home!

Que faire? / What is to be done?

Quel temps fait-il? / What's the weather like?

With *mieux*

aimer mieux / to prefer, like better

aller mieux / to feel better (person's health): *Êtes-vous toujours malade?* / Are you still sick? *Je vais mieux, merci.* / I'm feeling better, thank you.

de son mieux / one's best

faire de son mieux / to do one's best

tant mieux / so much the better

valoir mieux / to be better (worth more), to be preferable

With *non*

Je crois que non. / I don't think so.

Mais non! / Of course not!

Non merci! / No, thank you!

J'espère bien que non. / I hope not.

With *par*

par bonheur / fortunately

par-ci; par-là / here and there

par conséquent / consequently, therefore

par exemple / for example

par hasard / by chance

par ici / through here, this way, in this direction

par jour / per day, daily

par la fenêtre / out, through the window

par-là / through there, that way, in that direction

par malheur / unfortunately

par mois / per month, monthly

par semaine / per week, weekly

par tous les temps / in all kinds of weather

apprendre par cœur / to learn by heart, memorize

finir par + infinitive / to end up + present participle: *Ils ont fini par se marier.* / They ended up by getting married.

jeter l'argent par la fenêtre / to waste money

With *plus*

de plus / furthermore, besides, in addition

de plus en plus / more and more

n'en pouvoir plus / to be exhausted, not to be able to go on any longer: *Je n'en peux plus!* / I can't go on any longer!

Plus ça change plus c'est la même chose. / The more it changes, the more it remains the same.

une fois de plus / once more, one more time

With *quel*

Quel âge avez-vous? / How old are you?

Quel garçon! / What a boy!

Quel jour est-ce aujourd'hui? / What day is it today?

With *quelle*

De quelle couleur est (sont) . . . ? / What color is (are) . . . ?

Quelle fille! / What a girl!

Quelle heure est-il? / What time is it?

Quelle chance! / What luck!

With *quelque chose*

quelque chose à + infinitive / something + infinitive: *J'ai quelque chose à lui dire.* / I have something to say to him (to her).	*quelque chose de* + adjective / something + adjective: *J'ai quelque chose d'intéressant à vous dire.* / I have something interesting to tell you.

With *quoi*

à quoi bon? / what's the use? *avoir de quoi* + infinitive / to have something (enough) + infinitive: *Avez-vous de quoi écrire?* / Do you have something to write with?	*avoir de quoi manger* / to have something to eat *Il n'y a pas de quoi!* / You're welcome! *Quoi de neuf?* / What's new?

With *rien*

Cela ne fait rien. / That doesn't matter. *Cela ne sert à rien.* / That serves no purpose.	*de rien* / you're welcome, don't mention it *Rien de neuf!* / Nothing's new!

With *tant*

tant bien que mal / so-so *tant mieux* / so much the better *tant pis* / so much the worse *J'ai tant de travail!* / I have so much work!	*Je t'aime tant!* / I love you so much! *tant de choses* / so many things

With *tous*

tous (les) deux / both (m. plural)	*tous les soirs* / every evening
tous les ans / every year	*tous les mois* / every month
tous les jours / every day	
tous les matins / every morning	

With *tout*

après tout / after all	*tout d'un coup* / all of a sudden
en tout cas / in any case, at any rate	*tout de même!* / all the same! just the same!
pas du tout / not at all	*tout de suite* / immedi- ately, at once, right away
tout à coup / suddenly	
tout à fait / completely, entirely	
tout à l'heure / a little while ago, in a little while	*tout le monde* / everybody
tout d'abord / first of all	*tout le temps* / all the time

With *toute*

en toute hâte / with all possible speed, in great haste	*toutes (les) deux* / both (f. plural)
toute chose / everything	*toutes les nuits* / every night
de toutes ses forces / with all one's might	

With *y*

il y a + length of time / ago: *il y a un mois* / a month ago	*Il n'y a pas de quoi.* / You're welcome.
il y a / there is, there are	*y compris* / including
il y avait . . . / there was (there were) . . .	

§13.

Dates, Days, Months, Seasons

Dates

Quelle est la date aujourd'hui? / What's the date today?
Quel jour sommes-nous aujourd'hui? / What's the date today?

C'est aujourd'hui le premier octobre. / Today is October first.
C'est aujourd'hui le deux novembre. / Today is November second.

C'est lundi. / It's Monday.
C'est aujourd'hui mardi. / Today is Tuesday.

Quand êtes-vous né(e)? / When were you born?
Je suis né(e) le vingt-deux août, mil neuf cent soixante-six. / I was born on August 22, 1966.

Use the cardinal numbers for dates, except "the first," which is *le premier.*

Days

The days of the week, which are all masculine, are:

dimanche / Sunday
lundi / Monday
mardi / Tuesday
mercredi / Wednesday

jeudi / Thursday
vendredi / Friday
samedi / Saturday

Months

The months of the year, which are all masculine, are:

janvier / January
février / February
mars / March
avril / April
mai / May
juin / June

juillet / July
août / August
septembre / September
octobre / October
novembre / November
décembre / December

To say "in" + the name of the month, use *en: en janvier, en février;* OR *au mois de janvier, au mois de février* / in the month of January, etc.

§13.4

Seasons

The seasons of the year, which are all masculine, are:

le printemps / spring   *l'automne* / fall
l'été / summer   *l'hiver* / winter

| Mnemonic tip | *En hiver,* you shiver. |

To say "in" + the name of the season, use *en* except with *printemps: au printemps, en été, en automne, en hiver* / in spring, in summer, etc.

§14.

Telling Time

Il est une heure et demie.

§14.1
TIME EX-
PRESSIONS
YOU OUGHT
TO KNOW

Quelle heure est-il? / What time is it?
Il est une heure. / It is one o'clock.
Il est une heure dix. / It is ten minutes after one.
Il est une heure et quart. / It is a quarter after one.
Il est deux heures et demie. / It is half past two; it is
two thirty.
Il est trois heures moins vingt. / It is twenty minutes to
three.
Il est trois heures moins le quart. / It is a quarter to three.
Il est midi. / It is noon.
Il est minuit. / It is midnight.
à quelle heure? / at what time?
à une heure / at one o'clock
à une heure précise / at exactly one o'clock
à deux heures précises / at exactly two o'clock
à neuf heures du matin / at nine in the morning
à trois heures de l'après-midi / at three in the afternoon
à dix heures du soir / at ten in the evening
à l'heure / on time
à temps / in time
vers trois heures / around three o'clock; about three
o'clock
un quart d'heure / a quarter of an hour; a quarter hour
une demi-heure / a half hour
Il est midi et demi / It is twelve thirty; It is half past
twelve (noon).
Il est minuit et demi. / It is twelve thirty; It is half past
twelve (midnight).

- In telling time, *Il est* + the hour is used, whether it is one or
  more than one, e.g., *Il est une heure. Il est deux heures.*

- If the time is after the hour, state the hour, then the minutes:
  Il est une heure dix.

- The conjunction *et* is used with *quart* after the hour and
  with *demi* or *demie: Il est une heure et quart. Il est une
  heure et demie. Il est midi et demi.*

139

The masculine form *demi* is used after a masculine noun: *Il est midi et demi.* The feminine form *demie* is used after a feminine noun: *Il est deux heures et demie.*

Demi remains *demi* when before a feminine or masculine noun, and is joined to the noun with a hyphen: *une demi-heure.*

- If the time expressed is before the hour, *moins* is used: *Il est trois heures moins vingt.*

- A quarter after the hour is *et quart;* a quarter to the hour is *moins le quart.*

- To express A.M. use *du matin;* to express P.M. use *de l'après-midi* if the time is in the afternoon; *du soir* if in the evening.

§14.2 "OFFICIAL" TIME EXPRESSIONS

Another way to tell time is the official time used by the French government on radio and TV, in railroad and bus stations, and at airports.

- It is the twenty-four-hour system.

- In this system, *quart, demi, demie, moins,* and *et* are not used.

- When you hear or see the stated time, subtract twelve from the number you hear or see. If the number is less than twelve, it is A.M. time, except for *24 heures,* which is midnight; *zéro heure* is also midnight.

EXAMPLES

> *Il est treize heures.* / It is 1:00 P.M.
> *Il est quinze heures.* / It is 3:00 P.M.
> *Il est vingt heures trente.* / It is 8:30 P.M.
> *Il est minuit.* / It is midnight.
> *It est seize heures trente.* / It is 4:30 P.M.
> *Il est dix-huit heures quinze.* / It is 6:15 P.M.
> *Il est vingt heures quarante-cinq.* / It is 8:45 P.M.
> *Il est vingt-deux heures cinquante.* / It is 10:50 P.M.

The abbreviation for *heure* or *heures* is *h.*

EXAMPLES

> *Il est 20 h. 20.* / It is 8:20 P.M.
> *Il est 15 h. 50.* / It is 3:50 P.M.
> *Il est 23 h. 30.* / It is 11:30 P.M.

Talking About the Weather

Quel temps fait-il? / What's the weather like?

WITH *Il fait* . . .

Il fait beau. / The weather is fine. The weather is beautiful.
Il fait beau temps. / The weather is beautiful.
Il fait chaud. / It's warm.
Il fait clair. / It is clear.
Il fait doux. / It's mild.
Il fait du soleil. / It's sunny. (You can also say *Il fait soleil.*)
Il fait du tonnerre. / It's thundering. (OR: *Il tonne.*)
Il fait du vent. / It's windy.
Il fait frais. / It is cool.
Il fait froid. / It's cold.
Il fait humide. / It's humid.
Il fait mauvais. / The weather is bad.

WITH *Il fait un temps* . . .

Il fait un temps affreux. / The weather is frightful.
Il fait un temps calme. / The weather is calm.
Il fait un temps couvert. / The weather is cloudy.
Il fait un temps lourd. / It's muggy.
Il fait un temps magnifique. / The weather is magnificent.
Il fait un temps superbe. / The weather is superb.

WITH *Le temps* + VERB . . .

Le temps menace. / The weather is threatening.
Le temps se gâte. / The weather is getting bad.
Le temps se met au beau. / The weather is getting beautiful.
Le temps se met au froid. / It's getting cold.
Le temps se rafraîchit. / The weather is getting cool.

WITH *Le ciel est* . . .

Le ciel est bleu. / The sky is blue.
Le ciel est calme. / The sky is calm.
Le ciel est couvert. / The sky is cloudy.
Le ciel est gris. / The sky is gray.

WITH OTHER VERBS

Il gèle. / It's freezing.
Il grêle. / It's hailing.
Il neige. / It's snowing.
Il pleut. / It's raining.
Il tombe de la grêle. / It's hailing.

§16.

Numbers

Cardinal Numbers: 1 to 1000

0 *zéro* 1 *un, une* 2 *deux* 3 *trois*	70 *soixante-dix* 71 *soixante et onze* 72 *soixante-douze*, etc.
4 *quatre* 5 *cinq* 6 *six* 7 *sept*	80 *quatre-vingts* 81 *quatre-vingt-un* 82 *quatre-vingt-deux*, etc.
8 *huit* 9 *neuf* 10 *dix* 11 *onze* 12 *douze*	90 *quatre-vingt-dix* 91 *quatre-vingt-onze* 92 *quatre-vingt-douze*, etc.
13 *treize* 14 *quatorze* 15 *quinze*	100 *cent* 101 *cent un* 102 *cent deux*, etc.
16 *seize* 17 *dix-sept* 18 *dix-huit* 19 *dix-neuf*	200 *deux cents* 201 *deux cent un* 202 *deux cent deux*, etc.
20 *vingt* 21 *vingt et un* 22 *vingt-deux*, etc.	300 *trois cents* 301 *trois cent un* 302 *trois cent deux*, etc.
30 *trente* 31 *trente et un* 32 *trente-deux*, etc.	400 *quatre cents* 401 *quatre cent un* 402 *quatre cent deux*, etc.
40 *quarante* 41 *quarante et un* 42 *quarante-deux*, etc.	500 *cinq cents* 501 *cinq cent un* 502 *cinq cent deux*, etc.
50 *cinquante* 51 *cinquante et un* 52 *cinquante-deux*, etc.	600 *six cents* 601 *six cent un* 602 *six cent deux*, etc.
60 *soixante* 61 *soixante et un* 62 *soixante-deux*, etc.	700 *sept cents* 701 *sept cent un* 702 *sept cent deux*, etc.

800 *huit cents* 801 *huit cent un* 802 *huit cent deux*, etc.	**Mnemonic tip** If you're not sure that *vingt* is spelled with *ng* or *gn*, note this:
900 *neuf cents* 901 *neuf cent un* 902 *neuf cent deux*, etc.	*V I* | *N* | *G T* T W E | N | T Y
1000 *mille*	

Mnemonic tip Pronounce *seize* (16) as in English "**Says who?**"

Simple Arithmetical Expressions

deux et deux font quatre	$2 + 2 = 4$
trois fois cinq font quinze	$3 \times 5 = 15$
douze moins dix font deux	$12 - 10 = 2$
dix divisés par deux font cinq	$10 \div 2 = 5$

Fractions

½	*un demi*	a (one) half
⅓	*un tiers*	a (one) third
¼	*un quart*	a (one) fourth
⅕	*un cinquième*	a (one) fifth

Approximate Amounts

une dizaine	about ten
une quinzaine	about fifteen
une vingtaine	about twenty
une trentaine	about thirty
une quarantaine	about forty
une cinquantaine	about fifty
une soixantaine	about sixty
une centaine	about a hundred
un millier	about a thousand

Mnemonic tip You can remember that *une quarantaine* is about 40 because there are 40 days in a "quarantine."

Ordinal Numbers: First to Twentieth

first	premier, première	1st	1er, 1re
second	deuxième (second, seconde)	2d	2^{e}
third	troisième	3d	3^{e}
fourth	quatrième	4th	4^{e}
fifth	cinquième	5th	5^{e}
sixth	sixième	6th	6^{e}
seventh	septième	7th	7^{e}
eighth	huitième	8th	8^{e}
ninth	neuvième	9th	9^{e}
tenth	dixième	10th	10^{e}
eleventh	onzième	11th	11^{e}
twelfth	douzième	12th	12^{e}
thirteenth	treizième	13th	13^{e}
fourteenth	quatorzième	14th	14^{e}
fifteenth	quinzième	15th	15^{e}
sixteenth	seizième	16th	16^{e}
seventeenth	dix-septième	17th	17^{e}
eighteenth	dix-huitième	18th	18^{e}
nineteenth	dix-neuvième	19th	19^{e}
twentieth	vingtième	20th	20^{e}

Some observations:

- You must learn the difference between cardinal and ordinal numbers. If you have trouble distinguishing between the two, just remember that we use cardinal numbers most of the time: *un, deux, trois* (one, two, three), and so on.

- Use ordinal numbers to express a certain order: *premier* (*première,* if the noun following is feminine), *deuxième, troisième* (first, second, third), and so on.

- *Premier* is the masculine singular form and *première* is the feminine singular form. Examples: *le premier homme* / the first man, *la première femme* / the first woman.

- The masculine singular form *second,* or the feminine singular form *seconde,* is used to mean "second" when there are only two. When there are more than two, *deuxième* is used: *le Second Empire,* because there were only two empires in France, but *la Deuxième République,* because there have been more than two republics in France.

- The raised letters in *1er* are the last two letters in the word *premier;* it is equivalent to our "st" in 1st. The raised letters in *1ʳᵉ* are the last two letters in the word *première,* which is the feminine singular form of "first."

The raised letter *e* after an ordinal number (for example, *2ᵉ*) stands for the *-ième* ending of a French ordinal number.

• When referring to sovereigns or rulers, the only ordinal number used is *premier.* For all other designations, the cardinal numbers are used. The definite article "the" is used in English but not in French. Examples:

François 1ᵉʳ	*François Premier*	Francis the First
	BUT	
Louis XIV	*Louis Quatorze*	Louis the Fourteenth

§17.

Synonyms (similar meanings)

aide n.f., *secours* n.m.	aid, help
aimer mieux v., *préférer*	to like better, prefer
aliment n.m., *nourriture* n.f.	food, nourishment
anneau n.m., *bague* n.f.	ring (on finger)
arriver v., *se passer*	to happen, occur
aussitôt que conj., *dès que*	as soon as
auteur n.m. *écrivain* n.m.	author, writer
bâtiment n.m., *édifice,* n.m.	building, edifice
bâtir v., *construire*	to build, construct
beaucoup de adv., *bien des*	many
bref. brève adj., *court, courte*	brief, short
casser v., *rompre, briser*	to break
causer v., *parler*	to chat, talk
centre n.m., *milieu,* n.m.	center, middle
certain (certaine) adj., *sûr, sûre*	certain, sure
cesser v., *arrêter*	to cease, to stop
chagrin n.m., *souci* n.m.	sorrow, trouble, care, concern
chemin n.m., *route* n.f.	road, route
commencer à + infinitive, v., *se mettre à* + infinitive	to commence, begin, start
conseil n.m., *avis* n.m.	counsel, advice, opinion
content, (contente) adj., *heureux (heureuse)*	content, happy
de façon que conj., *de manière que*	so that, in such a way
décéder v., *mourir*	to die
dégoût n.m., *répugnance* n.f.	disgust, repugnance
dérober v., *voler*	to rob, steal
désirer v., *vouloir*	to desire, want
disputer v., *contester*	to dispute, argue, contest
docteur n.m., *médecin,* n.m.	doctor, physician
embrasser v., *donner un baiser*	to embrace, hug; to give a kiss
employer v., *se servir de*	to employ, use, make use of
épouvanter v., *effrayer*	to frighten, terrify, scare
erreur n.f., *faute,* n.f.	error, fault, mistake
espèce n.f., *sorte,* n.f.	species, type, kind, sort

adj.: adjective; adv.: adverb; conj.: conjunction; f.: feminine; m.: masculine; n.: noun; prep.: preposition; v.: verb

essayer de + infinitive, v., *tâcher de* + infinitive	to try, to attempt + infinitive
étrennes n.f., *cadeau* n.m.	Christmas gifts, present, gift
façon n.f., *manière,* n.f.	way, manner
fameux, (fameuse) adj., *célèbre*	famous, celebrated
fatigué, (fatiguée) adj., *épuisé, (épuisée)*	tired, fatigued, exhausted
favori, (favorite) adj., *préféré (préférée)*	favorite, preferred
fin n.f., *bout* n.m.	end
finir v., *terminer*	to finish, end, terminate
frémir v., *trembler*	to shiver, quiver, tremble
galette n.f., *gâteau* n.m.	cake
gaspiller v., *dissiper*	to waste, dissipate
gâter v., *abîmer*	to spoil, ruin, damage
glace n.f., *miroir* n.m.	hand mirror, mirror
grossier, grossière adj., *vulgaire*	gross, vulgar, cheap, common
habiter v., *demeurer*	to live (in), dwell, inhabit
haïr v., *détester*	to hate, detest
image n.f., *tableau* n.m.	image, picture
indiquer v., *montrer*	to indicate, show
jadis adv., *autrefois*	formerly, in times gone by
jeu n.m., *divertissement,* n.m.	game, amusement
labourer v, *travailler*	to labor, work
laisser v., *permettre*	to allow, permit
lier v., *attacher*	to tie, attach
lieu n.m., *endroit,* n.m.	place, spot, location
logis n.m. *habitation* n.f.	lodging, dwelling
lutter v., *combattre*	to struggle, fight, combat
maître n.m. *instituteur,* n.m.	master, teacher, instructor
maîtresse n.f. *institutrice,* n.f.	mistress, teacher, instructor
mauvais (mauvaise) adj., *méchant (méchante)*	bad, mean, nasty
mener v., *conduire*	to lead; to take (someone)
mince adj., *grêle*	thin, slender, skinny
naïf (naïve) adj., *ingénu (ingénue)*	naive, simple, innocent
net (nette) adj., *propre*	neat, clean
noces n.f., *mariage* n.m.	wedding, marriage
œuvre n.f., *travail* n.m.	work
ombre n.f., *obscurité* n.f.	shade, shadow, darkness
ombrelle n.f., *parasol* n.m.	sunshade, parasol, beach umbrella

parce que conj., *car*	because, for
pareil (pareille) adj., *égal (égale)*	similar, equivalent, equal
parvenir à v., *réussir à*	to succeed, to attain
pays n.m., *nation* n.f.	country, nation
pensée n.f., *idée,* n.f.	thought, idea
penser v., *réfléchir*	to think, reflect
penser à v., *songer à*	to think of; to dream of
professeur n.m., *maître,* n.m., *maîtresse,* n.f.	professor, teacher
puis adv., *ensuite*	then, afterwards
quand conj., *lorsque*	when
quelquefois adv., *parfois*	sometimes, at times
se rappeler v., *se souvenir de*	to recall, to remember
rester v., *demeurer*	to stay, to remain
sérieux (sérieuse) adj., *grave*	serious, grave
seulement adv., *ne* + verb + *que*	only
soin n.m., *attention* n.f.	care, attention
soulier n.m., *chaussure* n.f.	shoe, footwear
tout de suite adv., *immédiatement*	right away, immediately
triste adj., *malheureux (malheureuse)*	sad, unhappy
vêtements n.m., *habits,* n.m.	clothes, clothing
visage n.m., *figure* n.f.	face
vite adv., *rapidement*	quickly, rapidly

Mnemonic tip	*Bref* is brief and *court* is short because it contains the English word "curt" (brief, short).
Mnemonic tip	*Une chaussure* is a shoe because it contains *sur* / on, and you put it on your foot.
Mnemonic tip	*Une chaussette* is a sock because it's something like an anklet(te) sock.
Mnemonic tip	*Une parole* is a spoken word because when a prisoner is on "*parole*" he gives his word that he will behave in a civil manner.
Mnemonic tip	When you give someone *conseil,* you give him counsel, advice.
Mnemonic tip	When you *embrasser* a person, you put your *bras* / arms around that person.

§18.

Antonyms (opposites)

absent (absente) adj., absent	*présent (présente)* adj., present
acheter v., to buy	*vendre* v., to sell
agréable adj., pleasant, agreeable	*désagréable* adj., unpleasant, disagreeable
aimable adj., kind	*méchant (méchante)* adj., mean, nasty
aller v., to go	*venir* v., to come
ami (amie) n., friend	*ennemi (ennemie)* n., enemy
s'amuser refl. v., to enjoy oneself, to have a good time	*s'ennuyer* refl. v., to be bored
ancien (ancienne) adj., old, ancient	*nouveau (nouvel, nouvelle)* adj., new
avant prep., before	*après* prep., after
bas (basse) adj., low	*haut (haute)* adj., high
beau (bel, belle) adj., beautiful, handsome	*laid (laide)* adj., ugly
beaucoup (de) adv., much, many	*peu (de)* adv., little, some
beauté n.f., beauty	*laideur* n.f., ugliness
bête adj., stupid	*intelligent (intelligente)* adj., intelligent
bon (bonne) adj., good	*mauvais (mauvaise)* adj., bad
bonheur n.m., happiness	*malheur* n.m., unhappiness
chaud (chaude) adj., hot, warm	*froid (froide)* adj., cold
cher (chère) adj., expensive	*bon marché* cheap
content (contente) adj., glad, pleased	*mécontent (mécontente)* adj., displeased
court (courte) adj., short	*long (longue)* adj., long
debout adv., standing	*assis (assise)* adj., seated, sitting
dedans adv., inside	*dehors* adv., outside
demander v., to ask	*répondre* v., to reply
dernier (dernière) adj., last	*premier (première)* adj., first
derrière adv., prep., behind, in back of	*devant* adv., prep., in front of
dessous adv., prep., below, underneath	*dessus* adv., prep., above, over
différent (différente) adj., different	*pareil (pareille)* adj., same, similar

adj.: adjective; adv.: adverb; conj.: conjunction; f.: feminine; m.: masculine; n.: noun; prep.: preposition; v.: verb

difficile adj., difficult

facile adj., easy

domestique adj., domestic

sauvage adj., wild

donner v., to give

recevoir v., to receive

droite n.f., right

gauche n.f., left

emprunter v., to borrow

prêter v., to lend

entrer (dans) v., to enter (in, into)

sortir (de) v., to go out (of, from)

est n.m., east

ouest n.m., west

étroit (étroite) adj., narrow

large adj., wide

faible adj., weak

fort (forte) adj., strong

fermer v., to close

ouvrir v., to open

fin n.f., end

commencement n.m., beginning

finir v., to finish

commencer v., to begin; se mettre à v., to begin + inf.

gagner v., to win

perdre v., to lose

gai (gaie) adj., gay, happy

triste adj., sad

grand (grande) adj., large, tall, big

petit (petite) adj., small, little

gros (grosse) adj., fat

maigre adj., thin

grossier (grossière) adj., coarse, impolite

poli (polie) adj., polite

heureux (heureuse) adj., happy

malheureux (malheureuse) adj., unhappy

ici adv., here

là-bas adv., there

inutile adj., useless

utile adj., useful

jamais adv., never

toujours adv., always

jeune adj., young

vieux (vieil, vieille) adj., old

jeunesse n.f., youth

vieillesse n.f., old age

joli (jolie) adj., pretty

laid (laide) adj., ugly

jour n.m., day

nuit n.f., night

léger (légère) adj., light

lourd (lourde) adj., heavy

lentement adv., slowly

vite adv., quickly

mal adv., badly

bien adv., well

moderne adj., modern

ancien (ancienne) adj., ancient, old

moins adv., less

plus adv., more

monter v., to go up

descendre v., to go down

mourir v., to die

naître v., to be born

né (née) adj., past part., born

mort (morte) adj., past part., died, dead

nord n.m., north

sud n.m., south

nouveau (nouvel, nouvelle) adj., new

vieux (vieil, vieille) adj., old

obéir (à) v., to obey	*désobéir (à)* v., to disobey
ôter v., to remove, to take off	*mettre* v., to put, to put on
oui adv., yes	*non* adv., no
paix n.f., peace	*guerre* n.f., war
paraître v., to appear	*disparaître* v., to disappear
paresseux (paresseuse) adj., lazy	*travailleur (travailleuse)* adj., diligent
partir v., to leave	*arriver* v., to arrive
pauvre adj., poor	*riche* adj., rich
perdre v., to lose	*trouver* v., to find
plancher n.m., floor	*plafond* n.m., ceiling
plein (pleine) adj., full	*vide* adj., empty
poli (polie) adj., polite	*impoli (impolie) adj., impolite*
possible adj., possible	*impossible* adj., impossible
prendre v., to take	*donner* v., to give
près (de) adv., prep., near	*loin (de)* adv., prep., far (from)
propre adj., clean	*sale* adj., dirty
quelque chose pron., something	*rien* pron., nothing
quelqu'un pron., someone, somebody	*personne* pron., nobody, no one
question n.f., question	*réponse* n.f., answer, reply, response
refuser v., to refuse	*accepter* v., to accept
réussir (à) v., to succeed (at, in)	*échouer (à)* v., to fail (at, in)
rire v., to laugh	*pleurer* v., to cry, to weep
sans prep., without	*avec* prep., with
silence n.m., silence	*bruit* n.m., noise
souvent adv., often	*rarement* adv., rarely
sur prep., on	*sous* prep., under
sûr (sûre) adj., sure, certain	*incertain (incertaine)* adj., unsure, uncertain
tôt adv., early	*tard* adv., late
travailler v., to work	*jouer* v., to play
travailleur (travailleuse) adj., diligent, hardworking	*paresseux (paresseuse)* adj., lazy
vie n.f., life	*mort* n.f., death
vivre v., to live	*mourir* v., to die
vrai (vraie) adj., true	*faux (fausse)* adj., false

Mnemonic tip The verb *mourir* (to die) has one *r* because a person dies once; *nourrir* (to nourish) has two *r*'s because a person is nourished more than once.

Mnemonic tip	The word *dessous* (below, underneath) contains *sous* (under).

Mnemonic tip	The word *dessus* (above, over) contains *sus,* which reminds you of *sur* (on).

Mnemonic tip	*Perdre* means "to lose" because perdition is a place for lost souls.

Mnemonic tip	Detroit, a city in Michigan, is on the Detroit River, which is narrow *(étroit)* in spots.

Mnemonic tip	A floor *(le plancher)* was originally made of wooden planks.

Mnemonic tip	Pronounce *bonne* as in the English word "bun."

Mnemonic tip	You "mount" a mountain when you *monter une montagne.*

Mnemonic tip	You go **a**way when you *p**a**rtir* and you go **o**ut when you *s**o**rtir. Partir* and "away" contain **a**'s. *Sortir* and "go out" contain **o**'s.

Mnemonic tip	If you don't know your right from your left, *droite* contains "it" and so does "right."

§19.

Cognates

In addition to studying synonyms in §17. and antonyms in §18., another good way to increase your vocabulary is to become aware of cognates. A *cognate* is a word whose origin is the same as another word in another language. There are many cognates in French and English whose spelling is sometimes identical or very similar. Most of the time, the meaning is the same or similar; sometimes they appear to be related because of similar spelling, but they are not true cognates. You will find a list of these "false cognates" or "tricky words" in §20.

Generally speaking, certain endings, or suffixes, of French words have English equivalents.

EXAMPLES

French Suffix	Equivalent English Suffix	French Word	English Word
-able	-able	*adorable*	adorable
		aimable	amiable (likeable)
-aire	-ary	*le dictionnaire*	dictionary
-eux	-ous	*fameux*	famous
-euse		*fameuse*	
-ieux	-ous	*gracieux*	gracious
-ieuse		*gracieuse*	
-iste	-ist	*le (la) dentiste*	dentist
-ité	-ity	*la qualité*	quality
-ment	-ly	*correctement*	correctly
-mettre	-mit	*admettre*	admit
-oire	-ory	*la mémoire*	memory
-phie	-phy	*la photographie*	photography
-scrire	-scribe	*transcrire*	transcribe

A French word that contains the circumflex accent (^) over a vowel means that there used to be an *s* right after that vowel.

EXAMPLES

hâte / haste	*hôtel* / hostel	*bête* / beast	*île* / isle
pâte / paste	*honnête* / honest	*fête* / feast	*vêpres* / vespers
bâtard / bastard	*plâtre* / plaster	*mât* / mast	*prêtre* / priest

But you don't always get a cognate if you insert an *s* right after the vowel that contains a circumflex.

EXAMPLES

gâteau / cake   *bêler* / to bleat   *bâtiment* / building   *âme* / soul

Mnemonic tip | If you confuse *le gâteau* (cake) with *le bateau* (boat) because you can't remember which one contains the circumflex accent, remember that the ˆ in *gâteau* is the icing on top of the cake!

§20.

Tricky Words

"False friends" are look-alikes but have different meanings.

actualités n.f., pl. news reports

actuel adj. present, present-day

actuellement adv. at present

addition n.f. bill (check)

attendre v. to wait

belle adj., fem. beautiful

bénir v. to bless

blesser v. to wound

bras n.m. arm

but n.m. goal

cabinet n.m. office; study

car conj. because

causer v. to chat; to cause

cave n.f. cellar, basement

chair n.f. flesh

chat n.m. cat

chose n.f. thing

coin n.m. corner

comment adv. how

conférence n.f. lecture

crâne n.m. skull

crayon n.m. pencil

dent n.f. tooth

dire v. to say, to tell

dot n.f. dowry

éditeur n.m. publisher

essence n.f. gasoline

fin n.f. end

flèche n.f. arrow

fort adj., n. strong

four n.m. oven

front n.m. forehead

grand adj., m. tall, big, large

grave adj. serious

haïr v. to hate

journal n.m. newspaper

large adj. wide, broad

lecture n.f. reading

librairie n.f. bookstore

magasin n.m. store

main n.f. hand

marine n.f. navy; seascape

médecin n.m. doctor, physician

médecine n.f. medicine (study of)

médicament n.m. medicine

mine n.f. facial appearance

monnaie n.f. change (coins)

on pers. pron. one, someone, they

ours n.m. bear (animal)

pain n.m. bread

pal n.m. pale, stake (for punishment)

par prep. by

personnel adj. personal

pie n.f. magpie (bird)

pile n.f. battery; pile, heap

place n.f. plaza, place

plate adj., fem. flat

pour prep. for

prune n.f. plum

pruneau n.m. prune

raisin n.m. grape

raisin sec n.m. raisin

râpe n.f. grater (cheese)

rose adj. pink

rose n. rose

rue n.f. street

sable n.m. sand

sale adj. dirty, soiled

sensible adj. sensitive

son n.m. sound

stage n.m. training course of study

stylo n.m. pen

tôt adv. early

vent n.m. wind (air)

vie n.f. life

§21.

How to Ask a Question

- To ask a question, put **est-ce que** in front of the subject.

Est-ce que vous parlez français?	Do you speak French?
À quelle heure **est-ce que** le train part?	At what time does the train leave?

- If the first letter of the subject is a vowel or silent *h*, drop **e** in **que** and add an apostrophe.

Est-ce qu'il joue?	Is he playing?
Est-ce qu'Hélène est jolie?	Is Helen pretty?

- If your question is in the negative, put **ne** in front of the verb and **pas** after it.

Est-ce que tu **ne** travailles **pas**?	Aren't you working?
Est-ce que vous **n'**avez pas d'argent?	Don't you have any money?

- Instead of using **est-ce que**, you may use the inverted form. Move the subject pronoun and put it after the verb, joining it with a hyphen.

Parlez-vous français?	Do you speak French?
Ne parlez-vous **pas** anglais?	Don't you speak English?

- If the subject pronoun is **je**, do not use the inverted form. Use **est-ce que**. The inverted form with **je** is used only with certain verbs, for example:

Que sais-je?	What do I know?
Où suis-je?	Where am I?
Ai-je assez d'argent?	Do I have enough money?

- In the inverted form, if the last letter of the verb is a vowel in the third person singular, insert **-t-** between the verb and the subject pronouns **il**, **elle**, or **on**.

Danse-**t**-il?	Does he dance? Is he dancing?
À quelle heure arrive-**t**-elle?	At what time is she arriving?
Où va-**t**-on?	Where is one going?

- In the inverted form, if the subject is a noun, mention the noun first and use the pronoun of the noun.

Le docteur va-**t**-il venir bientôt?	Is the doctor going to come soon?

LET'S REVIEW

§22.

Test Yourself

**§1.
PRONOUNC-
ING FRENCH
SOUNDS**

Choose the correct answer by circling the letter.

1. The vowel *a* in the French word *la* is pronounced as in the English word
   A. lolly   B. ate   C. father   D. ago

2. The vowel *a* in the French word *pas* is pronounced as in the English word
   A. father   B. at   C. ate   D. bare

3. The vowel *é* in the French word *thé* is pronounced as in the English word
   A. ate   B. less   C. week   D. the

4. The vowel *i* in the French word *ici* is pronounced as in the English word
   A. see   B. it   C. idea   D. lie

5. The semiconsonant sound in the French word *oui* is pronounced as in the English word
   A. week   B. ouch   C. pooch   D. pouch

6. The consonant *ç* in the French word *ça* is pronounced as in the English word
   A. sorry   B. cat   C. pack   D. church

7. The vowel *è* in the French word *père* is pronounced as in the English word
   A. egg   B. week   C. the   D. say

8. The vowel *e* in the French word *le* is pronounced as in the English word
   A. ago   B. less   C. weak   D. lay

9. The sound of *ch* in the French word *chose* is pronounced as in the English word
   A. choose   B. chair   C. share   D. character

10. The sound of *u* in the French word *tu* is pronounced as in the English word
    A. tuck   B. push   C. much   D. cute

§2.
CAPITALIZA-
TION, PUNC-
TUATION
MARKS,
WORD
DIVISION

I. Divide the following French words into syllables.

   EXAMPLE: *beaucoup   beau / coup*

   1. *école*____   2. *important*____   3. *après*____

II. Match the French words for punctuation marks with their English equivalents.

   1. *le point*   ____ semicolon
   2. *la virgule*   ____ question mark
   3. *deux points*   ____ period
   4. *les guillemets*   ____ ellipses
   5. *le point d'interrogation*   ____ quotation marks
   6. *points de suspension*   ____ comma
   7. *point virgule*   ____ colon

§3.
ARTICLES

I. Write the appropriate definite article in front of each noun.

   1. __ *garçon*   2. __ *jeune fille*   3. __ *arbre*
   4. __ *livres*

II. Write the appropriate indefinite article in front of each noun.

   5. __ *frère*   6. __ *sœur*   7. __ *frères*
   8. __ *sœurs*

III. Write the French for the following phrases.

   9. to Canada _____
   10. to the United States _____
   11. to the library _____
   12. to the airport _____
   13. from the United States _____
   14. from Canada _____
   15. the boy's book _____
   16. the boys' books _____

IV. Write the French for the following sentences.

   17. I have some coffee. _____
   18. I don't have any coffee. _____
   19. I have some meat. _____
   20. I don't have any candies. _____

§4.
NOUNS

I. Write the definite article in front of each noun.

1. _____ homme   6. _____ chapeau
2. _____ femme   7. _____ chat
3. _____ coq   8. _____ gâteau
4. _____ vache   9. _____ âge
5. _____ poule 10. _____ sucette

II. Write the following nouns in the plural with the definite article.

11. le livre _____
12. l'étudiant _____
13. le journal _____
14. le bras _____
15. le bureau _____
16. l'œil _____
17. la voix _____
18. la maison _____
19. le ciel _____
20. le feu _____

§5.
ADJECTIVES

I. Supply the missing letters.

    EXAMPLE: les cie _ _   Answer: les cieux

1. Ce cra _ on est mauv _ _ _.
2. Janine est aussi grand _ que Monique.
3. Jacqueline est plu _ joli _ que Simone.
4. Anne est absent _.

II. Complete each sentence with ce, cet, cette, or ces.

5. _____ garçon est beau. 6. _____ arbre est beau.
7. _____ livres sont beaux. 8. _____ femme est belle.

III. Complete each sentence with belle, bel, beau, or beaux.

9. Janine est une _____ jeune fille.
10. C'est un _____ arbre.
11. Jacques est un _____ jeune homme.
12. Ces livres sont _____.

IV. Supply the missing letters.

13. Joseph est acti _ et Joséphine est acti _ _.
14. Joseph et Joséphine jouent dans le jardin publi _ et dans cette long _ _ rue.
15. Joseph est heur _ _ _. Joséphine est heure _ _ _.
16. Il est genti _ et elle est gent _ _ _ _.

V. Complete the sentence with *vieux, vieil, vieille,* or *veille.*

La ―――――― dame a passé la ―――――― de Noël avec
     17.   18.

son ―――――― ami dans un ―――――― cabaret.
    19.   20.

§6.
PRONOUNS

I. *Mots-croisés* (Crossword Puzzle)

Verticalement

1. 1st person singular direct and indirect object pronoun.
3. 3d person plural indirect object pronoun.
6. Preposition used with adverbs of quantity, e.g., *beaucoup, trop.*
7. Masculine plural demonstrative pronoun.
8. Masculine singular demonstrative pronoun.
9. 3d person masculine singular direct object pronoun.
11. Pronoun that takes the place of the partitive and serves as a direct object.

Horizontalement

2. Feminine singular subject pronoun.
4. Pronoun commonly used in an interrogative sentence, as in *Est-ce qu'il...a?*
5. 3d person singular indirect object pronoun.
8. Feminine singular demonstrative pronoun.
10. 1st person singular subject pronoun.
12. 1st person plural direct and indirect object pronoun.

II. *La Roue de Fortune* (The Wheel of Fortune)
Complete each of the following by writing in the missing letters. Some letters are given to get you started. They are all pronouns.

1. A _ C _ _   4. _ _ Q _ _ L L _

2. Q _ _ C _ _ Q _ _   5. _ A M _ _ N _ _

3. _ _ Q _ _ L

§7.
VERBS

I. *Mots-croisés* (Crossword Puzzle)

Write the past participle for each of the following verbs.

Verticalement

1. devoir	5. prendre	14. finir
2. naître	6. dire	16. mourir
3. lire	7. falloir	17. être
4. vendre	12. user	20. avoir

Horizontalement

1. donner	10. taire	18. naître
5. pouvoir	11. savoir	19. rire (à l'envers)*
7. fuir	13. lire	21. taire
8. rire	15. savoir	22. tuer
9. devoir (à l'envers)*		

  * à l'envers / **backwards**

II. *Dans le potage* / In the soup. In this word puzzle, find the present participle of each of the verbs listed below and draw a line around each one. The first verb on the list *(aller)* whose present participle is *allant* is already done, to get you started. The words are written horizontally, vertically, or backwards.

C	H	A	N	T	A	N	T	A	T
H	F	Y	T	N	V	E	A	P	N
O	A	A	N	A	E	F	V	R	A
I	I	N	A	N	A	I	E	E	Y
S	S	T	Y	E	N	N	N	N	O
I	A	A	O	T	T	I	D	A	V
S	N	N	R	D	I	S	A	N	T
S	T	T	C	T	É	S	N	T	N
A	L	L	A	N	T	A	T	O	A
N	A	I	S	S	A	N	T	S	N
T	N	O	S	A	N	T	F	A	E
L	I	S	A	N	T	T	A	N	V

aller
avoir
chanter
choisir
croire
dire
être
faire
finir
lire
naître
oser
prendre
tenir
vendre
venir
voir

III. *Dans le potage.* In this word puzzle, find the verb form in the present indicative tense for each verb in the sentences below. When you find them, draw a line around each one. The verb form in the present tense of *faire* in the first statement given below is *faites,* and it has already been done to get you started. The words are written horizontally, vertically, diagonally, or backwards.

A	I	M	E	B	A	L	I	T	A
C	D	A	L	O	S	E	T	I	D
O	O	E	F	I	O	A	E	G	I
U	I	E	A	A	L	L	O	N	S
R	S	V	S	I	O	U	E	A	U
S	A	I	R	E	U	Ê	T	E	S
I	L	N	A	P	S	U	V	L	O
A	E	I	P	E	U	V	E	N	T
E	O	N	T	N	E	D	N	E	V
L	U	I	A	L	L	E	Z	O	N
F	A	T	E	Z	V	A	V	A	I
F	I	N	I	S	S	O	N	S	S

Que (faire)-vous ce soir?
Que me (dire)-vous?
J' (aimer) danser.
Moi, je (aller) chez moi.
Les garçons (avoir)-ils
    assez d'argent pour
    aller au cinéma?
Nous (aller) en France
    l'été prochain.
Quand (partir)-tu?
Et vous, (être)-vous
    heureux?
Tes parents (pouvoir)-ils
    venir avec nous?
Que (devoir)-tu faire
    maintenant?
Pourquoi (courir)-tu?
(Vendre)-ils leur maison?
Est-ce que nous (finir) le
    travail aujourd'hui?

IV. *Dans le potage.* Find the verb form in the imperfect indicative tense for each verb in the sentences below. When you find them, draw a line around each one. The verb form in the imperfect tense of *avoir* in the first statement given below is *avais,* and it is already done for you to get you started. The words are written horizontally and vertically.

A	V	A	I	S	É	T	I	E	Z
A	V	I	E	Z	É	T	A	I	T
F	A	I	S	I	E	Z	E	A	V
M	A	N	G	I	O	N	S	L	D
A	É	M	A	L	L	A	I	S	I
F	T	A	O	L	I	S	A	I	S
A	I	R	B	U	V	A	I	S	I
I	O	C	D	I	S	A	I	T	E
S	N	H	A	V	A	I	T	T	Z
A	S	A	L	L	I	O	N	S	S
I	A	I	P	A	R	L	A	I	S
S	I	T	R	O	U	V	A	I	T

Autrefois, lorsque j'
(avoir) dix ans, j'étais
très heureux.

Quand ma mère (être)
jeune, elle était belle.

Que (faire)-vous quand je
vous ai téléphoné?

Mon frère jouait pendant
que je (lire).

Nous (aller) à la plage
quand il a commencé à
pleuvoir.

Autrefois, je (boire) du vin
mais maintenant je
bois de l'eau.

Où (aller)-tu ce matin
quand je t'ai vu?

Dites-moi, lorsque Marie
(avoir) dix ans, allait-
elle souvent à la plage
avec ses copines?

Que (faire)-tu quand je
t'ai appelé?

L'homme (marcher)
lentement.

Que (dire)-vous quand
Robert vous a interrompu?

Nous (être) heureux
quand nous étions enfants.

La maison se (trouver) au
pied d'une montagne.

Nous (manger) quand tu
es arrivé.

Je (parler) souvent à
Jean mais je ne lui
parle plus maintenant.

Où (être)-vous à 20 h.
précises le soir du 15
novembre?

Que (dire) l'élève de
moi quand je suis entré
dans la salle de classe?

V. *Mots-croisés.* This activity tests your knowledge of the past indefinite tense. The missing words are the present tense of *avoir* or *être* or the correct form of the past participle, or a subject pronoun.

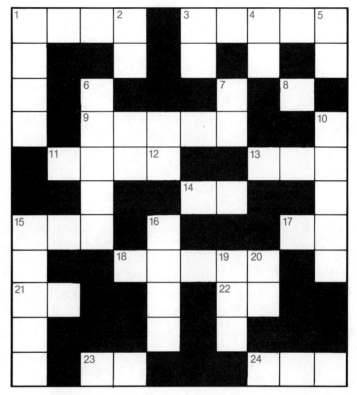

Horizontalement

1. *Hier, je* _____ *allé au cinéma.*
3. *Martine est* _____ *(aller) aux grands magasins.*
8. *Pierre* _____ *lu un livre.*
9. *Ils ont* _____ *(vouloir) partir.*
11. _____ *avez parlé assez.*
13. *La lettre? Je l'ai* _____ *(lire).*
14. *Pierre s'est* _____ *(taire).*
15. *J'ai* _____ *(mettre) du sucre dans le café.*

17. *J'ai* _____ *(devoir) (à l'envers)* partir.*
18. *Les lettres? Je les ai* _____ *(mettre) sur le bureau.*
21. *Nous avons bien* _____ *(rire).*
22. *Avez-vous* _____ *(savoir) la réponse?*
23. *Paul a-t-*_____ *compris?*
24. *Qu'a-t-elle* _____ *(dire)?*

* *à l'envers* / backwards

Verticalement

1. Je _____ tombé en montant dans le bus.
2. J'ai _____ (savoir) la réponse.
3. Hier soir, j' _____ beaucoup mangé.
4. Ma camarade a _____ (lire) un livre intéressant.
5. Ce matin j'ai _____ (avoir) un petit accident.
6. Nous _____ pris le train.
7. Les enfants ont _____ (pouvoir) manger.

10. Nous avons _____ (vendre) la maison.
12. A-t-il _____ (savoir) (à l'envers)* répondre à la question?
15. Madame Durand est _____ (mourir) la semaine dernière.
16. Tu as _____ (finir) la leçon?
19. Jacqueline _____ restée à la maison.
20. Tu as _____ (savoir) cela, n'est-ce pas?

*A l'envers/backwards

§8.
ADVERBS

I. Change the following adjectives into adverbs using the *-ment* ending in French.

1. gentil _____   3. affreux _____
2. franc _____   4. amer _____

II. Write at least ten common adverbs in French that do not end in *-ment*.

1. ____ 3. ____ 5. ____ 7. ____ 9. ____
2. ____ 4. ____ 6. ____ 8. ____ 10. ____

III. Unscramble the following letters to find an adverb in French. Then write it on the line provided.

| A H U E S M N M L E R U E E T | _____

IV. In this dialogue, Janine and you are talking about the exams in June and your summer vacation. Complete the conversation by choosing the appropriate French adverb from those given here.

bien   rapidement   récemment   toujours
aussi

Janine: Es-tu prêt pour tes examens?
Vous: Oui, je suis _____ prêt pour mes examens.
Janine: Demain j'ai encore un autre examen, et puis les vacances commencent.

> Vous: Les jours de vacances vont passer ＿＿＿.
> Janine: Nous avons passé l'été passé dans les montagnes.
> Vous: Ma famille et moi allons ＿＿＿ dans les montagnes.
> Janine: En juillet nous allons faire un voyage en Australie.
> Vous: Ma famille et moi ＿＿＿! Nous allons à Melbourne!
> Janine: Si tu me donnes ton adresse, je vais t'envoyer une carte postale de Sydney.
> Vous: Mais je t'ai donné ＿＿＿ mon adresse! L'as-tu perdue?

§9. PREPOSI- TIONS

Hidden words. Among the following prepositions numbered 1 to 6, some are hidden in the block of words given below, but some are not. Which of these prepositions are not in the block of words?

1. *dans*　　　2. *en*　　　3. *vers*
4. *envers*　　5. *pour*　　6. *pendant*

> POURQUOI LA PORTE UNE HEURE AIMER AVEC SOIR CHAQUE PAR ENVERS SANS DE DENT OU PARCE QUE VERS AN PENDANT PROBABLEMENT

Solution: The prepositions that are not in the block of words are the ones numbered: ＿＿＿＿＿＿＿＿＿＿

§10. CONJUNC TIONS

I. In the following paragraph, underline all the conjunctions that you find and write them on the lines below.

> Je ne peux pas aller à la surprise-partie chez Jim ce soir parce que j'ai beaucoup de devoirs à faire et, comme mon père est malade, je dois rester à la maison; mais demain c'est possible ou dans trois jours.

＿＿＿＿＿＿＿＿＿＿＿＿＿＿＿＿＿＿＿＿＿

＿＿＿＿＿＿＿＿＿＿＿＿＿＿＿＿＿＿＿＿＿

II. Complete the following French conjunctions.

1. *à moins* ＿＿＿＿ / unless
2. *de* ＿＿＿＿ *que* / for fear that
3. *en même* ＿＿＿＿ *que* / at the same time as
4. *jusqu'à* ＿＿＿＿ *que* / until
5. ＿＿＿＿ *que* / whereas

III. A Letter Clock. Three conjunctions in French are hidden in this clock; one conjunction from 12 to 6; one from 4 to 6; and another from 6 to 11. Note that the same letter can be common to the one that follows. This clock has no hands because it's a "word clock." Write the missing letters on the lines.

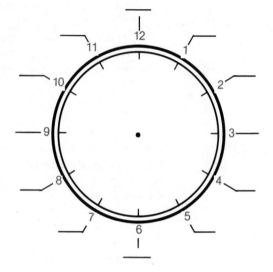

CLUES:

From 12 to 6, give the French for the conjunction "when" that is a synonym of *quand.*

From 4 to 6, give the French for the conjunction "that."

From 6 to 11, give the French for the conjunction "at the same time as."

(There was no more room in the clock to write *temps que* to complete that conjunction!)

§11.
ORDER OF ELEMENTS IN FRENCH SENTENCES

I. Unscramble the words to form a coherent sentence.

1. *me / ne / donne / les / Elle / pas* _____
2. *pas / ne / leur / le / Je / donne* _____
3. *leur / Ne / les / pas / donnez* _____
4. *s' / pas / est / lavée / ne / Elle* _____
5. *pas / ai / lui / donné / Je / le / ne* _____

§12.
IDIOMS

I. Each of the following sentences contains a blank. Of the three choices given, select the one that can be inserted in the blank to form a grammatically correct sentence and circle the letter of your choice.

1. _____ quand habitez-vous cet appartement?
   A. *Pour*   **B.** *Depuis*   **C.** *Combien de temps*

2. J'habite cet appartement _____ le vingt-deux août, 1966.
   A. *depuis*   **B.** *pour*   **C.** *il y a*

3. _____ quand êtes-vous malade?
   A. *Depuis*   **B.** *Combien de temps*   **C.** *Pour*

4. Je suis malade _____ samedi.
   A. *combien*   **B.** *depuis*   **C.** *de*

5. J'habitais l'appartement _____ le cinq avril 1987 quand j'ai déménagé.
   A. *pour*   **B.** *depuis combien de temps*   **C.** *depuis*

II. Write the missing word or words in order to complete each of the following basic idiomatic expressions. Choose from among the following:

à   au   aux   aller   avoir   d'   de   du   être   faire

1. _____ vélo
2. _____ téléphone
3. _____ pommes frites
4. _____ pied
5. _____ faim
6. comme _____ habitude
7. changer _____ train
8. _____ en retard
9. _____ un voyage
10. _____ une promenade
11. _____ lieu de
12. _____ partir de
13. _____ chercher
14. _____ besoin de
15. _____ soif
16. _____ bonne heure
17. **tout** _____ un coup
18. _____ en train de + infinitive
19. _____ les valises
20. Que _____ ?

§13.
DATES,
DAYS,
MONTHS,
SEASONS

I. Each of the following sentences contains a blank. Of the four choices given, select the one that can be inserted in the blank to form a sensible and grammatically correct sentence and circle the letter of your choice.

1. Quelle est la date aujourd'hui? C'est aujourd'hui _____ février.
   A. *l'un*   **B.** *le premier de*   **C.** *le premier*
   D. *la première*

2. *Quel jour précède lundi? C'est* _____ .
   A. *samedi*   **B.** *dimanche*   **C.** *mardi*
   D. *jeudi*

3. *Il y a* _____ *saisons dans l'année.*
   A. *cinq*   **B.** *quart*   **C.** *quatre*   **D.** *quarante*

4. *Les fleurs poussent* _____ *printemps.*
   A. *en*   **B.** *dans*   **C.** *dans le*   **D.** *au*

5. *En général,* _____ *hiver il fait froid à New York.*
   A. *en*   **B.** *dans*   **C.** *dans l'*   **D.** *à l'*

§14.
TELLING TIME

I. Study the clocks and below each one write the time that is given in French words.

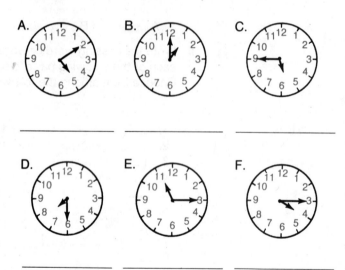

§15.
TALKING ABOUT THE WEATHER

I. Read the statement in English and then select the correct equivalent in French by drawing a circle around the letter of your choice.

1. What's the weather like today?
   A. *Fait-il beau temps aujourd'hui?*
   B. *Quel temps fait-il aujourd'hui?*
   C. *Fait-il un temps affreux aujourd'hui?*
   D. *Quelle heure est-il?*

2. It's very warm today.
   A. *Il fait très beau aujourd'hui.*
   B. *Il fait chaud aujourd'hui.*
   C. *Il fait très chaud aujourd'hui.*
   D. *Il fait très froid aujourd'hui.*

3. It's muggy.
   A. *Il fait un temps couvert.*
   B. *Le temps menace.*
   C. *Le temps se met au beau.*
   D. *Il fait un temps lourd.*

4. It's windy.
   A. *Il fait du tonnerre.*
   B. *Il fait du vent.*
   C. *Il grêle.*
   D. *Il pleut.*

5. It's raining.
   A. *Il neige.*
   B. *Il fait mauvais.*
   C. *Il gèle.*
   D. *Il pleut.*

II. Weather Announcement. Place the four numbered blocks vertically in the right spot next to the second column of letters, and you will read the weather announcement. The announcement reads vertically.

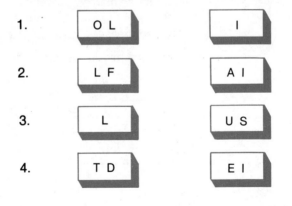

1. O L   I
2. L F   A I
3. L   U S
4. T D   E I

§16.
NUMBERS

I. Each of the following sentences contains a blank. Of the four choices given, select the one that can be inserted in the blank to form a sensible and grammatically correct sentence and circle the letter of your choice.

1. *Douze et treize font _____.*
   A. *vingt-deux*   B. *quinze*
   C. *cinquante-deux*   D. *vingt-cinq*

2. *Dix* _____ *quatre font six.*
   A. *et*   B. *fois*   C. *moins*   D. *divisés par*

3. *Cinq* _____ *seize font quatre-vingts.*
   A. *et*   B. *fois*   C. *moins*   D. *divisés par*

4. *Seize* _____ *huit font deux.*
   A. *et*   B. *fois*   C. *moins*   D. *divisés par*

5. *Cinq cents* _____ *deux font deux cent cinquante.*
   A. *et*   B. *fois*   C. *moins*   D. *divisés par*

II. Match the following.

1. *un quart*   _____ *one-fourth*
2. *un demi*   _____ *one-fifth*
3. *un cinquième*   _____ *one-half*
4. *un tiers*   _____ *one-third*

§17. SYNONYMS

I. Match the following synonyms.

1. *aide*   _____ *docteur*
2. *anneau*   _____ *avis*
3. *souci*   _____ *détester*
4. *médecin*   _____ *chaussure*
5. *haïr*   _____ *favori*
6. *préféré*   _____ *car*
7. *conseil*   _____ *secours*
8. *parce que*   _____ *chagrin*
9. *soulier*   _____ *donner un baiser*
10. *embrasser*   _____ *bague*

II. Write the missing letters on the lines.

1. __ R __ V __ __ L __ E R
2. D __ S __ R __ R
3. P __ __ F __ S __ E __ R
4. B __ T __ __ E __ T
5. M I __ I __ U
6. H __ B __ T E __

§18. ANTONYMS

I. Several words in one. Using the letters in the word *PARESSEUSE*, how many words can you find within it? Write at least six.

| P A R E S S E U S E |

1. _____   3. _____   5. _____
2. _____   4. _____   6. _____

II. Several words in one. Using the letters in the word *MAISON,* how many words can you find within it? Write at least six.

1. _____ 3. _____ 5. _____
2. _____ 4. _____ 6. _____

Now rearrange all the letters in the word *MAISON* and find another French word that contains the same letters. The new word is: _____

III. Match the following. They are all antonyms.

1. *étroit*   _____ *derrière*
2. *grand*   _____ *dehors*
3. *gai*   _____ *fausse*
4. *dedans*   _____ *petit*
5. *beauté*   _____ *naître*
6. *vraie*   _____ *laideur*
7. *ami*   _____ *sur*
8. *devant*   _____ *large*
9. *sous*   _____ *ennemi*
10. *mourir*   _____ *triste*

§19.
COGNATES

I. Write the English word for the following French words.

1. *honnête* _____   6. *bâtiment* _____
2. *pâte* _____   7. *gâteau* _____
3. *bête* _____   8. *âme* _____
4. *forêt* _____   9. *aimable* _____
5. *prêtre* _____   10. *permettre* _____

II. Alphabet Soup. Find the French words for the English cognates given below and circle each one. They are horizontal, vertical, and backwards.

A	E	L	B	A	M	I	A	P
P	A	T	P	L	Â	T	R	E
A	D	M	E	T	T	R	E	A
E	T	Â	P	E	T	Â	H	A

admit   mast   amiable   plaster   paste   haste

§20.
TRICKY
WORDS

I. Write the French word and its definite article for each of the following.

EXAMPLE: pen   You write: *le stylo*

1. sound _____
2. news reports _____
3. plum _____
4. thing _____
5. goal _____

6. prune _____
7. bread _____
8. store _____
9. arrow _____
10. bear (animal) _____

II. Match the following tricky French words with their English equivalents.

1. *le chat*
2. *causer*
3. *le front*
4. *large*
5. *la chair*
6. *blesser*
7. *bénir*
8. *le cabinet*
9. *sale*
10. *le sable*

_____ dirty
_____ flesh
_____ sand
_____ wide
_____ to wound
_____ forehead
_____ office or study
_____ cat
_____ to bless
_____ to chat

§21.
HOW TO ASK
A QUESTION

I. Write the following questions in French using **est-ce que**.
1. Do you speak French? (use **vous**) _____
2. At what time does the train leave? _____
3. Aren't you working? (use **tu**) _____

II. Write the following questions in French using the inverted form.
1. Do you speak French? (use **vous**) _____
2. Don't you speak English? (use **vous**) _____
3. What do I know? _____

III. Write the following questions in French using either **est-ce que** or the inverted form.
1. Where can I buy a newspaper? _____
2. Do you know what time it is? (use **tu**)_____
3. What are you saying? (use **vous**) _____

II. Several words in one. Using the letters in the word *MAISON,* how many words can you find within it? Write at least six.

1. _____   3. _____   5. _____
2. _____   4. _____   6. _____

Now rearrange all the letters in the word *MAISON* and find another French word that contains the same letters. The new word is: _____

III. Match the following. They are all antonyms.

1. *étroit*   _____ *derrière*
2. *grand*   _____ *dehors*
3. *gai*   _____ *fausse*
4. *dedans*   _____ *petit*
5. *beauté*   _____ *naître*
6. *vraie*   _____ *laideur*
7. *ami*   _____ *sur*
8. *devant*   _____ *large*
9. *sous*   _____ *ennemi*
10. *mourir*   _____ *triste*

§19.
COGNATES

I. Write the English word for the following French words.

1. *honnête* _____   6. *bâtiment* _____
2. *pâte* _____   7. *gâteau* _____
3. *bête* _____   8. *âme* _____
4. *forêt* _____   9. *aimable* _____
5. *prêtre* _____   10. *permettre* _____

II. Alphabet Soup. Find the French words for the English cognates given below and circle each one. They are horizontal, vertical, and backwards.

A	E	L	B	A	M	I	A	P
P	A	T	P	L	Â	T	R	E
A	D	M	E	T	T	R	E	A
E	T	Â	P	E	T	Â	H	A

admit   mast   amiable   plaster   paste   haste

§20. TRICKY WORDS

I. Write the French word and its definite article for each of the following.

EXAMPLE: pen You write: *le stylo*

1. sound _____
2. news reports _____
3. plum _____
4. thing _____
5. goal _____

6. prune _____
7. bread _____
8. store _____
9. arrow _____
10. bear (animal) _____

II. Match the following tricky French words with their English equivalents.

1. *le chat* _____ dirty
2. *causer* _____ flesh
3. *le front* _____ sand
4. *large* _____ wide
5. *la chair* _____ to wound
6. *blesser* _____ forehead
7. *bénir* _____ office or study
8. *le cabinet* _____ cat
9. *sale* _____ to bless
10. *le sable* _____ to chat

§21. HOW TO ASK A QUESTION

I. Write the following questions in French using **est-ce que**.
1. Do you speak French? (use **vous**) _____
2. At what time does the train leave? _____
3. Aren't you working? (use **tu**) _____

II. Write the following questions in French using the inverted form.
1. Do you speak French? (use **vous**) _____
2. Don't you speak English? (use **vous**) _____
3. What do I know? _____

III. Write the following questions in French using either **est-ce que** or the inverted form.
1. Where can I buy a newspaper? _____
2. Do you know what time it is? (use **tu**)_____
3. What are you saying? (use **vous**) _____

Answers

§1. PRONOUNCING FRENCH SOUNDS

1. A.   2. A.   3. A.   4. A.   5. A.   6. A.
7. A.   8. A.   9. C.   10. D.
Review §1.

§2. CAPITALIZA- TION, PUNC- TUATION MARKS, WORD DIVISION

I. 1. *é / cole*   2. *im / por / tant*   3. *a / près*

II. 7, 5, 1, 6, 4, 2, 3   Review §2.

§3. ARTICLES

I. 1. *le*   2. *la*   3. *l'*   4. *les*   Review §3.1.

II. 5. *un*   6. *une*   7. *des*   8. *des*   Review §3.2.

III. 9. *au Canada*
10. *aux Etats-Unis*
11. *à la bibliothèque*
12. *à l'aéroport*
13. *des Etats-Unis*
14. *du Canada*
15. *le livre du garçon*
16. *les livres des garçons*
Review §3.1.

IV. 17. *J'ai du café.*
18. *Je n'ai pas de café.*
19. *J'ai de la viande.*
20. *Je n'ai pas de bonbons.*
Review §3.3.

§4.
NOUNS

I. 1. *l'*   2. *la*   3. *le*   4. *la*   5. *la*   6. *le*
  7. *le*   8. *le*   9. *l'*   10. *la*   Review §4.1.

II. 11. *les livres*   17. *les voix*
   12. *les étudiants*   18. *les maisons*
   13. *les journaux*   19. *les cieux*
   14. *les bras*   20. *les feux*
   15. *les bureaux*   Review §4.2.
   16. *les yeux*

§5.
ADJECTIVES

I. 1. *y; a, i, s*   2. *e*   3. *s; e*   4. *e*
  Review §5.1 & §5.2.

II. 5. *ce*   6. *cet*   7. *ces*   8. *cette*
  Review §5.4 – 2.

III. 9. *belle*   10. *bel*   11. *beau*   12. *beaux*
  Review §5.1.

IV. 13. *f; v, e*   14. *c; u, e*   15. *e, u, x; u, s, e*
  16. *l; i, l, l, e*   Review §5.1.

V. 17. *vieille*   18. *veille*   19. *vieil*   20. *vieux*
  Review §5.1.

§6.
PRONOUNS

I. Review §6. – §6.1 – 8 for this crossword puzzle.

II. 1. U, U, N *(aucun)* Review §6.1 – 9.
  2. U, I, O, N, U, E *(quiconque)* Review §6.1 – 9.
  3. L, E, U, E *(lequel)* Review §6.1 – 10.
  4. L, A, U, E, E *(laquelle)* Review §6.1 – 10.
  5. L,   I, E, N, E *(la mienne)* Review §6.1 – 11.

§7.
VERBS

I. Review §7.2 for this crossword puzzle.

¹D	O	N	²N	E	■	³L	■	⁴V
Û	■		E		⁵P	U		E
■	⁶D	■		R		■		N
⁷F	U	I	⁸R	I		⁹Û		D
A		¹⁰T	U	¹¹S	¹²U			U
¹³L	U		¹⁴F		¹⁵S	U		■
L	¹⁶M		I		É			¹⁷É
U		O	¹⁸N	E				T
	¹⁹I	R		I		E		É
■	²¹T	U		²²T	U	É	■	■

II. Review §7.4 for the present participles in this word puzzle.

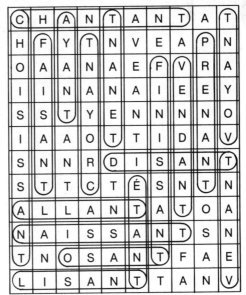

C	H	A	N	T	A	N	T	A	T
H	F	Y	T	N	V	E	A	P	N
O	A	A	N	A	E	F	V	R	A
I	I	N	A	N	A	I	E	E	Y
S	S	T	Y	E	N	N	N	N	O
I	A	A	O	T	T	I	D	A	V
S	N	N	R	D	I	S	A	N	T
S	T	T	C	T	É	S	N	T	N
A	L	L	A	N	T	A	T	O	A
N	A	I	S	S	A	N	T	S	N
T	N	O	S	A	N	T	F	A	E
L	I	S	A	N	T	T	A	N	V

III. Review §7.8–1 & §7.17 for the present indicative tense of verbs in this word puzzle.

A	I	M	E	B	A	L	I	T	A
C	D	A	L	O	S	E	T	I	D
O	O	E	F	I	O	A	E	G	I
U	I	E	A	A	L	L	O	N	S
R	S	V	S	I	O	U	E	A	U
S	A	I	R	E	U	Ê	T	E	S
I	L	N	A	P	S	U	V	L	O
A	E	I	P	E	U	V	E	N	T
E	O	N	T	N	E	D	N	E	V
L	U	I	A	L	L	E	Z	O	N
F	A	T	E	Z	V	A	V	A	I
F	I	N	I	S	S	O	N	S	S

IV. Review §7.8–2 & §7.17 for the imperfect indicative tense of verbs in this word puzzle.

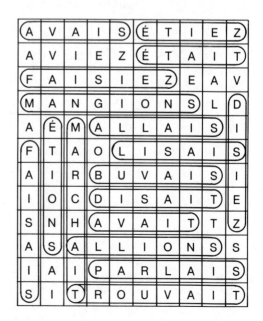

A	V	A	I	S	É	T	I	E	Z
A	V	I	E	Z	É	T	A	I	T
F	A	I	S	I	E	Z	E	A	V
M	A	N	G	I	O	N	S	L	D
A	É	M	A	L	L	A	I	S	I
F	T	A	O	L	I	S	A	I	S
A	I	R	B	U	V	A	I	S	I
I	O	C	D	I	S	A	I	T	E
S	N	H	A	V	A	I	T	T	Z
A	S	A	L	L	I	O	N	S	S
I	A	I	P	A	R	L	A	I	S
S	I	T	R	O	U	V	A	I	T

V. Review §7.1, §7.2, §7.3–1, §7.8–8, §7.17 for the past indefinite *(passé composé)* of verbs in this crossword puzzle.

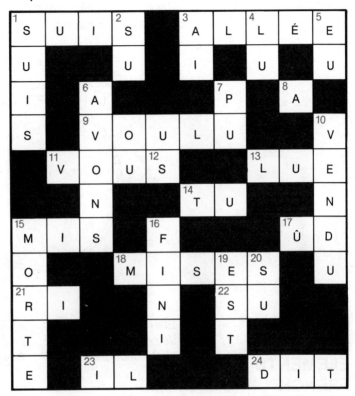

§8.
ADVERBS

I. 1. *gentiment*   2. *franchement*   3. *affreusement*
   4. *amèrement*   Review §8.1.

II. 1. *bien*   2. *mal*   3. *vite*   4. *combien*
   5. *comment*   6. *pourquoi*   7. *où*
   8. *quand*   9. *beaucoup*   10. *assez*
   Review §8.1, §8.3–1.

III. *malheureusement*   Review §8.1, §8.2.

IV. *bien; rapidement; toujours; aussi; récemment*
   Review §8.–§8.3.

§9.
PREPOSI-
TIONS—
SPECIAL USES

1, 2, 5. Review §9.

§10. CONJUNCTIONS

I. *parce que; et; comme; mais; ou*   Review §10.

II. 1. *que*   2. *peur (crainte)*   3. *temps*   4. *ce*
5. *tandis*   Review §10.

III.

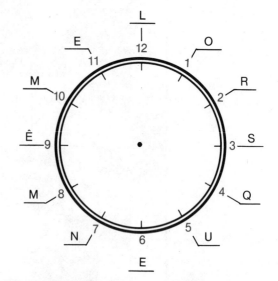

§11. ORDER OF ELEMENTS IN FRENCH SENTENCES

I. 1. *Elle ne me les donne pas.*   4. *Elle ne s'est pas lavée.*
2. *Je ne le leur donne pas.*   5. *Je ne le lui ai pas donné.*
3. *Ne les leur donnez pas.*   Review §11.

§12. IDIOMS

I. 1. B   2. A   3. A   4. B   5. C
Review §12.1.

II. 1. *à*   2. *au*   3. *aux*   4. *à*   5. *avoir*
6. *d'*   7. *de*   8. *être*   9. *faire*   10. *faire*
11. *au*   12. *à*   13. *aller*   14. *avoir*
15. *avoir*   16. *de*   17. *d'*   18. *être*
19. *faire*   20. *faire*   Review §12.2.

§13. DATES, DAYS, MONTHS, SEASONS

I. 1. C   2. B   3. C   4. D   5. A
Review §13.

§14.
TELLING TIME

A.

Il est cinq heures dix.

B.

Il est une heure.

C.

Il est six heures moins le quart.

D.

Il est sept heures et demie.

E.

Il est onze heures et quart.

F.

Il est quatre heures et quart.

Review §14.

§15.
TALKING ABOUT THE WEATHER

I. 1. B   2. C   3. D   4. B   5. D

II. *Il fait du soleil.*

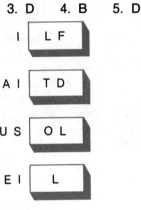

I   L F

A I   T D

U S   O L

E I   L

Review §15.

§16.
NUMBERS

I. 1. D   2. C   3. B   4. D   5. D

II. 1, 3, 2, 4

Review §16.

§17.
SYNONYMS

I. 4, 7, 5, 9, 6, 8, 1, 3, 10, 2

II. 1. T, A, A, I, L *(travailler)*   4. Â, I, M, N *(bâtiment)*
    2. É, I, E *(désirer)*   5. L, E *(milieu)*
    3. R, O, E, S, U *(profes-   6. A, I, R *(habiter)*
       seur)*

Review §17.

§18.
ANTONYMS

I. 1. *par*   2. *eu*   3. *se*   4. *rue*   5. *su*
   6. *paresse*

II. 1. *ma*   2. *si*   3. *son*   4. *mais*   5. *nom*
    6. *ai*

The new word is *AIMONS* (Let's love.)

III. 8, 4, 6, 2, 10, 5, 9, 1, 7, 3

§19.
COGNATES

I. 1. honest   2. paste   3. beast   4. forest
   5. priest   6. building   7. cake   8. soul
   9. amiable (likeable)   10. to permit

II.

A	E	L	B	A	M	I	A	P
P	A	T	P	L	Â	T	R	E
A	D	M	E	T	T	R	E	A
E	T	Â	P	E	T	Â	H	A

Review §19.

§20.
TRICKY
WORDS

I. 1. *le son*   2. *les actualités*   3. *la prune*
   4. *la chose*   5. *le but*   6. *le pruneau*   7. *le
   pain*   8. *le magasin*   9. *la flèche*   10. *l'ours*

II. 9, 5, 10, 4, 6, 3, 8, 1, 7, 2
Review §20.

§21.
HOW TO ASK
A QUESTION

I. 1. Est-ce que vous parlez français?
   2. À quelle heure est-ce que le train part?
   3. Est-ce que tu ne travailles pas?

II. 1. Parlez-vous français?
    2. Ne parlez-vous pas anglais?
    3. Que sais-je?

III. 1. Où est-ce que je peux acheter un journal? *or*
     Où puis-je acheter un journal?
     2. Est-ce que tu sais quelle heure il est? *or*
     Sais-tu quelle heure il est?
     3. Qu'est-ce que vous dites? *or* Que dites-vous?

Review §21. See **pouvoir**, **savoir**, **dire** in the verb tables
beginning on page 214.

PART TWO

GRAMMAR PRACTICE

§23.

Reading Comprehension

A. Paragraphs

Directions. Read each of the following paragraphs at least twice before selecting an answer to the question. The answers to these exercises are on page 201. After checking your answers, consult the vocabulary list beginning on page 291 so you can strengthen your knowledge of basic French vocabulary.

1. Des statistiques récentes ont révélé que les émissions de télévision consacrées aux animaux étaient celles qui avaient le plus de succès auprès des téléspectateurs de n'importe quel âge. Quand on combine le charme d'un beau paysage avec celui des bêtes sauvages, on a un spectacle apprécié de tout le monde.

   1. Quelle sorte de programme de télévision est très populaire?
      A. les programmes sur les statistiques
      B. les programmes de jeux télévisés
      C. les programmes policiers
      D. les programmes sur la nature

2. Les touristes canadiens qui achètent à Hong Kong des bijoux en jade ont souvent la surprise de leur vie. De retour chez eux, ils découvrent, la plupart du temps, que ces "souvenirs d'Orient" ont été fabriqués avec du jade venant d'une province canadienne, la Colombie Britannique.

   2. Qu'est-ce que ces touristes découvrent?
      A. Le jade vient souvent du Canada.
      B. Les bijoux sont très chers en Asie.
      C. Le jade n'a pas beaucoup de valeur.
      D. Les bijoux en vrai jade n'existent pas.

3. Dès le premier juillet, sur les autoroutes de France, les voitures avancent très lentement: vingt-cinq millions de Français partent en vacances. C'est que, pour les Français, les vacances d'été sont devenues une tradition et une obligation. Elles répondent aussi à un besoin de liberté d'action et de mouvement. Si on demandait à l'un de ces automobilistes pourquoi il se jette ainsi sur les routes dangereuses, il répondrait probablement: "Il faut que je me repose."

3. Pourquoi voit-on des millions de Français sur les routes en juillet?
   A. Ils veulent échapper aux chaleurs de l'été.
   B. Ils vont travailler à l'étranger.
   C. Ils aiment conduire dangereusement.
   D. Ils veulent être libres et se reposer.

4. On remarque depuis quelques années que les jeunes Français apprennent en anglais les chansons de Frank Sinatra et d'autres Américains, sans avoir appris l'anglais à l'école. Ils semblent le faire avec plaisir car ils sont passionnés par les thèmes de ces chansons. En cherchant à imiter ces artistes, ils arrivent parfois à un accent très authentique.

4. Comment ces jeunes Français apprennent-ils un peu d'anglais?
   A. en allant à l'école
   B. en rencontrant des artistes
   C. en apprenant des chansons
   D. en parlant à des Américains

5. Monsieur Pillet, un épicier de Paris, a eu un très joyeux Noël cette année. Il a décidé de manger les huîtres qu'il n'avait pas vendues avant les fêtes. Pendant qu'il en mangeait une, il s'est cassé une dent sur un petit objet rond et dur. Cet objet était une perle, qui a été estimée à trois mille francs. M. Pillet croit de nouveau au Père Noël!

5. Pourquoi cet épicier est-il content?
   A. Il a reçu beaucoup de cadeaux de Noël.
   B. Il est allé chez le dentiste.
   C. Il a mangé beaucoup d'huîtres.
   D. Il a trouvé un objet de grande valeur.

6. À Paris, la meilleure saison pour les amateurs de musique classique correspond à peu près à l'année scolaire. L'hiver, par exemple, est une période de l'année qui n'est pas recherchée par les touristes. C'est pourtant à ce moment-là qu'il y a de nombreux concerts donnés toutes les semaines par plusieurs grands orchestres français. On peut y assister à des prix modérés.

    6. Quand faut-il aller à Paris pour assister aux meilleurs concerts?
      A. entre septembre et juin
      B. pendant les grandes vacances
      C. le quatorze juillet
      D. pendant les fins de semaine

7. Un guide vendu chez tous les marchands de journaux a été publié pour tous les étudiants de l'université. Dans ce livre, on montre aux étudiants comment vivre avec peu d'argent, comment emprunter de l'argent aux banques, et où trouver un emploi. On leur parle aussi, bien entendu, du système universitaire français.

    7. Pourquoi ce livre est-il tellement apprécié des étudiants?
      A. Il donne les réponses aux questions des examens.
      B. Il contient un plan du métro.
      C. Il ne coûte pas cher.
      D. Il offre des renseignements pratiques.

8. Nous avons débarqué ce matin vers onze heures après une traversée assez mouvementée. On avait plusieurs heures de retard. D'abord, le moteur ne marchait pas bien. Ensuite, il y a eu du brouillard, puis du vent, enfin, il a plu. La mer était très agitée et beaucoup de voyageurs étaient malades. Moi aussi, naturellement. Je t'assure que le mal de mer, ça n'est pas agréable du tout!

    8. Comment cette personne a-t-elle fait le voyage?
      A. en avion
      B. en train
      C. en bateau
      D. en voiture

9. Maintenant, il va falloir faire ses courses le panier à la main, comme nos grands-parents. Les sacs en papier donnés dans les grands magasins sont de plus en plus rares. Le papier est devenu, comme le plastique, une marchandise très chère. En un an, le prix du papier a augmenté de soixante pour cent. Maintenant, les magasins sont forcés de vendre les sacs en papier qu'ils donnaient gratuitement l'année dernière.

9. Pourquoi faudra-t-il apporter un panier pour faire ses courses?
   A. Les magasins n'ont plus de sacs en papier.
   B. Les sacs en papier coûtent trop cher.
   C. Les paniers sont plus solides que les sacs en papier.
   D. Les sacs en papier ne sont plus assez grands.

10. Parmi les causes qui nous prédisposent aux accidents, viennent en premier lieu nos émotions, l'inquiétude ou la colère, par exemple, et la fatigue. Lorsque notre esprit fonctionne mal, l'émotion nous mène tout droit vers la catastrophe. L'émotion peut paralyser la raison et peut nous rendre vraiment indifférents aux dangers. La mauvaise humeur est donc un état d'esprit dangereux.

10. Qu'est-ce qui cause souvent les accidents?
    A. des conditions psychologiques extrêmes
    B. le manque d'expérience des jeunes
    C. la circulation intense dans les villes
    D. des voitures qui roulent trop lentement

11. Cet été, la petite ville de Saint-Tropez sera réservée aux piétons. Seuls les gens à pied auront accès à la plupart des rues de la ville et les voitures n'auront pas le droit d'y circuler. Cette mesure a été prise pour éviter les embouteillages dans Saint-Tropez. Cette petite ville, qui compte six mille habitants le reste de l'année, en a près de cent mille en été.

11. Qu'est-ce qu'on a décidé de faire à Saint-Tropez?
    A. limiter le nombre des touristes dans la ville
    B. construire de nouvelles autoroutes
    C. ouvrir d'immenses parcs de stationnement
    D. interdire la circulation automobile dans certaines rues

12. Hans, un petit Allemand de onze ans, a bien peur de voir ses vacances en France se terminer dès le premier jour. L'auto de ses parents, une Opel blanche, a été volée, avec tous leurs bagages, devant un hôtel de la banlieue de Paris. Alors, si vous voyez une Opel blanche, pensez à Hans.

   12. Pourquoi les vacances de Hans risquent-elles d'être interrompues?
      A. Il est tombé malade.
      B. Il a perdu ses parents.
      C. Des voleurs ont pris la voiture de la famille.
      D. Ses parents ont eu un accident.

13. Dimanche dernier, Paris ressemblait à une ville transformée. Toutes les rues de la capitale, en effet, étaient recouvertes d'une couche de glace où les enfants s'amusaient à patiner. Par une température de zéro degré centigrade, les Parisiens ont préféré rester chez eux.

   13. Qu'est-ce qui a forcé les Parisiens à rester chez eux?
      A. la réparation des rues
      B. un désastre national
      C. un froid glacial
      D. les ordres de la police

14. Pendant un arrêt de travail des employés du métro, les malheureux Parisiens ont voulu prendre leur voiture. Alors, tout le monde s'est trouvé bloqué aux carrefours. On allait plus vite à pied qu'en voiture. Et, cependant, le meilleur moyen d'aller à son travail était encore la bicyclette.

   14. Quel était le moyen de transport le plus pratique?
      A. le métro
      B. le vélo
      C. l'autobus
      D. la voiture

15. Bien que les feuilles sèches soient une bonne protection pour le sol, les feuilles qui se décomposent sont très malfaisantes. Il est nécessaire de tout nettoyer avec soin. L'accumulation de feuilles en temps pluvieux peut provoquer des maladies assez graves pour les plantes.

15. Pourquoi faut-il enlever toutes les feuilles mortes?
   A. Elles font du mal à la végétation.
   B. Elles ne sont pas belles.
   C. Elles causent des incendies.
   D. Elles souffrent de la pluie.

B. Long Selections

Directions. In the following passages, each blank space represents a missing word or expression. For each blank space, four possible completions are provided. Only one of them makes sense in the context of the passage. First, read the passage in its entirety to determine its general meaning. Then read it a second time. For each blank space choose the completion that makes the best sense. The answers to these exercises appear on page 201. After checking your answers, consult the vocabulary list beginning on page 291 so you can strengthen your knowledge of basic French vocabulary.

Selection Number 1

Six jeunes Québécois âgés de dix-huit à vingt-quatre ans vont partir du Nord de l'Alberta pour Montréal en canot à la dure route des "voyageurs." Ils vont refaire exactement le chemin que parcouraient de 1780 à 1820 les courageux "voyageurs" qui transportaient les fourrures pour la Compagnie de la Baie d'Hudson.

Ce sera _____ de 4.400 kilomètres de lacs,

1. A. un film
   B. un voyage
   C. une exploitation
   D. une description

de rivières, et de rapides dans les forêts. Le groupe a commencé ses préparatifs il y a plusieurs mois. Les jeunes ont déjà _____ un régime alimentaire composé

2. A. préparé
   B. inventé
   C. publié
   D. mangé

de 190 kilos de viande et d'une grande variété de légumes et de fruits. Puisqu'il leur est impossible de _____ une telle quantité de nourriture dans

3. A. servir
   B. vendre
   C. transporter
   D. boire

le canot, ils ont prévu six points de ravitaillement où ils trouveront des provisions laisées là à l'avance.

L'équipe compte faire quarante kilomètres par jour. Une fois par semaine, pour rassurer leurs familles, ils transmettront _____ par radio à

4. A. de la musique
   B. leurs félicitations
   C. des SOS
   D. de leurs nouvelles

l'école Richelieu-Quatre Saisons qui suivra de près leurs progrès. Cette école se spécialise dans ce genre de projet. Elle a pour objectif d'encourager les adolescents à _____ des expéditions en canot-camping.

5. A. financer
   B. faire
   C. imaginer
   D. décrire

Il n'est pas étonnant qu'aujourd'hui beaucoup de jeunes s'intéressent à ces activités.

Selection Number 2

L'hiver est peut-être la saison où se pratiquent le plus de sports au Québec. Il y a d'abord le patinage sur glace. À peu près tous les enfants en âge de marcher apprennent à _____. Durant l'hiver chaque cour

6. A. courir
   B. parler
   C. lire
   D. patiner

d'école, chaque parc public possède sa patinoire à la surface bien glacée et bien lisse où on va avec ses amis. Ces patinoires servent aussi à la pratique du sport national, le hockey. Tous les petits Québécois rêvent de devenir un jour des étoiles de ce _____ .

7. A. sport
   B. film
   C. cours
   D. ciel

Le ski alpin est aussi très pratiqué. Ses régions de montagnes ont permis au Québec d'établir de nombreuses stations de ski et de produire des champions internationaux. Le ski de fond et la raquette sont de plus en plus populaires. La raquette est un instrument inventé par les Indiens. C'est un cadre de bois sur lequel sont tendues des bandes de peau. On fixe les raquettes sous ses chaussures et on peut ainsi _____ sur la neige sans grand effort.

8. A. marcher
   B. peindre
   C. dormir
   D. conduire

Le sport d'hiver le plus nouveau, c'est la motoneige, sorte de véhicule sur skis d'invention québécoise, qui permet de se déplacer rapidement sur toute surface enneigée. Ce véhicule rend aussi de grands services dans le Grand Nord où il _____ maintenant les

9. A. guide
   B. remplace
   C. cache
   D. aide

traîneaux tirés par des chiens qui étaient autrefois le seul moyen de transport dans cette région. Mais il cause aussi beaucoup d'ennuis. Il est très bruyant, il fait fuir les animaux sauvages, et il brise les plantes. Malgré tout, à la campagne, il n'est pas rare de voir une ou plusieurs motoneiges à la porte des maisons. D'autre part, quand il y a des tempêtes de neige particulièrement
_____ , et que les routes sont

10. A. pittoresques
     B. courtes
     C. amusantes
     D. violentes

bloquées, c'est la motoneige qui permet de secourir les automobilistes en détresse.

Selection Number 3

Il y a des changements notables dans les habitudes alimentaires des Français. L'image traditionnelle du Français typique grand mangeur de pain ne correspond plus à la réalité. La _____ de pain par personne a diminué.

11. A. conservation
     B. consommation
     C. perte
     D. tranche

La consommation de pommes de terre a diminué aussi. Cependant, le "steak pommes frites" reste le plat populaire. Les portions de frites sont peut-être moins copieuses, mais les tranches de _____ demeurent

12. A. pain
     B. viande
     C. fromage
     D. gâteau

aussi grandes. La consommation de boeuf a augmenté légèrement malgré son prix élevé. Le porc et le poulet sont aussi très appréciés et les Français en _____

13. A. mangent
     B. boivent
     C. exportent
     D. expliquent

beaucoup. Par contre, la viande de cheval se vend de moins en moins et les boucheries chevalines avec leurs enseignes bien particulières deviennent de plus en plus _____ .

14. A. pittoresques
    B. célèbres
    C. rares
    D. mystérieuses

Curieusement, les Français mangent moins de légumes frais. Il y a une diminution du même ordre pour les légumes en conserves et pour les fruits frais dont la consommation par personne baisse considérablement. On n'y voit aucune raison évidente et on se demande _____

15. A. où
    B. à qui
    C. quand
    D. comment

expliquer cette situation qui pourrait avoir des résultats sérieux.

C. Pictures

Directions: In this section there are seven pictures. Under each picture there is a question. Look at the picture carefully, read the question, and select the best answer from choices A, B, C, or D. Answers appear on page 201.

Picture Number 1

1. Qu'est-ce que la religieuse regarde?
   A. des chaussures
   B. des chaussettes
   C. des robes
   D. des sacs

Picture Number 2

2. Que vend-on ici sous le parasol?
   A. des journaux
   B. des fleurs
   C. des livres
   D. des magazines

Picture Number 3

3. Que font les clients ici sur la terrasse d'un restaurant?
   A. Ils se battent
   B. Ils mangent et ils boivent
   C. Ils dorment
   D. Ils courent

Picture Number 4

4. Quel temps fait-il aujourd'hui?
   A. Il pleut
   B. Il neige
   C. Il fait un temps splendide
   D. Il est presque cinq heures et demie

Picture Number 5

5. Qu'est-ce qui flotte sur l'eau?
   A. le petit garçon
   B. la petite fille
   C. le voilier miniature
   D. les deux enfants

Picture Number 6

6. Quel genre de magasin est-ce?
   A. une librairie
   B. une bibliothèque
   C. une charcuterie
   D. un café

Picture Number 7

7. Qu'est-ce qu'on peut acheter ici?
   A. des tickets
   B. des repas
   C. des quais
   D. des livres de poche et des journaux

Answers

A. Paragraphs

1. **D**	4. **C**	7. **D**	10. **A**	13. **C**
2. **A**	5. **D**	8. **C**	11. **D**	14. **B**
3. **D**	6. **A**	9. **B**	12. **C**	15. **A**

B. Long Selections

1. **B**	4. **D**	7. **A**	10. **D**	13. **A**
2. **A**	5. **B**	8. **A**	11. **B**	14. **C**
3. **C**	6. **D**	9. **B**	12. **B**	15. **D**

C. Pictures

1. **D**	3. **B**	5. **C**	7. **D**
2. **B**	4. **A**	6. **A**	

§24.

Writing

A. Lists of Words to Write on Given Topics

Directions. In this section, various topics are presented to encourage you to write lists of words and expressions in French to enrich your vocabulary. If you need any help, consult Part One of this book and the vocabulary list beginning on page 291. Sample answers appear on page 211. If the word or expression you would like to write in French is not in Part One or the vocabulary list, consult a standard dictionary.

I. You have been invited to a wedding. You are planning to give the bride and groom a present. Write a list of four things you are considering.

1. _____ 3. _____
2. _____ 4. _____

II. Your friend is making plans to go to the circus with you. You prefer to go to the movies. Write four words or expressions you would use in the conversation to persuade your friend to go to the movies instead of the circus.

1. _____ 3. _____
2. _____ 4. _____

III. You are in a stationery shop **(une papeterie)** because you want to buy a pen. Write four words or expressions you would use in this conversation.

1. _____ 3. _____
2. _____ 4. _____

IV. Write six words in French for things you like to eat or drink for breakfast.

1. _____ 4. _____
2. _____ 5. _____
3. _____ 6. _____

202

V. You are in a French restaurant. Write the words for four vegetables that are on the menu.
   1. _____   3. _____
   2. _____   4. _____

VI. Now you are looking at the list of fish. Write four that are on the menu.
   1. _____   3. _____
   2. _____   4. _____

VII. Write the words for two kinds of cheese on the menu.
   1. _____   2. _____

VIII. Write four words in French for things in your house that sometimes need to be repaired.
   1. _____   3. _____
   2. _____   4. _____

IX. You are in a hospital visiting a friend who broke an arm and a leg. Write four words or expressions you would use in your conversation.
   1. _____   3. _____
   2. _____   4. _____

X. Write four words or expressions you would use while talking to a desk clerk at the airport.
   1. _____   3. _____
   2. _____   4. _____

B. Simple Guided Composition for Expression

Directions. Various situations are presented here to encourage you to write simple sentences in French. If you need any help, consult Part One of this book, in particular §12.2, the formation of verb forms in §7., and the vocabulary list beginning on page 291. Sample sentences appear on page 211.

1. You are talking to the desk clerk in a hotel. Make the following three statements: Tell the clerk your name, say that you have a reservation, and present your passport.

   _____
   _____
   _____
   _____
   _____

2. You are in a bookstore. Write three sentences saying that you want to buy a book on modern art, that you don't want to pay much, and that it is a present for a friend.

_____

_____

_____

_____

_____

3. You are talking to a friend. Write two sentences saying that you are going to the movies this evening. Ask your friend to come with you.

_____

_____

_____

_____

_____

4. You are in a restaurant. Tell the waiter that you would like a cheese omelet, French fries, and a tomato salad. Then ask him to bring you a cup of coffee.

_____

_____

_____

_____

_____

5. You don't feel well today. Tell the doctor you are sick, that you have a headache, a stomachache, and a pain in the neck.

_____

_____

_____

_____

_____

6. You are on a tourist bus in Paris. Tell the person next to you that you're going to Versailles, that you are going to take a walk in the gardens, and that you are going to have dinner with some friends.

_____

_____

_____

_____

7. Tell your French teacher where you are going to spend the summer, with whom, and how many weeks you will be there.

_____
_____
_____
_____
_____

8. Your friends gave you a surprise birthday party. Write that you received many presents, that you ate cake and ice cream, and you danced and sang.

_____
_____
_____
_____
_____

9. Your best friend asked you where you went yesterday. Say that you went to the beach, you swam, and you played ball.

_____
_____
_____
_____
_____

10. Another friend wants to know what you did last night. Say that you watched television, that you saw a good French film, and that you liked it a lot.

_____
_____
_____
_____
_____

C. Word Games to Increase Your Vocabulary

Directions. In this section there are ten word games. Follow the directions for each game. If you need any help, consult Part One of this book and the vocabulary lists beginning on page 291. Check your answers and solutions in the answers section on page 212.

I. Parts of the body

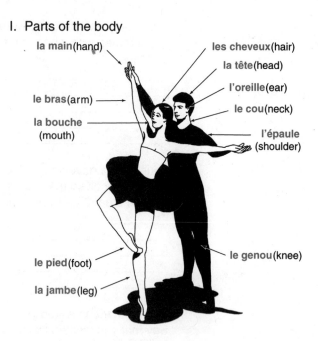

la main (hand)

les cheveux (hair)

la tête (head)

l'oreille (ear)

le bras (arm)

le cou (neck)

la bouche (mouth)

l'épaule (shoulder)

le pied (foot)

le genou (knee)

la jambe (leg)

These two dancers posed for a moment to give you a chance to learn some of the parts of the body. In the grid, find five of the words in the picture and draw a line around each of them. They are written horizontally, vertically, diagonally, and backwards.

M	A	I	N	E	B	M	N	Z
O	A	J	E	B	R	I	E	E
R	N	A	C	M	S	A	L	O
E	I	M	O	A	E	L	O	R
I	R	B	R	J	I	N	A	L
M	A	B	E	E	P	R	T	S
E	Z	P	R	Q	C	H	E	V
J	E	O	L	E	G	C	O	U

II. Drop one letter in each of the following words to find new words. Write the new word on the line.

1. **moins**/less   > le _____ /month
2. le **mois**/month   > _____ /me
3. le **cours**/course   > la _____ /yard
4. le **fils**/son   > le _____ /thread
5. **prendre**/to take   > _____ /to give back
6. la **fleur**/flower   > _____ /their
7. le **coussin**/cushion > le _____ /cousin
8. le **poisson**/fish   > le _____ /poison
9. la **porte**/door   > le _____ /port
10. **faible**/weak   > la _____ /fable

III. The letters of the following words are scrambled. Put them in the correct order to find the word. Then write it on the line. The clues will help you.

1. | O A U R N J L | _____

   Clue: It's something you read.

2. | S S O I P N O | _____

   Clue: It's something you eat, usually as an entrée.

3. | P O U S E | _____

   Clue: It's something you eat in a bowl or cup.

4. | L O T Y S | _____

   Clue: You write with it.

5. | I L A B A | _____

   Clue: You sweep the floor with it.

IV. Choose a word in column B to complete the statement in column A. The English meanings of the French words are given below.

A	**B**
1. Je peux boire _____ .	une omelette
2. Je peux jeter _____ .	une personne
3. Je peux regarder _____ .	une piscine
4. Je peux lire _____ .	la musique
5. Je peux nager dans_____ .	une balle
6. Je peux accepter_____ .	un cadeau
7. Je peux écouter _____ .	la télé
8. Je peux acheter _____ .	une invitation
9. Je peux aider _____ .	un livre
10. Je peux faire _____ .	un café

accepter to accept
acheter to buy, to purchase
aider to help
balle ball
boire to drink
cadeau gift, present
café coffee
dans in
écouter to listen (to)
faire to make, to do
invitation invitation
je peux I can, I am able

jeter to throw
lire to read
livre book
musique music
nager to swim
omelette omelet
personne person
piscine swimming pool
regarder to look at, to watch
télé TV

V. Add the appropriate accent mark to one vowel in each of the following words to get another word, another meaning. The accent marks are: **accent aigu (´)**, **accent grave (`)**, **accent circonflexe (^)**, **tréma (¨)**.

1. sur/on	> _____/sure
2. ou/or	> _____/where
3. mais/but	> le _____/corn
4. des/of the, from the	> _____/since
5. de/of, from	> le _____/thimble
6. la/the	> _____/there
7. a/has	> _____/at, to

VI. Match the articles of clothing with the parts of the
body where the articles are worn by writing the
corresponding number on the line. You learned these
parts of the body in game I.

Les Vêtements/Clothing   Les Parties du corps
                            humain/Parts of the
                            human body

1. la chaussure/shoe   _____ la jambe
2. le gant/glove   _____ la tête
3. l'écharpe/scarf   _____ le pied
4. le chapeau/hat   _____ les épaules
5. le bas/stocking   _____ le cou
6. le châle/shawl   _____ la main

VII. Change one letter to another letter in a French word
and get another word, another meaning.

1. je sais/I know   je _____ /I am
2. je lis/I'm reading   je _____ /I'm saying
3. je vais/I'm going   je _____ /I'm doing,
                                           I'm making
4. il suit/he is following il _____ /he knows
5. nous savons/we know   nous _____ /we wash
6. vous levez/you raise   vous _____ /you wash
7. laisser/to let, to allow _____ /to lower
8. le pain/bread   le _____ /bath
9. la tête/head   la _____ /beast
10. le bain/bath   la _____ /hand
11. les cheveux/hair   les _____ /horses
12. lire/to read   _____ /to say,
                                         to tell
13. tonner/to thunder   _____ /to give
14. les jeux/games   _____ /two
15. la maison/house   la _____ /reason

VIII. Arrange these money bags **(les sacs d'argent)**
according to the letter on each bag to find the amount
of French francs they contain. Then write the French
word on the line below them.

IX. **Quel temps fait-il aujourd'hui?**/What's the weather like today? To find out, arrange these blocks of letters so that they spell out today's weather forecast. Then write the four French words on the line below them.

X. Have you ever played a word game in English combining two words to get a new word with a new meaning? For example, extra + ordinary = extraordinary. Here are some in French for you to combine. Write the new French word on the line. In just this game, you are learning twenty-six French words!

1. **main**/hand
   tenant/holding
   } _____ /now

2. **autre**/other
   fois/time
   } _____ /formerly

3. **de**/of, from
   dans/in
   } _____ /inside, within

4. **de**/of, from
   hors/out
   } _____ /outside

5. **de**/of, from
   bout/tip, end
   } _____ /standing

6. **pour**/for
   quoi/what
   } _____ /why

7. **pour**/for
   tant/so much, so many
   } _____ /however

8. **sur**/on
   tout/all
   } _____ /especially

9. **quoi**/what
   que/that
   } _____ /although

10. **si**/if
    non/no
    } _____ /if not

Answers

A. Lists of Words to Write on Given Topics

Note: The French words and expressions given here are not the only answers. They are samples. If you do not know their meanings, consult the vocabulary beginning on page 291.

I.   1. un vase   3. une couverture
     2. une lampe   4. cent dollars

II. 1. Je préfère   3. un film intéressant
     2. au cinéma   4. une histoire d'amour

III. 1. Je désire   3. un stylo
     2. acheter   4. à bon marché

IV. 1. du café   4. un oeuf
     2. du lait   5. un croissant
     3. du jus d'orange   6. une brioche

V.   1. les carottes   3. les haricots verts
     2. les épinards   4. les petits pois

VI. 1. le saumon   3. la truite
     2. la sole   4. la morue

VII. 1. le camembert   2. le roquefort

VIII. 1. l'aspirateur   3. le lave-vaisselle
      2. le robinet   4. le lave-linge

IX. 1. se casser le bras   3. comment
     2. la jambe   4. aller mieux

X.   1. à quelle heure   3. partir
     2. c'est combien?   4. arriver

B. Simple Guided Composition for Expression

1. Mon nom est ... J'ai une réservation. Voici mon passeport.
2. Je désire acheter un livre sur l'art moderne. Je ne veux pas payer beaucoup. C'est un cadeau pour un ami.
3. Je vais au cinéma ce soir. Veux-tu venir avec moi? (or: Est-ce que tu veux venir avec moi?)
4. J'aimerais une omelette au fromage, des frites, et une salade de tomates. Apportez-moi une tasse de café, s'il vous plaît.
5. Je suis malade. J'ai mal à la tête, mal à l'estomac, et mal au cou.

6. Je vais à Versailles. Je vais faire une promenade dans les jardins. Je vais dîner avec des amis.
7. Je vais passer l'été à Paris avec ma famille. Nous allons rester à Paris trois semaines.
8. J'ai reçu beaucoup de cadeaux pour mon anniversaire. J'ai mangé du gâteau et de la glace. J'ai dansé et j'ai chanté.
9. Hier je suis allé(e) à la plage. J'ai nagé et j'ai joué à la balle.
10. Hier soir j'ai regardé la télé. J'ai vu un bon film français. Je l'ai beaucoup aimé.

C. Word Games to Increase Your Vocabulary

I. Parts of the body

M	A	I	N	E	B	M	N	Z
O	A	J	E	B	R	I	E	E
R	N	A	C	M	S	A	L	O
E	I	M	O	A	E	L	O	R
I	R	B	R	J	I	N	A	L
M	A	B	E	E	P	R	T	S
E	Z	P	R	Q	C	H	E	V
J	E	O	L	E	G	C	O	U

II.
1. mois
2. moi
3. cour
4. fil
5. rendre
6. leur
7. cousin
8. poison
9. port
10. fable

III.
1. JOURNAL
2. POISSON
3. SOUPE
4. STYLO
5. BALAI

IV.
1. un café
2. une balle
3. la télé
4. un livre
5. une piscine
6. une invitation
7. la musique
8. un cadeau
9. une personne
10. une omelette

V.
1. sûr
2. où
3. maïs
4. dès
5. dé
6. là
7. à

VI. 5, 4, 1, 6, 3, 2

VII.
1. suis	6. lavez	11. chevaux
2. dis	7. baisser	12. dire
3. fais	8. bain	13. donner
4. sait	9. bête	14. deux
5. lavons	10. main	15. raison

VIII. MILLE (one thousand)

IX. il fait du soleil. (It's sunny.)

X.
1. maintenant	5. debout	8. surtout
2. autrefois	6. pourquoi	9. quoique
3. dedans	7. pourtant	10. sinon
4. dehors		

§25.

French Verb Conjugation Tables

Review the section on verbs in **§7.** in this book, in particular, **§7.6** through **§7.19**. For an in-depth and extensive presentation of French verb tenses and their uses, consult Barron's *501 French Verbs Fully Conjugated in All the Tenses.*

In French there are fourteen verb tenses. There are seven simple tenses identified below as tense numbers 1–7. A simple tense contains one verb form. There are seven compound tenses identified as tense numbers 8–14. A compound tense contains one verb form and a past participle. There is also the Imperative, which is not a tense but a mood.

There are three major types of regular verbs. In the infinitive form, they end in either **-er**, **-ir** or **-re**. For example, **parler**, **finir**, **vendre**.

FORMATION OF THE SEVEN SIMPLE TENSES NUMBERS 1 THROUGH 7 FOR REGULAR VERBS

TENSE NO. 1 *PRÉSENT DE L'INDICATIF* (Present Indicative)

For **-er** type verbs, drop **er** from the infinitive form. What is left is called the stem. Then add the following endings to the stem:

Singular: **e, es, e**;
Plural: **ons, ez, ent**

---

parler to talk, to speak
Singular: **je parle, tu parles, il/elle/on parle**
Plural: **nous parlons, vous parlez, ils/elles parlent**

For **-ir** type verbs, drop **ir** from the infinitive form. What is left is called the stem. Then add the following endings to the stem:

Singular: **is, is, it**;
Plural: **issons, issez, issent**

---

finir to finish
Singular: **je finis, tu finis, il/elle/on finit**
Plural: **nous finissons, vous finissez, ils/elles finissent**

For **-re** type verbs, drop **re** from the infinitive form. What is left is called the stem. Then add the following endings to the stem. Note that there is no ending to add to the third person singular.

Singular: **s, s, —**;
Plural: **ons, ez, ent**

---

vendre to sell
Singular: **je vends, tu vends, il/elle/on vend**
Plural: **nous vendons, vous vendez, ils/elles vendent**

Refer to the above patterns of formation for the following regular **-er**, **-ir**, **-re** verbs in the present indicative tense.

Note that at times some of the verb forms in this tense require the addition of an accent mark or one that is different from the one in the infinitive. Also, note that some verb forms change in spelling in other ways, for example, **c** to **ç**, **l** to **ll**, **g** to **ge**, and others as in the forms given below. These changes in spelling are called Orthographical Changing verbs. Nevertheless, the endings added to the stems of the verbs are regular, as given above. The changes in spelling indicate proper pronunciation. See **§7.17** in this book.

---

accepter to accept
Singular: **j'accepte, tu acceptes, il/elle/on accepte**
Plural: **nous acceptons, vous acceptez, ils/elles acceptent**

acheter to buy, to purchase
Singular: **j'achète, tu achètes, il/elle/on achète**
Plural: **nous achetons, vous achetez, ils/elles achètent**

admirer to admire
Singular: **j'admire, tu admires, il/elle/on admire**
Plural: **nous admirons, vous admirez, ils/elles admirent**

agacer to annoy, to pester
Singular: **j'agace, tu agaces, il/elle/on agace**
Plural: **nous agaçons, vous agacez, ils/elles agacent**

aimer to love, to like
Singular: **j'aime, tu aimes, il/elle/on aime**
Plural: **nous aimons, vous aimez, ils/elles aiment**

s'amuser to have a good time, to enjoy oneself, to amuse oneself
Singular: **je m'amuse, tu t'amuses, il/elle/on s'amuse**
Plural: **nous nous amusons, vous vous amusez, ils/elles s'amusent**

appeler to call
Singular: **j'appelle, tu appelles, il/elle/on appelle**
Plural: **nous appelons, vous appelez, ils/elles appellent**

s'appeler to call oneself, to be named
Singular: **je m'appelle, tu t'appelles, il/elle/on s'appelle**
Plural: **nous nous appelons, vous vous appelez, ils/elles s'appellent**

apporter to bring
Singular: **j'apporte, tu apportes, il/elle/on apporte**
Plural: **nous apportons, vous apportez, ils/elles apportent**

attendre to wait, to wait for, to expect
Singular: **j'attends, tu attends, il/elle/on attend**
Plural: **nous attendons, vous attendez, ils/elles attendent**

bâtir to build
Singular: **je bâtis, tu bâtis, il/elle/on bâtit**
Plural: **nous bâtissons, vous bâtissez, ils/elles bâtissent**

bouger to budge, to move
Singular: **je bouge, tu bouges, il/elle/on bouge**
Plural: **nous bougeons, vous bougez, ils/elles bougent**

casser to break
Singular: **je casse, tu casses, il/elle/on casse**
Plural: **nous cassons, vous cassez, ils/elles cassent**

se casser to break (a part of one's body, *e.g.,* arm, leg, nose)
Singular: **je me casse, tu te casses, il/elle/on se casse**
Plural: **nous nous cassons, vous vous cassez, ils/elles se cassent**

choisir to choose, to select
Singular: **je choisis, tu choisis, il/elle/on choisit**
Plural: **nous choisissons, vous choisissez, ils/elles choisissent**

commencer to begin, to start, to commence
Singular: **je commence, tu commences, il/elle/on commence**
Plural: **nous commençons, vous commencez, ils/elles commencent**

se coucher to go to bed
Singular: **je me couche, tu te couches, il/elle/on se couche**
Plural: **nous nous couchons, vous vous couchez, ils/elles se couchent**

danser to dance
Singular: **je danse, tu danses, il/elle/on danse**
Plural: **nous dansons, vous dansez, ils/elles dansent**

défendre to defend, to forbid, to prohibit
Singular: **je défends, tu défends, il/elle/on défend**
Plural: **nous défendons, vous défendez, ils/elles défendent**

descendre to go down, to descend
Singular: **je descends, tu descends, il/elle/on descend**
Plural: **nous descendons, vous descendez, ils/elles descendent**

désirer to desire
Singular: **je désire, tu désires, il/elle/on désire**
Plural: **nous désirons, vous désirez, ils/elles/ désirent**

donner to give
Singular: **je donne, tu donnes, il/elle/on donne**
Plural: **nous donnons, vous donnez, ils/elles donnent**

entendre to hear, to understand
Singular: **j'entends, tu entends, il/elle/on entend**
Plural: **nous entendons, vous entendez, ils/elles entendent**

entrer to enter
Singular: **j'entre, tu entres, il/elle/on entre**
Plural: **nous entrons, vous entrez, ils/elles entrent**

envoyer to send
Singular: **j'envoie, tu envoies, il/elle/on envoie**
Plural: **nous envoyons, vous envoyez, ils/elles envoient**

grandir to grow (up, taller), to increase
Singular: **je grandis, tu grandis, il/elle/on grandit**
Plural: **nous grandissons, vous grandissez, ils/elles grandissent**

maigrir to lose weight
Singular: **je maigris, tu maigris, il/elle/on maigrit**
Plural: **nous maigrissons, vous maigrissez, ils/elles maigrissent**

manger to eat
Singular: **je mange, tu manges, il/elle/on mange**
Plural: **nous mangeons, vous mangez, ils/elles mangent**

nager to swim
Singular: **je nage, tu nages, il/elle/on nage**
Plural: **nous nageons, vous nagez, ils/elles nagent**

passer to spend (time)
Singular: **je passe, tu passes, il/elle/on passe**
Plural: **nous passons, vous passez, ils/elles passent**

perdre to lose
Singular: **je perds, tu perds, il/elle/on perd**
Plural: **nous perdons, vous perdez, ils/elles perdent**

réfléchir to think, to reflect, to ponder
Singular: **je réfléchis, tu réfléchis, il/elle/on réfléchit**
Plural: **nous réfléchissons, vous réfléchissez, ils/elles réfléchissent**

regarder to look (at), to watch
Singular: **je regarde, tu regardes, il/elle/on regarde**
Plural: **nous regardons, vous regardez, ils/elles regardent**

rendre to give back, to return (something), to render; to vomit
Singular: **je rends, tu rends, il/elle/on rend**
Plural: **nous rendons, vous rendez, ils/elles rendent**

répondre to respond, to reply, to answer
Singular: **je réponds, tu réponds, il/elle/on répond**
Plural: **nous répondons, vous répondez, ils/elles répondent**

rester to stay, to remain
Singular: **je reste, tu restes, il/elle/on reste**
Plural: **nous restons, vous restez, ils/elles restent**

réussir to succeed
Singular: **je réussis, tu réussis, il/elle/on réussit**
Plural: **nous réussissons, vous réussissez, ils/elles réussissent**

rougir to blush, to redden
Singular: **je rougis, tu rougis, il/elle/on rougit**
Plural: **nous rougissons, vous rougissez, ils/elles rougissent**

voyager to travel
Singular: **je voyage, tu voyages, il/elle/on voyage**
Plural: **nous voyageons, vous voyagez, ils/elles voyagent**

For the uses of this tense, see §7.8—1 in this book.

TENSE NO. 2 *IMPARFAIT DE L'INDICATIF* (Imperfect Indicative)

For **-er, -ir, -re** verbs, take the **nous** form in the present indicative as shown in Tense No. 1, drop the ending **ons** and add the following endings:

Singular: **ais, ais, ait**;
Plural: **ions, iez, aient**

---

parler to talk, to speak
Singular: **je parlais, tu parlais, il/elle/on parlait**
Plural: **nous parlions, vous parliez, ils/elles parlaient**

---

finir to finish
Singular: **je finissais, tu finissais, il/elle/on finissait**
Plural: **nous finissions, vous finissiez, ils/elles finissaient**

---

vendre to sell
Singular: **je vendais, tu vendais, il/elle/on vendait**
Plural: **nous vendions, vous vendiez, ils/elles vendaient**

For an English translation of French verb tenses, see the model verbs in French and English in all the tenses in **§7.6** and **§7.7** in this book.

---

acheter to buy, to purchase
Singular: **j'achetais, tu achetais, il/elle/on achetait**
Plural: **nous achetions, vous achetiez, ils/elles achetaient**

---

se casser to break (a part of one's body, *e.g.*, arm, leg, nose)
Singular: **je me cassais, tu te cassais, il/elle/on se cassait**
Plural: **nous nous cassions, vous vous cassiez, ils/elles se cassaient**

---

choisir to choose, to select
Singular: **je choisissais, tu choisissais, il/elle/on choisissait**
Plural: **nous choisissions, vous choisissiez, ils/elles choisissaient**

---

commencer to begin, to start, to commence
Singular: **je commençais, tu commençais, il/elle/on commençait**
Plural: **nous commencions, vous commenciez, ils/elles commençaient**

---

se coucher to go to bed
Singular: **je me couchais, tu te couchais, il/elle/on se couchait**
Plural: **nous nous couchions, vous vous couchiez, ils/elles se couchaient**

donner to give
Singular: **je donnais, tu donnais, il/elle/on donnait**
Plural: **nous donnions, vous donniez, ils/elles donnaient**

entendre to hear
Singular: **j'entendais, tu entendais, il/elle/on entendait**
Plural: **nous entendions, vous entendiez, ils/elles entendaient**

entrer to enter
Singular: **j'entrais, tu entrais, il/elle/on entrait**
Plural: **nous entrions, vous entriez, ils/elles entraient**

envoyer to send
Singular: **j'envoyais, tu envoyais, il/elle/on envoyait**
Plural: **nous envoyions, vous envoyiez, ils/elles envoyaient**

manger to eat
Singular: **je mangeais, tu mangeais, il/elle/on mangeait**
Plural: **nous mangions, vous mangiez, ils/elles mangeaient**

perdre to lose
Singular: **je perdais, tu perdais, il/elle/on perdait**
Plural: **nous perdions, vous perdiez, ils/elles perdaient**

réfléchir to think, to reflect, to ponder
Singular: **je réfléchissais, tu réfléchissais, il/elle/on réfléchissait**
Plural: **nous réfléchissions, vous réfléchissiez, ils/elles réfléchissaient**

regarder to look (at), to watch
Singular: **je regardais, tu regardais, il/elle/on regardait**
Plural: **nous regardions, vous regardiez, ils/elles regardaient**

rendre to give back, to return (something), to render; to vomit
Singular: **je rendais, tu rendais, il/elle/on rendait**
Plural: **nous rendions, vous rendiez, ils/elles rendaient**

répondre to respond, to reply, to answer
Singular: **je répondais, tu répondais, il/elle/on répondait**
Plural: **nous répondions, vous répondiez, ils/elles répondaient**

rester to stay, to remain
Singular: **je restais, tu restais, il/elle/on restait**
Plural: **nous restions, vous restiez, ils/elles restaient**

réussir to succeed
Singular: **je réussissais, tu réussissais, il/elle/on réussissait**
Plural: **nous réussissions, vous réussissiez, ils/elles réussissaient**

---

rougir to blush, to redden
Singular: **je rougissais, tu rougissais, il/elle/on rougissait**
Plural: **nous rougissions, vous rougissiez, ils/elles rougissaient**

---

voyager to travel
Singular: **je voyageais, tu voyageais, il/elle/on voyageait**
Plural: **nous voyagions, vous voyagiez, ils/elles voyageaient**

For the uses of this tense, see **§7.8—2** in this book.

TENSE NO. 3 *PASSÉ SIMPLE* (Past Definite or Simple Past)

For all **-er** verbs, drop **er** and add the following endings. Review the note about Orthographical Changing verbs above in Tense No. 1. See also **§7.17** in this book.

Singular: **ai, as, a**;
Plural: **âmes, âtes, èrent**

---

parler to talk, to speak
Singular: **je parlai, tu parlas, il/elle/on parla**
Plural: **nous parlâmes, vous parlâtes, ils/elles parlèrent**

For **-ir** and **-re** verbs, drop **ir** and **re** and add the following endings:

Singular: **is, is, it**;
Plural: **îmes, îtes, irent**

---

finir to finish
Singular: **je finis, tu finis, il/elle/on finit**
Plural: **nous finîmes, vous finîtes, ils/elles finirent**

---

vendre to sell
Singular: **je vendis, tu vendis, il/elle/on vendit**
Plural: **nous vendîmes, vous vendîtes, ils/elles vendirent**

---

acheter to buy, to purchase
Singular: **j'achetai, tu achetas, il/elle/on acheta**
Plural: **nous achetâmes, vous achetâtes, ils/elles achetèrent**

---

aller to go
Singular: **j'allai, tu allas, il/elle/on alla**
Plural: **nous allâmes, vous allâtes, ils/elles allèrent**

---

choisir to choose, to select
Singular: **je choisis, tu choisis, il/elle/on choisit**
Plural: **nous choisîmes, vous choisîtes, ils/elles choisirent**

---

commencer to begin, to start, to commence
Singular: **je commençai, tu commenças, il/elle/on commença**
Plural: **nous commençâmes, vous commençâtes, ils/elles commencèrent**

---

entendre to hear, to understand
Singular: **j'entendis, tu entendis, il/elle/on entendit**
Plural: **nous entendîmes, vous entendîtes, ils/elles entendirent**

---

manger to eat
Singular: **je mangeai, tu mangeas, il/elle/on mangea**
Plural: **nous mangeâmes, vous mangeâtes, ils/elles mangèrent**

---

perdre to lose
Singular: **je perdis, tu perdis, il/elle/on perdit**
Plural: **nous perdîmes, vous perdîtes, ils/elles perdirent**

For the uses of this tense, see **§7.8—3** in this book.

TENSE NO. 4 *FUTUR* (Future)

For **-er** and **-ir** verbs, add the following endings to the whole infinitive. For **-re** verbs, drop **e** in **re** before adding the future endings, which are as follows. Note that these endings are based on the present indicative tense of the irregular verb **avoir**/to have.

Singular: **ai**, **as**, **a**;
Plural: **ons**, **ez**, **ont**

parler to talk, to speak
Singular: **je parlerai, tu parleras, il/elle/on parlera**
Plural: **nous parlerons, vous parlerez, ils/elles parleront**

finir to finish
Singular: **je finirai, tu finiras, il/elle/on finira**
Plural: **nous finirons, vous finirez, ils/elles finiront**

vendre to sell
Singular: **je vendrai, tu vendras, il/elle/on vendra**
Plural: **nous vendrons, vous vendrez, ils/elles vendront**

acheter to buy, to purchase
Singular: **j'achèterai, tu achèteras, il/elle/on achètera**
Plural: **nous achèterons, vous achèterez, ils/elles achèteront**

Note the addition of the **accent grave (`)** on the first **e** in these forms.

apprendre to learn
Singular: **j'apprendrai, tu apprendras, il/elle/on apprendra**
Plural: **nous apprendrons, vous apprendrez, ils/elles apprendront**

choisir to choose, to select
Singular: **je choisirai, tu choisiras, il/elle/on choisira**
Plural: **nous choisirons, vous choisirez, ils/elles choisiront**

donner to give
Singular: **je donnerai, tu donneras, il/elle/on donnera**
Plural: **nous donnerons, vous donnerez, ils/elles donneront**

écouter to listen (to)
Singular: **j'écouterai, tu écouteras, il/elle/on écoutera**
Plural: **nous écouterons, vous écouterez, ils/elles écouteront**

entendre to hear, to understand
Singular: **j'entendrai, tu entendras, il/elle/on entendra**
Plural: **nous entendrons, vous entendrez, ils/elles entendront**

---

penser to think
Singular: **je penserai, tu penseras, il/elle/on pensera**
Plural: **nous penserons, vous penserez, ils/elles penseront**

---

réussir to succeed
Singular: **je réussirai, tu réussiras, il/elle/on réussira**
Plural: **nous réussirons, vous réussirez, ils/elles réussiront**

For the uses of this tense, see **§7.8—4** in this book.

TENSE NO. 5 *CONDITIONNEL PRÉSENT* (Conditional)

For **-er** and **-ir** verbs, add the following endings to the whole infinitive. For **-re** verbs, drop **e** in **re** before adding the conditional endings, which are as follows. Note that these endings are the same as those for the imperfect indicative (Tense No. 2).

Singular: **ais, ais, ait**;
Plural: **ions, iez, aient**

---

parler to talk, to speak
Singular: **je parlerais, tu parlerais, il/elle/on parlerait**
Plural: **nous parlerions, vous parleriez, ils/elles parleraient**

---

finir to finish
Singular: **je finirais, tu finierais, il/elle/on finirait**
Plural: **nous finirions, vous finiriez, ils/elles finiraient**

---

vendre to sell
Singular: **je vendrais, tu vendrais, il/elle/on vendrait**
Plural: **nous vendrions, vous vendriez, ils/elles vendraient**

---

acheter to buy, to purchase
Singular: **j'achèterais, tu achèterais, il/elle/on achèterait**
Plural: **nous achèterions, vous achèteriez, ils/elles achèteraient**

Note the addition of the **accent grave (`)** on the first **e** in these forms.

---

apprendre to learn
Singular: **j'apprendrais, tu apprendrais, il/elle/on apprendrait**
Plural: **nous apprendrions, vous apprendriez, ils/elles apprendraient**

---

choisir to choose, to select
Singular: **je choisirais, tu choisirais, il/elle/on choisirait**
Plural: **nous choisirions, vous choisiriez, ils/elles choisiraient**

---

donner to give
Singular: **je donnerais, tu donnerais, il/elle/on donnerait**
Plural: **nous donnerions, vous donneriez, ils/elles donneraient**

écouter to listen (to)
Singular: **j'écouterais, tu écouterais, il/elle/on écouterait**
Plural: **nous écouterions, vous écouteriez, ils/elles écouteraient**

---

entendre to hear, to understand
Singular: **j'entendrais, tu entendrais, il/elle/on entendrait**
Plural: **nous entendrions, vous entendriez, ils/elles entendraient**

réussir to succeed
Singular: **je réussirais, tu réussirais, il/elle/on réussirait**
Plural: **nous réussirions, vous réussiriez, ils/elles réussiraient**

For an English translation of French verb tenses, see the model verbs in French and English in all the tenses in **§7.6** and **§7.7** in this book. For the uses of this tense, see **§7.8—5**.

TENSE NO. 6 *PRÉSENT DU SUBJONCTIF* (Present Subjunctive)

To form this tense regularly, drop the ending **-ant** of the present participle of **-er**, **-ir**, **-re** verbs and add the following endings. Review the present participle in **§7.4** in this book.

Singular: **e**, **es**, **e**;
Plural: **ions**, **iez**, **ent**

---

parler to talk, to speak
Singular: **que je parle, que tu parles, qu'il/elle/on parle**
Plural: **que nous parlions, que vous parliez, qu'ils/elles parlent**

---

finir to finish
Singular: **que je finisse, que tu finisses, qu'il/elle/on finisse**
Plural: **que nous finissions, que vous finissiez, qu'ils/elles finissent**

---

vendre to sell
Singular: **que je vende, que tu vendes, qu'il/elle/on vende**
Plural: **que nous vendions, que vous vendiez, qu'ils/elles vendent**

---

acheter to buy, to purchase
Singular: **que j'achète, que tu achètes, qu'il/elle/on achète**
Plural: **que nous achetions, que vous achetiez, qu'ils/elles achètent**

Note the addition of the **accent grave (`)** where required.

---

choisir to choose, to select
Singular: **que je choisisse, que tu choisisses, qu'il/elle/on choisisse**
Plural: **que nous choisissions, que vous choisissiez, qu'ils/elles choisissent**

---

donner to give
Singular: **que je donne, que tu donnes, qu'il/elle/on donne**
Plural: **que nous donnions, que vous donniez, qu'ils/elles donnent**

écouter to listen (to)
Singular: **que j'écoute, que tu écoutes, qu'il/elle/on écoute**
Plural: **que nous écoutions, que vous écoutiez, qu'ils/elles écoutent**

---

entendre to hear, to understand
Singular: **que j'entende, que tu entendes, qu'il/elle/on entende**
Plural: **que nous entendions, que vous entendiez, qu'ils/elles entendent**

se laver to wash oneself
Singular: **que je me lave, que tu te laves, qu'il/elle/on se lave**
Plural: **que nous nous lavions, que vous vous laviez, qu'ils/elles se lavent**

réussir to succeed
Singular: **que je réussisse, que tu réussisses, qu'il/elle/on réussisse**
Plural: **que nous réussissions, que vous réussissiez, qu'ils/elles réussissent**

For an English translation of French verb tenses, see the model verbs in French and English in all the tenses in **§7.6** and **§7.7** in this book. For the uses of this tense, see **§7.8—6**.

TENSE NO. 7 *IMPARFAIT DU SUBJONCTIF* (Imperfect Subjunctive)

To form this tense regularly, drop the endings of the *passé simple* (Tense No. 3) for **-er**, **-ir**, **-re** verbs and add the following endings.

For **-er** verbs, add: Singular: **asse, asses, ât**; Plural: **assions, assiez, assent**

For **-ir** verbs, add: Singular: **isse, isses, ît**; Plural: **issions, issiez, issent**

For **-re** verbs, add: Singular: **usse, usses, ût**; Plural: **ussions, ussiez, ussent**

---

parler to talk, to speak
Singular: **que je parlasse, que tu parlasses, qu'il/elle/on parlât**
Plural: **que nous parlassions, que vous parlassiez, qu'ils/elles parlassent**

---

finir to finish
Singular: **que je finisse, que tu finisses, qu'il/elle/on finît**
Plural: **que nous finissions, que vous finissiez, qu'ils/elles finissent**

---

lire to read
Singular: **que je lusse, que tu lusses, qu'il/elle/on lût**
Plural: **que nous lussions, que vous lussiez, qu'ils/elles lussent**

---

acheter to buy, to purchase
Singular: **que j'achetasse, que tu achetasses, qu'il/elle/on achetât**
Plural: **que nous achetassions, que vous achetassiez, qu'ils/elles achetassent**

---

aller to go
Singular: **que j'allasse, que tu allasses, qu'il/elle/on allât**
Plural: **que nous allassions, que vous allassiez, qu'ils/elles allassent**

---

choisir to choose, to select
Singular: **que je choisisse, que tu choisisses, qu'il/elle/on choisît**
Plural: **que nous choisissions, que vous choisissiez, qu'ils/elles choisissent**

---

perdre to lose
Singular: **que je perdisse, que tu perdisses, qu'il/elle/on perdît**
Plural: **que nous perdissions, que vous perdissiez, qu'ils/elles perdissent**

---

réussir to succeed
Singular: **que je réussisse, que tu réussisses, qu'il/elle/on réussît**
Plural: **que nous réussissions, que vous réussissiez, qu'ils/elles réussissent**

---

vendre to sell
Singular: **que je vendisse, que tu vendisses, qu'il/elle/on vendît**
Plural: **que nous vendissions, que vous vendissiez, qu'ils/elles vendissent**

For an English translation of French verb tenses, see the model verbs in French and English in all the tenses in **§7.6** and **§7.7** in this book. For the uses of this tense, see **§7.8—7**.

FORMATION OF THE SEVEN COMPOUND TENSES NUMBERS 8 THROUGH 14

TENSE NO. 8 *PASSÉ COMPOSÉ* (Past Indefinite or Compound Past)

This commonly used compound past tense is based on Tense No. 1 of **avoir** or **être**. In other words, you form the *passé composé* by using the auxiliary (helping) verb **avoir** or **être** (whichever is appropriate) in the **présent de l'indicatif** plus the past participle of the verb you have in mind to use.

For the complete conjugation of **avoir** and **être** in the seven simple tenses, see **§7.19** in this book.

To learn how to form a past participle regularly and to learn the common irregular past participles, see **§7.2** in this book.

To know which verbs are conjugated with **avoir** or **être** to form the compound tenses, see **§7.3—1**

Samples of verbs conjugated with **avoir** in the *passé composé*:

donner to give
Singular: **j'ai donné, tu as donné, il/elle/on a donné**
Plural: **nous avons donné, vous avez donné, ils/elles ont donné**

---

finir to finish
Singular: **j'ai fini, tu as fini, il/elle/on a fini**
Plural: **nous avons fini, vous avez fini, ils/elles ont fini**

---

vendre to sell
Singular: **j'ai vendu, tu as vendu, il/elle/on a vendu**
Plural: **nous avons vendu, vous avez vendu, ils/elles ont vendu**

Samples of verbs conjugated with **être** in the *passé composé*:
Note that the past participle must agree in gender (masculine or feminine) and number (singular or plural) with the subject. The agreement is indicated by adding **e** if feminine and **s** if plural. If the gender and number of some of the subject pronouns are not known, **e** and **s** are shown in parentheses.

---

aller to go
Singular: **je suis allé(e), tu es allé(e), il est allé, elle est allée, on est allé(e)**
Plural: **nous sommes allé(e)s, vous êtes allé(e)(s), ils sont allés, elles sont allées**

partir to leave
Singular: **je suis parti(e), tu es parti(e), il est parti, elle est partie, on est parti(e)**
Plural: **nous sommes parti(e)(s), vous êtes parti(e)(s), ils sont partis, elles sont parties**

A reflexive verb is also known as a pronominal verb. It contains the reflexive pronouns **me, te, se, nous, vous**, as in **je me..., tu te..., il se..., elle se..., on se..., nous nous..., vous vous..., ils se..., elles se...**. In the infinitive form, a reflexive verb contains the pronoun **se**, as in **se laver**. Reflexive verbs are conjugated with **être** to form the seven compound tenses. See **§6.1—12** in this book.

Samples of pronominal verbs conjugated with **être** in the *passé composé:*

se laver to wash oneself
Singular: **je me suis lavé(e), tu t'es lavé(e), il s'est lavé, elle s'est lavée, on s'est lavé(e)**
Plural: **nous nous sommes lavé(e)s, vous vous êtes lavé(e)(s), ils se sont lavés, elles se sont lavées**

se blesser to hurt oneself, to injure oneself
Singular: **je me suis blessé(e), tu t'es blessé(e), il s'est blessé, elle s'est blessée, on s'est blessé(e)**
Plural: **nous nous sommes blessé(e)s, vous vous êtes blessé(e)(s), ils se sont blessés, elles se sont blessées**

For the uses of this tense, see **§7.8—8.**

TENSE NO. 9 *PLUS-QUE-PARFAIT DE L'INDICATIF* (Pluperfect Indicative)

This tense is based on Tense No. 2 of **avoir** or **être**. It is formed by using the required helping verb, **avoir** or **être**, in the **imparfait de l'indicatif** plus the past participle of the verb you have in mind to use.

Refer to **§6.1—12**, **§7.2**, **§7.3—1**, **§7.6**, **§7.7**, and **§7.19** in this book.

---

aller to go
Singular: **j'étais allé(e), tu étais allé(e), il était allé, elle était allée, on était allé(e)**
Plural: **nous étions allé(e)s, vous étiez allé(e)(s), ils étaient allés, elles étaient allées**

---

donner to give
Singular: **j'avais donné, tu avais donné, il/elle/on avait donné**
Plural: **nous avions donné, vous aviez donné, ils/elles avaient donné**

---

finir to finish
Singular: **j'avais fini, tu avais fini, il/elle/on avait fini**
Plural: **nous avions fini, vous aviez fini, ils/elles avaient fini**

---

se laver to wash oneself
Singular: **je m'étais lavé(e), tu t'étais lavé(e), il s'était lavé, elle s'était lavée, on s'était lavé(e)**
Plural: **nous nous étions lavé(e)s, vous vous étiez lavé(e)(s), ils s'étaient lavés, elles s'étaient lavées**

---

partir to leave
Singular: **j'étais parti(e), tu étais parti(e), il était parti, elle était partie, on était parti(e)**
Plural: **nous étions parti(e)s, vous étiez parti(e)(s), ils étaient partis, elles étaient parties**

---

vendre to sell
Singular: **j'avais vendu, tu avais vendu, il/elle/on avait vendu**
Plural: **nous avions vendu, vous aviez vendu, ils/elles avaient vendu**

For the uses of this tense, see **§7.8—9**.

TENSE NO. 10 *PASSÉ ANTÉRIEUR* (Past anterior)

This tense is based on Tense No. 3 of **avoir** or **être**. It is formed by using the required helping verb, **avoir** or **être**, in the **passé simple** plus the past participle of the verb you have in mind to use.

Refer to **§6.1—12**, **§7.2**, **§7.3—1**, **§7.6**, **§7.7**, and **§7.19** in this book. For the uses of this tense, see **§7.8—10**.

---

aller to go
Singular: **je fus allé(e), tu fus allé(e), il fut allé, elle fut allée, on fut allé(e)**
Plural: **nous fûmes allé(e)s, vous fûtes allé(e)(s), ils furent allés, elles furent allées**

---

donner to give
Singular: **j'eus donné, tu eus donné, il/elle/on eut donné**
Plural: **nous eûmes donné, vous eûtes donné, ils/elles eurent donné**

---

finir to finish
Singular: **j'eus fini, tu eus fini, il/elle/on eut fini**
Plural: **nous eûmes fini, vous eûtes fini, ils/elles eurent fini**

---

se laver to wash oneself
Singular: **je me fus lavé(e), tu te fus lavé(e), il se fut lavé, elle se fut lavée, on se fut lavé(e)**
Plural: **nous nous fûmes lavé(e)s, vous vous fûtes lavé(e)(s), ils se furent lavés, elles se furent lavées**

---

partir to leave
Singular: **je fus parti(e), tu fus parti(e), il fut parti, elle fut partie, on fut parti(e)**
Plural: **nous fûmes parti(e)s, vous fûtes parti(e)(s), ils furent partis, elles furent parties**

---

vendre to sell
Singular: **j'eus vendu, tu eus vendu, il/elle/on eut vendu**
Plural: **nous eûmes vendu, vous eûtes vendu, ils/elles eurent vendu**

TENSE NO. 11   *FUTUR ANTÉRIEUR* (Future Perfect)

This tense is based on Tense No. 4 of **avoir** or **être**. It is formed by using the required helping verb, **avoir** or **être**, in the **futur** plus the past participle of the verb you have in mind to use.

Refer to **§6.1—12**, **§7.2**, **§7.3—1**, **§7.6**, **§7.7**, and **§7.19** in this book. For the uses of this tense, see **§7.8—11**.

---

aller to go
Singular: **je serai allé(e), tu seras allé(e), il sera allé, elle sera allée, on sera allé(e)**
Plural: **nous serons allé(e)s, vous serez allé(e)(s), ils seront allés, elles seront allées**

---

donner to give
Singular: **j'aurai donné, tu auras donné, il/elle/on aura donné**
Plural: **nous aurons donné, vous aurez donné, ils/elles auront donné**

---

finir to finish
Singular: **j'aurai fini, tu auras fini, il/elle/on aura fini**
Plural: **nous aurons fini, vous aurez fini, ils/elles auront fini**

---

se laver to wash oneself
Singular: **je me serai lavé(e), tu te seras lavé(e), il se sera lavé, elle se sera lavée, on se sera lavé(e)**
Plural: **nous nous serons lavé(e)s, vous vous serez lavé(e)(s), ils se seront lavés elles se seront lavées**

---

partir to leave
Singular: **je serai parti(e), tu seras parti(e), il sera parti, elle sera partie, on sera parti(e)**
Plural: **nous serons parti(e)s, vous serez parti(e)(s), ils seront partis, elles seront parties**

---

vendre to sell
Singular: **j'aurai vendu, tu auras vendu, il/elle/on aura vendu**
Plural: **nous aurons vendu, vous aurez vendu, ils/elles auront vendu**

TENSE NO. 12 *CONDITIONNEL PASSÉ* (Conditional perfect)

This tense is based on Tense No. 5 of **avoir** or **être**. It is formed by using the required helping verb, **avoir** or **être**, in the **conditionnel présent** plus the past participle of the verb you have in mind to use.

Refer to §6.1—12, §7.2, §7.3—1, §7.6, §7.7, and §7.19 in this book. For the uses of this tense, see §7.8—12.

---

aller to go
Singular: **je serais allé(e), tu serais allé(e), il serait allé, elle serait allée, on serait allé(e)**
Plural: **nous serions allé(e)s, vous seriez allé(e)(s), ils seraient allés, elles seraient allées**

---

donner to give
Singular: **j'aurais donné, tu aurais donné, il/elle/on aurait donné**
Plural: **nous aurions donné, vous auriez donné, ils/elles auraient donné**

---

finir to finish
Singular: **j'aurais fini, tu aurais fini, il/elle/on aurait fini**
Plural: **nous aurions fini, vous auriez fini, ils/elles auraient fini**

---

se laver to wash oneself
Singular: **je me serais lavé(e), tu te serais lavé(e), il se serait lavé, elle se serait lavée, on se serait lavé(e)**
Plural: **nous nous serions lavé(e)s, vous vous seriez lavé(e)(s), ils se seraient lavés, elles se seraient lavées**

---

partir to leave
Singular: **je serais parti(e), tu serais parti(e), il serait parti, elle serait partie, on serait parti(e)**
Plural: **nous serions parti(e)s, vous seriez parti(e)(s), ils seraient partis, elles seraient parties**

---

vendre to sell
Singular: **j'aurais vendu, tu aurais vendu, il/elle/on aurait vendu**
Plural: **nous aurions vendu, vous auriez vendu, ils/elles auraient vendu**

TENSE NO. 13 *PASSÉ DU SUBJONCTIF* (Past subjunctive)

This tense is based on Tense No. 6 of **avoir** or **être**. It is formed by using the required helping verb, **avoir** or **être**, in the **présent du subjonctif** plus the past participle of the verb you have in mind to use.

Refer to §6.1—12, §7.2, §7.3—1, §7.6, §7.7, and §7.19 in this book. For the uses of this tense, see §7.8—13.

---

aller to go
Singular: **que je sois allé(e), que tu sois allé(e), qu'il soit allé, qu'elle soit allée, qu'on soit allé(e)**
Plural: **que nous soyons allé(e)s, que vous soyez allé(e)(s), qu'ils soient allés, qu'elles soient allées**

---

donner to give
Singular: **que j'aie donné, que tu aies donné, qu'il/elle/on ait donné**
Plural: **que nous ayons donné, que vous ayez donné, qu'ils/elles aient donné**

---

finir to finish
Singular: **que j'aie fini, que tu aies fini, qu'il/elle/on ait fini**
Plural: **que nous ayons fini, que vous ayez fini, qu'ils/elles aient fini**

---

se laver to wash oneself
Singular: **que je me sois lavé(e), que tu te sois lavé(e), qu'il se soit lavé, qu'elle se soit lavée, qu'on se soit lavé(e)**
Plural: **que nous nous soyons lavé(e)s, que vous vous soyez lavé(e)(s), qu'ils se soient lavés, qu'elles se soient lavées**

---

partir to leave
Singular: **que je sois parti(e), que tu sois parti(e), qu'il soit parti, qu'elle soit partie, qu'on soit parti(e)**
Plural: **que nous soyons parti(e)s, que vous soyez parti(e)(s), qu'ils soient partis, qu'elles soient parties**

---

vendre to sell
Singular: **que j'aie vendu, que tu aies vendu, qu'il/elle/on ait vendu**
Plural: **que nous ayons vendu, que vous ayez vendu, qu'ils/elles aient vendu**

TENSE NO. 14 *PLUS-QUE-PARFAIT DU SUBJONCTIF* (Pluperfect subjunctive)

This tense is based on Tense No. 7 of **avoir** or **être**. It is formed by using the required helping verb, **avoir** or **être**, in the **imparfait du subjonctif** plus the past participle of the verb you have in mind to use.

Refer to §6.1—12, §7.2, §7.3—1, §7.6, §7.7, and §7.19 in this book. For the uses of this tense, see §7.8—14.

---

aller to go
Singular: que je fusse allé(e), que tu fusses allé(e), qu'il fût allé, qu'elle fût
           allée, qu'on fût allé(e)
Plural: que nous fussions allé(e)s, que vous fussiez allé(e)(s), qu'ils fussent
           allés, qu'elles fussent allées

---

donner to give
Singular: que j'eusse donné, que tu eusses donné, qu'il/elle/on eût donné
Plural: que nous eussions donné, que vous eussiez donné, qu'ils/elles
           eussent donné

---

finir to finish
Singular: que j'eusse fini, que tu eusses fini, qu'il/elle/on eût fini
Plural: que nous eussions fini, que vous eussiez fini, qu'ils/elles eussent fini

---

se laver to wash oneself
Singular: que je me fusse lavé(e), que tu te fusses lavé(e), qu'il se fût lavé,
           qu'elle se fût lavée, qu'on se fût lavé(e)
Plural: que nous nous fussions lavé(e)s, que vous vous fussiez lavé(e)(s),
           qu'ils se fussent lavés, qu'elles se fussent lavées

---

partir to leave
Singular: que je fusse parti(e), que tu fusses parti(e), qu'il fût parti, qu'elle fût
           partie, qu'on fût parti(e)
Plural: que nous fussions parti(e)s, que vous fussiez parti(e)(s), qu'ils
           fussent partis, qu'elles fussent parties

---

vendre to sell
Singular: que j'eusse vendu, que tu eusses vendu, qu'il/elle/on eût vendu
Plural: que nous eussions vendu, que vous eussiez vendu, qu'ils/elles
           eussent vendu

§26.

Commonly Used Irregular Verbs in the Seven Simple Tenses and the Imperative

The names of the seven simple tenses for the seven tense numbers are given below. In the tables that follow, the tense number is used instead of the tense name. Refer to this list when you have to.

Tense Number
1 *Présent de l'indicatif* (Present indicative)
2 *Imparfait de l'indicatif* (Imperfect indicative)
3 *Passé Simple* (Past Definite or Simple Past)
4 *Futur* (Future)
5 *Conditionnel présent* (Conditional)
6 *Présent du Subjonctif* (Present Subjunctive)
7 *Imparfait du Subjonctif* (Imperfect Subjunctive)

The Imperative (Command) mood is used when telling someone to do or not to do something, *e.g.,* get up, don't get up, go, don't go, come in, don't come in. For the uses of the Imperative, consult **§7.8—15** in this book. The three forms of the Imperative given in the tables below are second person singular **(tu)**, first person plural **(nous)**, second person plural **(vous)**, as in this example: **va** go, **ne va pas** don't go; **allons** let's go, **n'allons pas** let's not go; **allez** go, **n'allez pas** don't go.

For the formation of the present participle and for irregular present participles, see **§7.4**.

For the formation of the past participle and for irregular past participles, see **§7.2**.

For the meanings of the seven simple tenses and the imperative, see **§7.6** and **§7.7**.

Refer to **§7.19** in this book for the complete forms of the irregular verbs **aller**/to go, **avoir**/to have, **être**/to be, **faire**/to do, to make.

In the following tables, the first line of verb forms is the singular: **je, j'**/I; **tu**/you *(fam.)*; **il**/he, it; **elle**/she, it; for the several meanings of the indefinite subject pronoun **on**, see **§6.1—9**.

The second line is the plural: **nous**/we; **vous**/you *(s. polite and pl.)*; **ils**/they *(m.)*; **elles**/they *(f.)*.

---

aller to go   *pr. part.* **allant**   *past part.* **allé**

For all the forms in the seven simple tenses, see **§7.19**.

---

apprendre to learn   *pr. part.* **apprenant**   *past part.* **appris**

1   j'apprends tu apprends, il/elle/on apprend
     nous apprenons, vous apprenez, ils/elles apprennent

2   j'apprenais, tu apprenais, il/elle/on apprenait
     nous apprenions, vous appreniez, ils/elles apprenaient

3   j'appris, tu appris, il/elle/on apprit
     nous apprîmes, vous apprîtes, ils/elles apprirent

4   j'apprendrai, tu apprendras, il/elle/on apprendra
     nous apprendrons, vous apprendrez, ils/elles apprendront

5   j'apprendrais, tu apprendrais, il/elle/on apprendrait
     nous apprendrions, vous apprendriez, ils/elles apprendraient

6   que j'apprenne, que tu apprennes, qu'il/elle/on apprenne
     que nous apprenions, que vous appreniez, qu'ils/elles apprennent

7   que j'apprisse, que tu apprisses, qu'il/elle/on apprît
     que nous apprissions, que vous apprissiez, qu'ils/elles apprissent

Imperative: **apprends, apprenons, apprenez**

---

s'asseoir to sit down   *pr. part.* **s'asseyant**   *past part.* **assis**

1   **je m'assieds, tu t'assieds, il/elle/on s'assied
    nous nous asseyons, vous vous asseyez, ils/elles s'asseyent**

2   **je m'asseyais, tu t'asseyais, il/elle/on s'asseyait
    nous nous asseyions, vous vous asseyiez, ils/elles s'asseyaient**

3   **je m'assis, tu t'assis, il/elle/on s'assit
    nous nous assîmes, vous vous assîtes, ils/elles s'assirent**

4   **je m'assiérai, tu t'assiéras, il/elle/on s'assiéra
    nous nous assiérons, vous vous assiérez, ils/elles s'assiéront**

5   **je m'assiérais, tu t'assiérais, il/elle/on s'assiérait
    nous nous assiérions, vous vous assiériez, ils/elles s'assiéraient**

6   **que je m'asseye, que tu t'asseyes, qu'il/elle/on s'asseye
    que nous nous asseyions, que vous vous asseyiez, qu'ils/elles s'asseyent**

7   **que je m'assisse, que tu t'assisses, qu'il/elle/on s'assît
    que nous nous assissions, que vous vous assissiez, qu'ils/elles s'assissent**

Imperative: **assieds-toi** sit down   **ne t'assieds pas** don't sit down
            asseyons-nous let's sit down **ne nous asseyons pas** let's not sit down
            asseyez-vous sit down   **ne vous asseyez pas** don't sit down

---

avoir to have   *pr. part.* **ayant**   *past part.* **eu**

For all the forms in the seven simple tenses, see **§7.19**.

---

boire to drink   *pr. part.* **buvant**   *past part.* **bu**

1   je bois, tu bois, il/elle/on boit
    nous buvons, vous buvez, ils/elles boivent

2   je buvais, tu buvais, il/elle/on buvait
    nous buvions, vous buviez, ils/elles buvaient

3   je bus, tu bus, il/elle/on but
    nous bûmes, vous bûtes, ils/elles burent

4   je boirai, tu boiras, il/elle/on boira
    nous boirons, vous boirez, ils/elles boiront

5   je boirais, tu boirais, il/elle/on boirait
    nous boirions, vous boiriez, ils/elles boiraient

6   que je boive, que tu boives, qu'il/elle/on boive
    que nous buvions, que vous buviez, qu'ils/elles boivent

7   que je busse, que tu busses, qu'il/elle/on bût
    que nous bussions, que vous bussiez, qu'ils/elles bussent

Imperative: **bois, buvons, buvez**

comprendre to understand   *pr. part.* **comprenant**   *past part.* **compris**

1   je comprends, tu comprends, il/elle/on comprend
    nous comprenons, vous comprenez, ils/elles comprennent

2   je comprenais, tu comprenais, il/elle/on comprenait
    nous comprenions, vous compreniez, ils/elles comprenaient

3   je compris, tu compris, il/elle/on comprit
    nous comprîmes, vous comprîtes, ils/elles comprirent

4   je comprendrai, tu comprendras, il/elle/on comprendra
    nous comprendrons, vous comprendrez, ils/elles comprendront

5   je comprendrais, tu comprendrais, il/elle/on comprendrait
    nous comprendrions, vous comprendriez, ils/elles comprendraient

6   que je comprenne, que tu comprennes, qu'il/elle/on comprenne
    que nous comprenions, que vous compreniez, qu'ils/elles comprennent

7   que je comprisse, que tu comprisses, qu'il/elle/on comprît
    que nous comprissions, que vous comprissiez, qu'ils/elles comprissent

Imperative: **comprends, comprenons, comprenez**

connaître to know, to be acquainted with *pr. part.* **connaissant** *past part.* **connu**

1 je connais, tu connais, il/elle/on connaît
nous connaissons, vous connaissez, ils/elles connaissent

2 je connaissais, tu connaissais, il/elle/on connaissait
nous connaissions, vous connaissiez, ils/elles connaissaient

3 je connus, tu connus, il/elle/on connut
nous connûmes, vous connûtes, ils/elles connurent

4 je connaîtrai, tu connaîtras, il/elle/on connaîtra
nous connaîtrons, vous connaîtrez, ils/elles connaîtront

5 je connaîtrais, tu connaîtrais, il/elle/on connaîtrait
nous connaîtrions, vous connaîtriez, ils/elles connaîtraient

6 que je connaisse, que tu connaisses, qu'il/elle/on connaisse
que nous connaissions, que vous connaissiez, qu'ils/elles connaissent

7 que je connusse, que tu connusses, qu'il/elle/on connût
que nous connussions, que vous connussiez, qu'ils/elles connussent

Imperative: **connais, connaissons, connaissez**

courir to run *pr. part.* **courant** *past part.* **couru**

1 je cours, tu cours, il/elle/on court
nous courons, vous courez, ils/elles courent

2 je courais, tu courais, il/elle/on courait
nous courions, vous couriez, ils/elles couraient

3 je courus, tu courus, il/elle/on courut
nous courûmes, vous courûtes, ils/elles coururent

4 je courrai, tu courras, il/elle/on courra
nous courrons, vous courrez, ils/elles courront

5 je courrais, tu courrais, il/elle/on courrait
nous courrions, vous courriez, ils/elles courraient

6 que je coure, que tu coures, qu'il/elle/on coure
que nous courions, que vous couriez, qu'ils/elles courent

7 que je courusse, que tu courusses, qu'il/elle/on courût
que nous courussions, que vous courussiez, qu'ils/elles courussent

Imperative: **cours, courons, courez**

---

croire to believe *pr. part.* **croyant** *past part.* **cru**

1 je crois, tu crois, il/elle/on croit
   nous croyons, vous croyez, ils/elles croient

2 je croyais, tu croyais, il/elle/on croyait
   nous croyions, vous croyiez, ils/elles croyaient

3 je crus, tu crus, il/elle/on crut
   nous crûmes, vous crûtes, ils/elles crurent

4 je croirai, tu croiras, il/elle/on croira
   nous croirons, vous croirez, ils/elles croiront

5 je croirais, tu croirais, il/elle/on croirait
   nous croirions, vous croiriez, ils/elles croiraient

6 que je croie, que tu croies, qu'il/elle/on croie
   que nous croyions, que vous croyiez, qu'ils/elles croient

7 que je crusse, que tu crusses, qu'il/elle/on crût
   que nous crussions, que vous crussiez, qu'ils/elles crussent

Imperative: **crois, croyons, croyez**

---

devenir to become *pr. part.* **devenant** *past part.* **devenu**

1 je deviens, tu deviens, il/elle/on devient
   nous devenons, vous devenez, ils/elles deviennent

2 je devenais, tu devenais, il/elle/on devenait
   nous devenions, vous deveniez, ils/elles devenaient

3 je devins, tu devins, il/elle/on devint
   nous devînmes, vous devîntes, ils/elles devinrent

4 je deviendrai, tu deviendras, il/elle/on deviendra
   nous deviendrons, vous deviendrez, ils/elles deviendront

5 je deviendrais, tu deviendrais, il/elle/on deviendrait
   nous deviendrions, vous deviendriez, ils/elles deviendraient

6 que je devienne, que tu deviennes, qu'il/elle/on devienne
   que nous devenions, que vous deveniez, qu'ils/elles deviennent

7 que je devinsse, que tu devinsses, qu'il/elle/on devînt
   que nous devinssions, que vous devinssiez, qu'ils/elles devinssent

Imperative: **deviens, devenons, devenez**

---

devoir to have to, ought, owe, should   *pr. part.* **devant**   *past part.* **dû (due)**

1   je dois, tu dois, il/elle/on doit
     nous devons, vous devez, ils/elles doivent

2   je devais, tu devais, il/elle/on devait
     nous devions, vous deviez, ils/elles devaient

3   je dus, tu dus, il/elle/on dut
     nous dûmes, vous dûtes, ils/elles durent

4   je devrai, tu devras, il/elle/on devra
     nous devrons, vous devrez, ils/elles devront

5   je devrais, tu devrais, il/elle/on devrait
     nous devrions, vous devriez, ils/elles devraient

6   que je doive, que tu doives, qu'il/elle/on doive
     que nous devions, que vous deviez, qu'ils/elles doivent

7   que je dusse, que tu dusses, qu'il/elle/on dût
     que nous dussions, que vous dussiez, qu'ils/elles dussent

Imperative: **dois, devons, devez**

---

dire to say, to tell   *pr. part.* **disant**   *past part.* **dit**

1   je dis, tu dis, il/elle/on dit
     nous disons, vous dites, ils/elles disent

2   je disais, tu disais, il/elle/on disait
     nous disions, vous disiez, ils/elles disaient

3   je dis, tu dis, il/elle/on dit
     nous dîmes, vous dîtes, ils/elles dirent

4   je dirai, tu diras, il/elle/on dira
     nous dirons, vous direz, ils/elles diront

5   je dirais, tu dirais, il/elle/on dirait
     nous dirions, vous diriez, ils/elles diraient

6   que je dise, que tu dises, qu'il/elle/on dise
     que nous disions, que vous disiez, qu'ils/elles disent

7   que je disse, que tu disses, qu'il/elle/on dît
     que nous dissions, que vous dissiez, qu'ils/elles dissent

Imperative: **dis, disons, dites**

dormir to sleep *pr. part.* **dormant** *past part.* **dormi**

1 je dors, tu dors, il/elle/on dort
nous dormons, vous dormez, ils/elles dorment

2 je dormais, tu dormais, il/elle/on dormait
nous dormions, vous dormiez, ils/elles dormaient

3 je dormis, tu dormis, il/elle/on dormit
nous dormîmes, vous dormîtes, ils/elles dormirent

4 je dormirai, tu dormiras, il/elle/on dormira
nous dormirons, vous dormirez, ils/elles dormiront

5 je dormirais, tu dormirais, il/elle/on dormirait
nous dormirions, vous dormiriez, ils/elles dormiraient

6 que je dorme, que tu dormes, qu'il/elle/on dorme
que nous dormions, que vous dormiez, qu'ils/elles dorment

7 que je dormisse, que tu dormisses, qu'il/elle/on dormît
que nous dormissions, que vous dormissiez, qu'ils/elles dormissent

Imperative: **dors, dormons, dormez**

écrire to write *pr. part.* **écrivant** *past part.* **écrit**

1 j'écris, tu écris, il/elle/on écrit
nous écrivons, vous écrivez, ils/elles écrivent

2 j'écrivais, tu écrivais, il/elle/on écrivait
nous écrivions, vous écriviez, ils/elles écrivaient

3 j'écrivis, tu écrivis, il/elle/on écrivit
nous écrivîmes, vous écrivîtes, ils/elles écrivirent

4 j'écrirai, tu écriras, il/elle/on écrira
nous écrirons, vous écrirez, ils/elles écriront

5 j'écrirais, tu écrirais, il/elle/on écrirait
nous écririons, vous écririez, ils/elles écriraient

6 que j'écrive, que tu écrives, qu'il/elle/on écrive
que nous écrivions, que vous écriviez, qu'ils/elles écrivent

7 que j'écrivisse, que tu écrivisses, qu'il/elle/on écrivît
que nous écrivissions, que vous écrivissiez, qu'ils/elles écrivissent

Imperative: **écris, écrivons, écrivez**

---

envoyer to send　　　　　　　　*pr. part.* **envoyant**　　　*past part.* **envoyé**

1　j'envoie, tu envoies, il/elle/on envoie
　　nous envoyons, vous envoyez, ils/elles envoient

2　j'envoyais, tu envoyais, il/elle/on envoyait
　　nous envoyions, vous envoyiez, ils/elles envoyaient

3　j'envoyai, tu envoyas, il/elle/on envoya
　　nous envoyâmes, vous envoyâtes, ils/elles envoyèrent

4　j'enverrai, tu enverras, il/elle/on enverra
　　nous enverrons, vous enverrez, ils/elles enverront

5　j'enverrais, tu enverrais, il/elle/on enverrait
　　nous enverrions, vous enverriez, ils/elles enverraient

6　que j'envoie, que tu envoies, qu'il/elle/on envoie
　　que nous envoyions, que vous envoyiez, qu'ils/elles envoient

7　que j'envoyasse, que tu envoyasses, qu'il/elle/on envoyât
　　que nous envoyassions, que vous envoyassiez, qu'ils/elles envoyassent

Imperative: **envoie, envoyons, envoyez**

être to be　　　　　　　　　　*pr. part.* **étant**　　　*past part.* **été**

For all the forms in the seven simple tenses, see **§7.19.**

---

faire to do, to make　　　　　　*pr. part.* **faisant**　　　*past part.* **fait**

For all the forms in the seven simple tenses, see **§7.19.**

---

falloir to be necessary　　　*pr. part.* (not in use)　　*past part.* **fallu**

This verb is impersonal, which means that it is used only in the third person singular with the subject **il**/it.

1	**il faut**	3	**il fallut**	5	**il faudrait**	7	**qu'il fallût**
2	**il fallait**	4	**il faudra**	6	**qu'il faille**		

Imperative: (not in use)

---

lire to read   *pr. part.* **lisant**   *past part.* **lu**

1   **je lis, tu lis, il/elle/on lit**
    nous lisons, vous lisez, ils/elles lisent

2   **je lisais, tu lisais, il/elle/on lisait**
    nous lisions, vous lisiez, ils/elles lisaient

3   **je lus, tu lus, il/elle/on lut**
    nous lûmes, vous lûtes, ils/elles lurent

4   **je lirai, tu liras, il/elle/on lira**
    nous lirons, vous lirez, ils/elles liront

5   **je lirais, tu lirais, il/elle/on lirait**
    nous lirions, vous liriez, ils/elles liraient

6   **que je lise, que tu lises, qu'il/elle/on lise**
    que nous lisions, que vous lisiez, qu'ils/elles lisent

7   **que je lusse, que tu lusses, qu'il/elle/on lût**
    que nous lussions, que vous lussiez, qu'ils/elles lussent

Imperative: **lis, lisons, lisez**

---

mettre to put, to place   *pr. part.* **mettant**   *past part.* **mis**

1   **je mets, tu mets, il/elle/on met**
    nous mettons, vous mettez, ils/elles mettent

2   **je mettais, tu mettais, il/elle/on mettait**
    nous mettions, vous mettiez, ils/elles mettaient

3   **je mis, tu mis, il/elle/on mit**
    nous mîmes, vous mîtes, ils/elles mirent

4   **je mettrai, tu mettras, il/elle/on mettra**
    nous mettrons, vous mettrez, ils/elles mettront

5   **je mettrais, tu mettrais, il/elle/on mettrait**
    nous mettrions, vous mettriez, ils/elles mettraient

6   **que je mette, que tu mettes, qu'il/elle/on mette**
    que nous mettions, que vous mettiez, qu'ils/elles mettent

7   **que je misse, que tu misses, qu'il/elle/on mît**
    que nous missions, que vous missiez, qu'ils/elles missent

Imperative: **mets, mettons, mettez**

mourir to die	pr. part. **mourant**	past part. **mort**

1 je meurs, tu meurs, il/elle/on meurt
nous mourons, vous mourez, ils/elles meurent

2 je mourais, tu mourais, il/elle/on mourait
nous mourions, vous mouriez, ils/elles mouraient

3 je mourus, tu mourus, il/elle/on mourut
nous mourûmes, vous mourûtes, ils/elles moururent

4 je mourrai, tu mourras, il/elle/on mourra
nous mourrons, vous mourrez, ils/elles mourront

5 je mourrais, tu mourrais, il/elle/on mourrait
nous mourrions, vous mourriez, ils/elles mourraient

6 que je meure, que tu meures, qu'il/elle/on meure
que nous mourions, que vous mouriez, qu'ils/elles meurent

7 que je mourusse, que tu mourusses, qu'il/elle/on mourût
que nous mourussions, que vous mourussiez, qu'ils/elles mourussent

Imperative: **meurs, mourons, mourez**

naître to be born	pr. part. **naissant**	past part. **né**

1 je nais, tu nais, il/elle/on naît
nous naissons, vous naissez, ils/elles naissent

2 je naissais, tu naissais, il/elle/on naissait
nous naissions, vous naissiez, ils/elles naissaient

3 je naquis, tu naquis, il/elle/on naquit
nous naquîmes, vous naquîtes, ils/elles naquirent

4 je naîtrai, tu naîtras, il/elle/on naîtra
nous naîtrons, vous naîtrez, ils/elles naîtront

5 je naîtrais, tu naîtrais, il/elle/on naîtrait
nous naîtrions, vous naîtriez, ils/elles naîtraient

6 que je naisse, que tu naisses, qu'il/elle/on naisse
que nous naissions, que vous naissiez, qu'ils/elles naissent

7 que je naquisse, que tu naquisses, qu'il/elle/on naquît
que nous naquissions, que vous naquissiez, qu'ils/elles naquissent

Imperative: **nais, naissons, naissez**

---

ouvrir to open   *pr. part.* **ouvrant**   *past part.* **ouvert**

1   j'ouvre, tu ouvres, il/elle/on ouvre
     nous ouvrons, vous ouvrez, ils/elles ouvrent

2   j'ouvrais, tu ouvrais, il/elle/on ouvrait
     nous ouvrions, vous ouvriez, ils/elles ouvraient

3   j'ouvris, tu ouvris, il/elle/on ouvrit
     nous ouvrîmes, vous ouvrîtes, ils/elles ouvrirent

4   j'ouvrirai, tu ouvriras, il/elle/on ouvrira
     nous ouvrirons, vous ouvrirez, ils/elles ouvriront

5   j'ouvrirais, tu ouvrirais, il/elle/on ouvrirait
     nous ouvririons, vous ouvririez, ils/elles ouvriraient

6   que j'ouvre, que tu ouvres, qu'il/elle/on ouvre
     que nous ouvrions, que vous ouvriez, qu'ils/elles ouvrent

7   que j'ouvrisse, que tu ouvrisses, qu'il/elle/on ouvrît
     que nous ouvrissions, que vous ouvrissiez, qu'ils/elles ouvrissent

Imperative: **ouvre, ouvrons, ouvrez**

---

partir to leave, to depart   *pr. part.* **partant**   *past part.* **parti**

1   je pars, tu pars, il/elle/on part
     nous partons, vous partez, ils/elles partent

2   je partais, tu partais, il/elle/on partait
     nous partions, vous partiez, ils/elles partaient

3   je partis, tu partis, il/elle/on partit
     nous partîmes, vous partîtes, ils/elles partirent

4   je partirai, tu partiras, il/elle/on partira
     nous partirons, vous partirez, ils/elles partiront

5   je partirais, tu partirais, il/elle/on partirait
     nous partirions, vous partiriez, ils/elles partiraient

6   que je parte, que tu partes, qu'il/elle/on parte
     que nous partions, que vous partiez, qu'ils/elles partent

7   que je partisse, que tu partisses, qu'il/elle/on partît
     que nous partissions, que vous partissiez, qu'ils/elles partissent

Imperative: **pars, partons, partez**

---

pleuvoir to rain   *pr. part.* **pleuvant**   *past part.* **plu**

This verb is impersonal, which means that it is used only in the third person singular with the subject **il**/it.

1	**il pleut**	3	**il plut**	5	**il pleuvrait**	7	**qu'il plût**
2	**il pleuvait**	4	**il pleuvra**	6	**qu'il pleuve**		

Imperative: (not in use)

---

pouvoir to be able, can   *pr. part.* **pouvant**   *past part.* **pu**

1   **je peux** or **je puis, tu peux, il/elle/on peut**
    nous pouvons, vous pouvez, ils/elles peuvent

2   **je pouvais, tu pouvais, il/elle/on pouvait**
    nous pouvions, vous pouviez, ils/elles pouvaient

3   **je pus, tu pus, il/elle/on put**
    nous pûmes, vous pûtes, ils/elles purent

4   **je pourrai, tu pourras, il/elle/on pourra**
    nous pourrons, vous pourrez, ils/elles pourront

5   **je pourrais, tu pourrais, il/elle/on pourrait**
    nous pourrions, vous pourriez, ils/elles pourraient

6   **que je puisse, que tu puisses, qu'il/elle/on puisse**
    que nous puissions, que vous puissiez, qu'ils/elles puissent

7   **que je pusse, que tu pusses, qu'il/elle/on pût**
    que nous pussions, que vous pussiez, qu'ils/elles pussent

Imperative: (not in use)

---

prendre to take   *pr. part.* **prenant**   *past part.* **pris**

1   je prends, tu prends, il/elle/on prend
    nous prenons, vous prenez, ils/elles prennent

2   je prenais, tu prenais, il/elle/on prenait
    nous prenions, vous preniez, ils/elles prenaient

3   je pris, tu pris, il/elle/on prit
    nous prîmes, vous prîtes, ils/elles prirent

4   je prendrai, tu prendras, il/elle/on prendra
    nous prendrons, vous prendrez, ils/elles prendront

5   je prendrais, tu prendrais, il/elle/on prendrait
    nous prendrions, vous prendriez, ils/elles prendraient

6   que je prenne, que tu prennes, qu'il/elle/on prenne
    que nous prenions, que vous preniez, qu'ils/elles prennent

7   que je prisse, que tu prisses, qu'il/elle/on prît
    que nous prissions, que vous prissiez, qu'ils/elles prissent

Imperative: **prends, prenons, prenez**

---

recevoir to receive   *pr. part.* **recevant**   *past part.* **reçu**

1   je reçois, tu reçois, il/elle/on reçoit
    nous recevons, vous recevez, ils/elles reçoivent

2   je recevais, tu recevais, il/elle/on recevait
    nous recevions, vous receviez, ils/elles recevaient

3   je reçus, tu reçus, il/elle/on reçut
    nous reçûmes, vous reçûtes, ils/elles reçurent

4   je recevrai, tu recevras, il/elle/on recevra
    nous recevrons, vous recevrez, ils/elles recevront

5   je recevrais, tu recevrais, il/elle/on recevrait
    nous recevrions, vous recevriez, ils/elles recevraient

6   que je reçoive, que tu reçoives, qu'il/elle/on reçoive
    que nous recevions, que vous receviez, qu'ils/elles reçoivent

7   que je reçusse, que tu reçusses, qu'il/elle/on reçût
    que nous reçussions, que vous reçussiez, qu'ils/elles reçussent

Imperative: **reçois, recevons, recevez**

rire to laugh   *pr. part.* **riant**   *past part.* **ri**

1 **je ris, tu ris, il/elle/on rit**
   nous rions, vous riez, ils/elles rient

2 **je riais, tu riais, il/elle/on riait**
   nous riions, vous riiez, ils/elles riaient

3 **je ris, tu ris, il/elle/on rit**
   nous rîmes, vous rîtes, ils/elles rirent

4 **je rirai, tu riras, il/elle/on rira**
   nous rirons, vous rirez, ils/elles riront

5 **je rirais, tu rirais, il/elle/on rirait**
   nous ririons, vous ririez, ils/elles riraient

6 **que je rie, que tu ries, qu'il/elle/on rie**
   que nous riions, que vous riiez, qu'ils/elles rient

7 **que je risse, que tu risses, qu'il/elle/on rît**
   que nous rissions, que vous rissiez, qu'ils/elles rissent

Imperative: **ris, rions, riez**

savoir to know (how)   *pr. part.* **sachant**   *past part.* **su**

1 **je sais, tu sais, il/elle/on sait**
   nous savons, vous savez, ils/elles savent

2 **je savais, tu savais, il/elle/on savait**
   nous savions, vous saviez, ils/elles savaient

3 **je sus, tu sus, il/elle/on sut**
   nous sûmes, vous sûtes, ils/elles surent

4 **je saurai, tu sauras, il/elle/on saura**
   nous saurons, vous saurez, ils/elles sauront

5 **je saurais, tu saurais, il/elle/on saurait**
   nous saurions, vous sauriez, ils/elles sauraient

6 **que je sache, que tu saches, qu'il/elle/on sache**
   que nous sachions, que vous sachiez, qu'ils/elles sachent

7 **que je susse, que tu susses, qu'il/elle/on sût**
   que nous sussions, que vous sussiez, qu'ils/elles sussent

Imperative: **sache, sachons, sachez**

---

sentir to feel, to smell   *pr. part.* **sentant**   *past part.* **senti**

1   **je sens, tu sens, ils/elle/on sent**
    nous sentons, vous sentez, ils/elles sentent

2   **je sentais, tu sentais, il/elle/on sentait**
    nous sentions, vous sentiez, ils/elles sentaient

3   **je sentis, tu sentis, il/elle/on sentit**
    nous sentîmes, vous sentîtes, ils/elles sentirent

4   **je sentirai, tu sentiras, il/elle/on sentira**
    nous sentirons, vous sentirez, ils/elles sentiront

5   **je sentirais, tu sentirais, il/elle/on sentirait**
    nous sentirions, vous sentiriez, ils/elles sentiraient

6   **que je sente, que tu sentes, qu'il/elle/on sente**
    que nous sentions, que vous sentiez, qu'ils/elles sentent

7   **que je sentisse, que tu sentisses, qu'il/elle/on sentît**
    que nous sentissions, que vous sentissiez, qu'ils/elles sentissent

Imperative: **sens, sentons, sentez**

---

servir to serve   *pr. part.* **servant**   *past part.* **servi**

1   **je sers, tu sers, il/elle/on sert**
    nous servons, vous servez, ils/elles servent

2   **je servais, tu servais, il/elle/on servait**
    nous servions, vous serviez, ils/elles servaient

3   **je servis, tu servis, il/elle/on servit**
    nous servîmes, vous servîtes, ils/elles servirent

4   **je servirai, tu serviras, il/elle/on servira**
    nous servirons, vous servirez, ils/elles serviront

5   **je servirais, tu servirais, il/elle/on servirait**
    nous servirions, vous serviriez, ils/elles serviraient

6   **que je serve, que tu serves, qu'il/elle/on serve**
    que nous servions, que vous serviez, qu'ils/elles servent

7   **que je servisse, que tu servisses, qu'il/elle/on servît**
    que nous servissions, que vous servissiez, qu'ils/elles servissent

Imperative: **sers, servons, servez**

---

sortir to go out   *pr. part.* **sortant**   *past part.* **sorti**

1   **je sors, tu sors, il/elle/on sort
nous sortons, vous sortez, ils/elles sortent**

2   **je sortais, tu sortais, il/elle/on sortait
nous sortions, vous sortiez, ils/elles sortaient**

3   **je sortis, tu sortis, il/elle/on sortit
nous sortîmes, vous sortîtes, ils/elles sortirent**

4   **je sortirai, tu sortiras, il/elle/on sortira
nous sortirons, vous sortirez, ils/elles sortiront**

5   **je sortirais, tu sortirais, il/elle/on sortirait
nous sortirions, vous sortiriez, ils/elles sortiraient**

6   **que je sorte, que tu sortes, qu'il/elle/on sorte
que nous sortions, que vous sortiez, qu'ils/elles sortent**

7   **que je sortisse, que tu sortisses, qu'il/elle/on sortît
que nous sortissions, que vous sortissiez, qu'ils/elles sortissent**

Imperative: **sors, sortons, sortez**

---

suivre to follow   *pr. part.* **suivant**   *past part.* **suivi**

1   **je suis, tu suis, il/elle/on suit
nous suivons, vous suivez, ils/elles suivent**

2   **je suivais, tu suivais, il/elle/on suivait
nous suivions, vous suiviez, ils/elles suivaient**

3   **je suivis, tu suivis, il/elle/on suivit
nous suivîmes, vous suivîtes, ils/elles suivirent**

4   **je suivrai, tu suivras, il/elle/on suivra
nous suivrons, vous suivrez, ils/elles suivront**

5   **je suivrais, tu suivrais, il/elle/on suivrait
nous suivrions, vous suivriez, ils/elles suivraient**

6   **que je suive, que tu suives, qu'il/elle/on suive
que nous suvions, que vous suiviez, qu'ils/elles suivent**

7   **que je suivisse, que tu suivisses, qu'il/elle/on suivît
que nous suivissions, que vous suivissiez, qu'ils/elles suivissent**

Imperative: **suis, suivons, suivez**

tenir to hold   *pr. part.* **tenant**   *past part.* **tenu**

1   je tiens, tu tiens, il/elle/on tient
    nous tenons, vous tenez, ils/elles tiennent

2   je tenais, tu tenais, il/elle/on tenait
    nous tenions, vous teniez, ils/elles tenaient

3   je tins, tu tins, il/elle/on tint
    nous tînmes, vous tîntes, ils/elles tinrent

4   je tiendrai, tu tiendras, il/elle/on tiendra
    nous tiendrons, vous tiendrez, ils/elles tiendront

5   je tiendrais, tu tiendrais, il/elle/on tiendrait
    nous tiendrions, vous tiendriez, ils/elles tiendraient

6   que je tienne, que tu tiennes, qu'il/elle/on tienne
    que nous tenions, que vous teniez, qu'ils/elles tiennent

7   que je tinsse, que tu tinsses, qu'il/elle/on tînt
    que nous tinssions, que vous tinssiez, qu'ils/elles tinssent

Imperative: **tiens, tenons, tenez**

venir to come   *pr. part.* **venant**   *past part.* **venu**

1   je viens, tu viens, il/elle/on vient
    nous venons, vous venez, ils/elles viennent

2   je venais, tu venais, il/elle/on venait
    nous venions, vous veniez, ils/elles venaient

3   je vins, tu vins, il/elle/on vint
    nous vînmes, vous vîntes, ils/elles vinrent

4   je viendrai, tu viendras, il/elle/on viendra
    nous viendrons, vous viendrez, ils/elles viendront

5   je viendrais, tu viendrais, il/elle/on viendrait
    nous viendrions, vous viendriez, ils/elles viendraient

6   que je vienne, que tu viennes, qu'il/elle/on vienne
    que nous venions, que vous veniez, qu'ils/elles viennent

7   que je vinsse, que tu vinsses, qu'il/elle/on vînt
    que nous vinssions, que vous vinssiez, qu'ils/elles vinssent

Imperative: **viens, venons, venez**

vivre to live   *pr. part.* **vivant**   *past part.* **vécu**

1   je vis, tu vis, il/elle/on vit
     nous vivons, vous vivez, ils/elles vivent

2   je vivais, tu vivais, il/elle/on vivait
     nous vivions, vous viviez, ils/elles vivaient

3   je vécus, tu vécus, il/elle/on vécut
     nous vécûmes, vous vécûtes, ils/elles vécurent

4   je vivrai, tu vivras, il/elle/on vivra
     nous vivrons, vous vivrez, ils/elles vivront

5   je vivrais, tu vivrais, il/elle/on vivrait
     nous vivrions, vous vivriez, ils/elles vivraient

6   que je vive, que tu vives, qu'il/elle/on vive
     que nous vivions, que vous viviez, qu'ils/elles vivent

7   que je vécusse, que tu vécusses, qu'il/elle/on vécût
     que nous vécussions, que vous vécussiez, qu'ils/elles vécussent

Imperative: **vis, vivons, vivez**

---

voir to see   *pr. part.* **voyant**   *past part.* **vu**

1   je vois, tu vois, il/elle/on voit
     nous voyons, vous voyez, ils/elles voient

2   je voyais, tu voyais, il/elle/on voyait
     nous voyions, vous voyiez, ils/elles voyaient

3   je vis, tu vis, il/elle/on vit
     nous vîmes, vous vîtes, ils/elles virent

4   je verrai, tu verras, il/elle/on verra
     nous verrons, vous verrez, ils/elles verront

5   je verrais, tu verrais, il/elle/on verrait
     nous verrions, vous verriez, ils/elles verraient

6   que je voie, que tu voies, qu'il/elle/on voie
     que nous voyions, que vous voyiez, qu'ils/elles voient

7   que je visse, que tu visses, qu'il/elle/on vît
     que nous vissions, que vous vissiez, qu'ils/elles vissent

Imperative: **vois, voyons, voyez**

vouloir to want   *pr. part.* **voulant**   *past part.* **voulu**

1   je veux, tu veux, il/elle/on veut
    nous voulons, vous voulez, ils/elles veulent

2   je voulais, tu voulais, il/elle/on voulait
    nous voulions, vous vouliez, ils/elles voulaient

3   je voulus, tu voulus, il/elle/on voulut
    nous voulûmes, vous voulûtes, ils/elles voulurent

4   je voudrai, tu voudras, il/elle/on voudra
    nous voudrons, vous voudrez, ils/elles voudront

5   je voudrais, tu voudrais, il/elle/on voudrait
    nous voudrions, vous voudriez, ils/elles voudraient

6   que je veuille, que tu veuilles, qu'il/elle/on veuille
    que nous voulions, que vous vouliez, qu'ils/elles veuillent

7   que je voulusse, que tu voulusses, qu'il/elle/on voulût
    que nous voulussions, que vous voulussiez, qu'ils/elles voulussent

Imperative: **veuille, veuillons, veuillez**

§27.

Definitions of Basic Grammatical Terms with Examples

active voice

When we speak or write in the active voice, the subject of the verb performs the action. The action falls on the direct object.

Example:
Everyone loves Janine / Tout le monde aime Janine.
The subject is *everyone.* The verb is *loves.* The direct object is *Janine.*

Review **§7.9.** See also *passive voice* in this list. Compare the above sentence with the example in the passive voice.

adjective

An adjective is a word that modifies a noun or a pronoun. In grammar, to modify a word means to describe, limit, expand, or make the meaning particular.

Examples:
a beautiful garden / un beau jardin; she is pretty / elle est jolie.
The adjective *beautiful/beau* modifies the noun *garden/jardin.* The adjective *pretty/jolie* modifies the pronoun *she/elle.*

In French there are different kinds of adjectives. *See also* comparative adjective, demonstrative adjective, descriptive adjective, interrogative adjective, limiting adjective, possessive adjective, superlative adjective.

Review **§5.**

adverb

An adverb is a word that modifies a verb, an adjective, or another adverb. An adverb says something about how, when, where, to what extent, or in what way.

Examples:
Jane runs swiftly / **Jeanne court rapidement**. The adverb
swiftly/***rapidement*** modifies the verb *runs*/*court*. The
adverb shows *how* she runs.

Jack is a very good friend / **Jacques est un très bon ami**.
The adverb *very*/***très*** modifies the adjective *good*/***bon***.
The adverb shows *how good a friend* he is.

The boy is eating too fast now / **Le garçon mange trop
vite maintenant**. The adverb *too*/***trop*** modifies the adverb
fast/***vite***. The adverb shows *to what extent* he is eating
fast. The adverb *now*/***maintenant*** tells us *when*.

The post office is there / **Le bureau de poste est là**. The
adverb *there*/***là*** modifies the verb *is*/*est*. It tells us *where*
the post office is.

Mary writes carefully / **Marie écrit soigneusement**. The
adverb *carefully*/***soigneusement*** modifies the verb
writes/***écrit***. It tells us *in what way* she writes.

Review **§8.**

affirmative statement, negative statement

A statement in the affirmative is the opposite of a statement
in the negative. To negate an affirmative statement is to
make it negative.

Examples:
In the affirmative: I like chocolate ice cream / **J'aime la
glace au chocolat.**
In the negative: I do not like chocolate ice cream / **Je
n'aime pas la glace au chocolat.**

Review **§7.18.**

agreement of adjective with noun

Agreement is made on the adjective with the noun it
modifies in gender (masculine or feminine) and number
(singular or plural).

Examples:
a white house / **une maison blanche**. The adjective
blanche is feminine singular because the noun **une
maison** is feminine singular.

two white houses / **deux maisons blanches**. The adjective **blanches** is feminine plural because the noun **maisons** is feminine plural.

Review **§5.1** and **§5.2.**

agreement of past participle of a reflexive verb with its reflexive pronoun

Agreement is made on the past participle of a reflexive verb with its reflexive pronoun in gender (masculine or feminine) and number (singular or plural) if that pronoun is the *direct object* of the verb. The agreement is determined by looking at the subject to see its gender and number, which is the same as its reflexive pronoun. If the reflexive pronoun is the *indirect object*, an agreement is *not* made.

Examples:
to wash oneself / **se laver**. For more reflexive verbs, see the verb tables.
She washed herself / **Elle s'est lavée**. There is a feminine agreement on the past participle **lavée** (added **e**) with the reflexive pronoun **se** (here, **s'**) because it serves as a direct object pronoun. What or whom did she wash? Herself, which is expressed in **se (s')**.

But:
She washed her hair / **Elle s'est lavé les cheveux**. There is no feminine agreement on the past participle **lavé** here because the reflexive pronoun **(se**, here, **s')** serves as an *indirect object*. The direct object is **les cheveux** and it is stated *after* the verb. What did she wash? She washed her hair *on herself **(s')**.*

Review **§6.1—12, §7.1, §7.3—1, §7.8—8,** and **§7.19.** *See also* reflexive pronoun and reflexive verb.

agreement of past participle with its direct object

Agreement is made on the past participle with its direct object in gender (masculine or feminine) and number (singular or plural) when the verb is conjugated with **avoir** in the compound tenses. Agreement is made when the direct object, if there is one, *precedes* the verb.

Examples:
Where are the little cakes? Paul ate them / **Où sont les petits gâteaux? Paul les a mangés**. The verb **a mangés**

is in the *passé composé*; **manger** is conjugated with **avoir**. There is a plural agreement on the past participle **mangés** (added **s**) because the *preceding* direct object *them* / *les* is masculine plural, referring to *les petits gâteaux*, which is masculine plural.

Who wrote the letters? Robert wrote them / **Qui a écrit les lettres? Robert les a écrites**. The verb **a écrites** is in the *passé composé*; **écrire** is conjugated with **avoir**. There is a feminine plural agreement on the past participle **écrites** (added **e** and **s**) because the *preceding* direct object *them* / *les* is feminine plural, referring to *les lettres*, which is feminine plural. A past participle functions as an adjective. An agreement in gender and number is *not* made with *an indirect object. See* indirect object noun, indirect object pronoun.

Review **§7.1, §7.3—1, §7.8—8.** *See also* direct object noun, direct object pronoun.

agreement of past participle with the subject

Agreement is made on the past participle with the subject in gender (masculine or feminine) and number (singular or plural) when the verb is conjugated with **être** in the compound tenses.

Examples:
She went to Paris / **Elle est allée à Paris**. The verb **est allée** is in the *passé composé*; **aller** is conjugated with **être**. There is a feminine agreement on the past participle **allée** (added **e**) because the subject **elle** is feminine singular.

The boys have arrived / **Les garçons sont arrivés**. The verb **sont arrivés** is in the *passé composé*; **arriver** is conjugated with **être**. There is a plural agreement on the past participle **arrivés** (added **s**) because the subject **les garçons** is masculine plural.

Review **§7.1, §7.3—1, §7.8—8, §7.19.** *See also* past participle and subject.

agreement of verb with its subject

A verb agrees in person (first, second, or third) and in number (singular or plural) with its subject.

Examples:
Does he always tell the truth? / **Dit-il toujours la vérité?**
The verb **dit** (of **dire**) is third person singular because the
subject *il* / *he* is third person singular.

Where are they going? / **Où vont-ils?** The verb **vont** (of
aller) is third person plural because the subject *ils* / *they* is
third person plural.

Review **§7.1.** *See also* **§6.1—1** for person and number.

antecedent

An antecedent is a word to which a relative pronoun refers.
It comes *before* the pronoun.

Examples:
The girl who is laughing over there is my sister / **La jeune
fille qui rit là-bas est ma soeur.** The antecedent is *girl* / *la
jeune fille*. The relative pronoun *who* / *qui* refers to the girl.

The car that I bought is expensive / **La voiture que j'ai
achetée est chère.** The antecedent is *car* / **la voiture.** The
relative pronoun *that* / *que* refers to the car. Note also that
the past participle **achetée** is fem. sing. because it refers to
la voiture (fem. sing.), which precedes the verb.

Review **§6.1—13.** *See also* relative pronoun.

auxiliary verb

An auxiliary verb is a helping verb. In English grammar it
is *to have.* In French grammar it is **avoir** (to have) or **être**
(to be). An auxiliary verb is used to help form the
compound tenses.

Examples:
I have eaten / **J'**ai* mangé**; she has left / **elle** *est* partie**.

Review **§7.3—1** to find out about verbs conjugated with
avoir or **être** as helping verbs.

cardinal number

A cardinal number is a number that expresses an amount,
such as *one, two, three,* and so on.

Review **§16.** *See also* ordinal number.

causative faire

In English grammar, a causative verb causes something to be done. In French grammar the idea is the same. The subject of the verb causes the action expressed in the verb to be carried out by someone else.

Examples:
Mrs. Roth makes her students work in French class /
Madame Roth fait travailler ses élèves dans la classe de français.

Mr. Smith is having a house built / **Monsieur Smith fait construire une maison.**

Review **§7.14.**

clause

A clause is a group of words that contains a subject and a predicate. A predicate may contain more than one word. A conjugated verb form is revealed in the predicate.

Example:
Mrs. Coty lives in a small apartment / Madame Coty **demeure dans un petit appartement.**
The subject is *Mrs. Coty/ Madame Coty.* The predicate is *lives in a small apartment/ demeure dans un petit appartement.* The verb is *lives/ demeure.*

See also dependent clause, independent clause.

comparative adjective

When making a comparison between two persons or things, an adjective is used to express the degree of comparison in the following ways.

Examples:
Of the same degree of comparison: Raymond is *as tall as* his father / **Raymond est *aussi grand que* son père.**

Of a lesser degree of comparison: Monique is *less intelligent than* her sister / **Monique est *moins intelligente que* sa soeur.**

Of a higher degree of comparison: This apple is *more delicious than* that apple / **Cette pomme-ci est *plus délicieuse que* cette pomme-là.**

Review **§5.4—5.** *See also* superlative adjective.

comparative adverb

An adverb is compared in the same way as an adjective is compared. *See* comparative adjective.

Examples:
Of the same degree of comparison: Mr. Bernard speaks *as fast as* Mr. Claude / **Monsieur Bernard parle** *aussi vite que* **Monsieur Claude.**

Of a lesser degree of comparison: Alice studies *less seriously than* her sister / **Alice étudie** *moins sérieusement que* **sa soeur.**

Of a higher degree of comparison: Albert works *more slowly than* his brother / **Albert travaille** *plus lentement que* **son frère.**

Review **§8.3—3.** *See also* superlative adverb.

complex sentence

A complex sentence contains one independent clause and one or more dependent clauses.

Examples:
One independent clause and one dependent clause: Jack is handsome but his brother isn't / **Jacques est beau mais son frère ne l'est pas.**
The independent clause is *Jack is handsome.* It makes sense when it stands alone because it expresses a complete thought. The dependent clause is *but his brother isn't.* The dependent clause, which is introduced by the conjunction *but*, does not make complete sense when it stands alone because it *depends* on the thought expressed in the independent clause.

One independent clause and two dependent clauses: Mary gets good grades in school because she studies but her sister never studies / **Marie reçoit de bonnes notes à l'école parce qu'elle étudie mais sa soeur n'étudie jamais.**
The independent clause is *Mary gets good grades in school.* It makes sense when it stands alone because it expresses a complete thought. The first dependent clause is *because she studies.* This dependent clause, which is introduced by the conjunction *because*, does not make complete sense when it stands alone because it *depends* on the thought expressed in the independent clause. The second dependent clause is *but her sister never studies.*

That dependent clause, which is introduced by the conjunction *but*, does not make complete sense either when it stands alone because it *depends* on the thought expressed in the independent clause.

Use the verb tables beginning on page 214.

See also dependent clause, independent clause.

compound sentence

A compound sentence contains two or more independent clauses.

Example:
Mrs. Dubois went to the supermarket, she bought some groceries, and then she returned home / **Madame Dubois est allée au supermarché, elle a acheté des provisions, et puis elle est rentrée chez elle**.

This compound sentence contains three independent clauses. They are independent because they make sense when they stand alone.

Review the *passé composé* in **§7.8—8.** *See also* independent clause. Use the verb tables beginning on page 214.

conditional perfect tense

In French grammar, the conditional used to be considered a mood. Grammarians now regard it as a tense of the indicative mood.

This tense is defined with examples in **§7.8—12.**

conditional present tense

In French grammar, the conditional used to be considered a mood. Grammarians now regard it as a tense of the indicative mood.

This tense is defined with examples in **§7.8—5.**

conjugation

The conjugation of a verb is the fixed order of all its forms showing their inflections (changes) in the three persons of the singular and plural in a particular tense.

For examples, review **§7.19** for the conjugation of **aller**, **avoir**, **être**, and **faire** in all their forms in the fourteen tenses and the imperative.

conjunction

A conjunction is a word that connects words or groups of words.

Examples:
and/**et**, or/**ou**, but/**mais**
You and I are going downtown / **Toi et moi, nous allons en ville**.
You can stay home or you can come with us / **Tu peux rester à la maison ou tu peux venir avec nous**.

Review **§10.** first, then **§7.15.**

declarative sentence

A declarative sentence makes a statement.

Example:
I have finished the work / **J'ai fini le travail**.

definite article

The definite article in French has four forms and they all mean *the*. To find out what they are, with examples using them, review **§3.1.**

demonstrative adjective

A demonstrative adjective is an adjective that points out. It is placed in front of a noun.

Examples:
this book/**ce livre**; these flowers/**ces fleurs**

To see them all in French and English, with examples using them, review **§5.4—2.**

demonstrative pronoun

A demonstrative pronoun is a pronoun that points out. It takes the place of a noun. It agrees in gender and number with the noun it replaces.

Examples:
I have two apples; do you prefer *this one* or *that one*? / **J'ai deux pommes; préférez-vous celle-ci ou celle-là?**
Sorry, but I prefer *those* / **Je regrette, mais je préfère celles-là**.

Do you like the ones that are on the table? / **Aimez-vous celles qui sont sur la table?**

Review **§6.1—8.** For demonstrative pronouns that are neuter, *see* neuter.

dependent clause

A dependent clause is a group of words that contains a subject and a predicate. It does not express a complete thought when it stands alone. It is called *dependent* because it depends on the independent clause for a complete meaning. Subordinate clause is another term for dependent clause.

Example:
Mary is absent today because she is sick / **Marie est absente aujourd'hui parce qu'elle est malade**.
The independent clause is *Mary is absent today.* The dependent clause is *because she is sick.*

See also clause, independent clause.

descriptive adjective

A descriptive adjective is an adjective that describes a person, place, or thing.

Examples:
a pretty girl / **une jolie jeune fille**; a handsome boy / **un beau garçon**; a small house / **une petite maison**; a big city / **une grande ville**; an expensive car / **une voiture chère**.

Review **§5.4—1.** *See also* adjective.

direct object noun

A direct object noun receives the action of the verb *directly.* That is why it is called a direct object, as opposed to an indirect object. A direct object noun is normally placed *after* the verb.

Example:
I am writing a letter / **J'écris une lettre**.
The subject is *I / Je.* The verb is *am writing / écris.* The direct object is the noun *letter / une lettre.*

Review **§6.1—2** and the examples in sentences. *See also* direct object pronoun.

direct object pronoun

A direct object pronoun receives the action of the verb *directly*. It takes the place of a direct object noun. In French a pronoun that is a direct object of a verb is ordinarily placed *in front of* the verb.

Examples:
I am writing it / **Je l'écris.**
A direct object pronoun is placed *after* the verb and joined with a hyphen *in the affirmative imperative.*

Write it now / **Écrivez-la maintenant.**

Review **§6.1—2** for all the direct object pronouns and examples in sentences. Also, review examples of an affirmative imperative sentence containing direct and indirect object pronouns in **§11**. *See also* imperative.

disjunctive pronoun

In French grammar a disjunctive pronoun is a pronoun that is stressed; in other words, emphasis is placed on it.

Example:
I speak well; *he* does not speak well / *Moi*, **je parle bien**; *lui*, **il ne parle pas bien.**

Review **§6.1—7** to see them all with examples of their uses.

ending of a verb

In French grammar the ending of a verb form changes according to the person and number of the subject and the tense of the verb.

Example:
To form the present indicative tense of a regular **-er** type verb like **parler**, drop **er** of the infinitive and add the following endings: **-e, -es, -e** for the first, second, and third persons of the singular; **-ons, -ez, -ent** for the first, second, and third persons of the plural.
You then get: **je parle, tu parles, il (elle, on) parle; nous parlons, vous parlez, ils (elles) parlent**

Review **§7.8.** Use the verb tables beginning on page 214.

See also stem of a verb.

feminine

In French grammar the gender of a noun, pronoun, or adjective is feminine or masculine, not male or female.

See also gender.

future perfect tense

This tense is defined with examples in **§7.8—11.**

future tense

This tense is defined with examples in **§7.8—4.**

gender

In French grammar gender means masculine or feminine.

Examples:
Masculine: the boy / **le garçon** he, it / **il** the rooster / **le coq**
the book / **le livre**
Feminine: the girl / **la jeune fille** she, it / **elle** the hen / **la poule** the house / **la maison**

Review **§4.1.**

gerund

In English grammar, a gerund is a word formed from a verb. It ends in *ing.* Actually, it is the present participle of a verb. But it is not used as a verb. It is used as a noun.

Examples:
Seeing is believing / **Voir c'est croire.**
However, in French grammar, the infinitive form of the verb is used, as in the above example, when the verb is used as a noun. In French, *seeing is believing* is expressed as *to see is to believe.*
The French gerund is also a word formed from a verb. It ends in **ant**. It is also the present participle of a verb. As a gerund, it is normally preceded by the preposition **en**.

En partant, il a fait ses excuses / While leaving, he made his excuses.

Review **§7.4.**

if (si) clause

An "if" clause is defined with examples in verb tenses in **§7.10.**

See also clause.

imperative

The imperative is a mood, not a tense. It is used to express a command. In French it is used in the second person of the singular **(tu)**, the second person of the plural **(vous)**, and in the first person of the plural **(nous)**.

Review **§7.8—15** for examples. *See also* person (first, second, third).

imperfect indicative tense

This tense is defined with examples in **§7.8—2.**

imperfect subjunctive tense

This tense is defined with examples in **§7.8—7.**

indefinite article

In English the indefinite articles are *a, an*, as in *a book, an apple.* They are indefinite because they do not refer to any definite or particular noun.

In French there are two indefinite articles in the singular: one in the masculine form **(un)** and one in the feminine form **(une)**.

Examples:
Masculine singular: un livre/*a book*

Feminine singular: une pomme/*an apple*
In French they both change to **des** in the plural.

I have a brother/J'ai un frère.   I have brothers/J'ai des frères.

I have a sister/J'ai une soeur.   I have sisters/J'ai des soeurs.

I have an apple/J'ai une pomme.   I have apples/J'ai des pommes.

Review **§3.2.** *See also* definite article.

indefinite pronoun

An indefinite pronoun is a pronoun that does not refer to any definite or particular noun.

Examples:
something / **quelque chose**   someone, somebody/
quelqu'un, quelqu'une;   each one / **chacun, chacune**
anything / **n'importe quoi**
Review **§6.1—9** for the basic indefinite pronouns.

independent clause

An independent clause is a group of words that contains a subject and a predicate. It expresses a complete thought when it stands alone.

Example:
The cat is sleeping under the bed / **Le chat dort sous le lit.**

See also clause, dependent clause, predicate.

indicative mood

The indicative mood is used in sentences that make a statement or ask a question. The indicative mood is used most of the time when we speak or write in English or French.

Examples:
I am going home now / **Je vais chez moi maintenant.**
Where are you going? / **Où allez-vous?**

indirect object noun

An indirect object noun receives the action of the verb *indirectly*.

Example:
I am writing a letter to Mary *or* I am writing Mary a letter /
J'écris une lettre à Marie.
The subject is *I* / *Je*. The verb is *am writing* / *écris*. The direct object noun is *a letter* / *une lettre*. The indirect object noun is *Mary* / *Marie*.
An agreement is not made with an indirect object noun.

Review **§6.1—3** and the examples in sentences. *See also* indirect object pronoun.

indirect object pronoun

An indirect object pronoun takes the place of an indirect object noun. It receives the action of the verb *indirectly*.

Example:
I am writing a letter to her *or* I am writing her a letter / Je lui écris une lettre.
The indirect object pronoun is *(to) her* / lui.
An agreement is not made with an indirect object pronoun.

Review **§6.1—3** for all the indirect object pronouns and examples in sentences. For the position of double object pronouns (direct and indirect), consult **§6.1—4.** *See also* indirect object noun.

infinitive

An infinitive is a verb form. In English, it is normally stated with the preposition *to,* as in *to talk, to finish, to sell.* In French, the infinitive form of a verb consists of three major types: those of the first conjugation that end in **-er**, the second conjugation that end in **-ir**, and the third conjugation that end in **-re**.

Examples:
parler/*to talk, to speak*   finir/*to finish*   vendre/*to sell*

Review **§7.13.** Use the verb tables beginning on page 214.

interjection

An interjection is a word that expresses emotion, a feeling of joy, of sadness, an exclamation of surprise, and other exclamations consisting of one or two words.

Examples:
Ah!/Ah!   Oh!/Oh!   Darn it!/Zut!   Whew!/Ouf!
My God!/Mon Dieu!

interrogative adjective

In French, an interrogative adjective is an adjective that is used in a question. It agrees in gender and number with the noun it modifies.

Examples:
What book do you want? / Quel livre désirez-vous?
What time is it? / Quelle heure est-il?

Review **§5.4—3.**

interrogative adverb

In French, an interrogative adverb is an adverb that introduces a question. As an adverb, it modifies the verb.

Examples:
How are you? / **Comment allez-vous?**
How much does this book cost? / **Combien coûte ce livre?**
When will you arrive? / **Quand arriverez-vous?**

Review **§8.3—1.**

interrogative pronoun

An interrogative pronoun is a pronoun that asks a question. There are interrogative pronouns that refer to persons and those that refer to things.

Examples:
Who is on the phone? / **Qui est à l'appareil?**
What are you saying? / **Que dites-vous?**

Review **§6.1—10.**

interrogative sentence

An interrogative sentence asks a question.

Example:
What are you doing? / **Que faites-vous?**

intransitive verb

An intransitive verb is a verb that does not take a direct object.

Examples:
The professor is talking loudly / **Le professeur parle fort.**
An intransitive verb takes an indirect object.

The professor is talking to us / **Le professeur nous parle.**

Review **§7.3—3.**

irregular verb

An irregular verb is a verb that does not follow a fixed pattern in its conjugation in the various verb tenses.

Examples of basic irregular verbs in French: **aller**/to go
avoir/to have   **être**/to be   **faire**/to do, to make

Use the tables of irregular verbs beginning on page 241. *See also* conjugation, regular verb.

limiting adjective

A limiting adjective is an adjective that limits a quantity.

Example:
three tickets / trois billets a few candies / quelques bonbons

main clause

Main clause is another term for independent clause. *See* independent clause.

masculine

In French grammar the gender of a noun, pronoun, or adjective is masculine or feminine, not male or female.

See also gender.

mood of verbs

Some grammarians use the term *the mode* instead of *the mood* of a verb. Either term means *the manner or way* a verb is expressed. In English and in French grammar a verb expresses an action or state of being in the following moods (modes, *ways*): the indicative mood, the imperative mood, and the subjunctive mood. In French grammar, there is also the infinitive mood when the whole infinitive is used, *e.g.,* **voir**, **croire**, as in Voir c'est croire / *Seeing is believing (to see is to believe).* Most of the time, in English and French, we speak and write in the indicative mood.

Review **§7.8.**

negative statement, affirmative statement

(*see* affirmative statement, negative statement)

neuter

A word that is neuter is neither masculine nor feminine. Common neuter demonstrative pronouns are ce (c') / *it*, ceci / *this*, cela / *that*, ça / *that*. They are invariable, which means they do not change in gender and number.

Examples:
It's not true / **Ce n'est pas vrai**   it is true / **c'est vrai**
this is true / **ceci est vrai**   that is true / **cela est vrai**
what is that? / **qu'est-ce que c'est que ça?**

Review **§6.1—8.** For demonstrative pronouns that are not neuter, *see* demonstrative pronoun.

There is also the neuter pronoun **le**, as in: **Je le crois** /
I believe it   **Je le pense** / I think so. Review **§6.1—15.**

noun

A noun is a word that names a person, animal, place, thing, condition or state, or quality.

Examples:
the man / **l'homme**   the woman / **la femme**   the horse / **le cheval**   the house / **la maison**   the book / **le livre**
happiness / **le bonheur**   excellence / **l'excellence** *(fem.)*
In French the noun **le nom** is the word for name and noun.

Review **§4.**

number

In English and French grammar, number means singular or plural.

Examples:
Masc. sing.: the boy / **le garçon**   the arm / **le bras**
the eye / **l'oeil**
Masc. pl.: the boys / **les garçons**   the arms / **les bras**
the eyes / **les yeux**

Fem. sing.: the girl / **la jeune fille**   the house / **la maison**
the hen / **la poule**
Fem. pl.: the girls / **les jeunes filles**
the houses / **les maisons**   the hens / **les poules**

Review **§4.1, §4.2.**

ordinal number

An ordinal number is a number that expresses position in a series, such as *first, second, third*, and so on. In English and French grammar we talk about first person, second person, third person singular or plural regarding subjects and verbs.

Review **§16.** *See also* cardinal number.

orthographical changes in verb forms

An orthographical change in a verb form is a change in spelling.

Examples:
The second letter **c** in the verb commencer/*to begin* changes to **ç** if the letter after it is **a**, **o**, or **u**, as in *nous commençons/we begin.* The reason for this spelling change is to preserve the sound of *s* as it is pronounced in the infinitive form **commencer**. When **a**, **o** or **u** follow the letter **c**, the **c** is pronounced as in the sound of **k**. The mark under the letter **ç** is called une cédille/*cedilla*. Some linguists say it is the lower part of the letter **s** and it tells you to pronounce **ç** as an **s** sound. Other linguists say that **ç** was borrowed from the Greek alphabet, where it represents the sound of **s** when it is the last letter of a Greek word.

The verb s'appeler/*to call oneself, to be named* contains a single **l**. When a verb form is stressed on the syllable containing one **l**, it doubles, as in je m'appelle... /*l call myself..., my name is....*

Review **§7.17.**

partitive

In French grammar the partitive denotes a *part* of a whole; in other words, *some.*

Review **§3.3** for examples. Also, review the use of **en** in **§6.1—5.**

passive voice

When we speak or write in the active voice and change to the passive voice, the direct object becomes the subject, the subject becomes the object of a preposition, and the verb becomes *to be* plus the past participle of the active verb. The past participle functions as an adjective.

Example:
Janine is loved by everyone / Janine est aimée de tout le monde.
The subject is *Janine.* The verb is *is.* The object of the preposition *by/de* is *everyone/tout le monde.*

Review **§7.9.** *See also* active voice. Compare the above sentence with the example in the active voice.

past anterior tense

This tense is defined with examples in **§7.8—10.**

past indefinite tense

This tense is defined with examples in **§7.8—8.** In French it is the *passé composé.*

past participle

A past participle is derived from a verb. It is used to form the compound tenses. Its auxiliary verb is **avoir** / *to have* or **être** / *to be.* It is part of the verb tense.

Examples:
With **avoir** as the auxiliary verb: **Elle a mangé** / She has eaten.
The subject is *elle/she.* The verb is **a mangé** / *has eaten.* The tense of the verb is the *passé composé.* The auxiliary verb is *a/has.* The past participle is *mangé/eaten.*

With **être** as the auxiliary verb: **Elle est arrivée** / She has arrived.
The verb is *est arrivée/has arrived.* The tense of the verb is the *passé composé.* The auxiliary verb is *est.* The past participle is *arrivée/arrived.*

Review **§7.2** for the regular formation of a past participle and a list of irregular past participles. Review **§7.3—1** and **§7.8—8.** *See also* agreement of past participle with the subject.

past perfect tense

This tense is also called the pluperfect indicative tense. *See* **§7.8—9** for a definition with examples.

past simple tense

This tense is defined with examples in **§7.8—3.** It is also called the simple past tense or past definite tense. In French it is the *passé simple.*

past subjunctive tense

This tense is defined with examples in **§7.8—13.**

person (first, second, third)

Verb forms in a particular tense are learned systematically according to person (first, second, third) and number (singular, plural).

Example, showing the present indicative tense of the verb aller / to go:

Singular
first person: **je vais**
second person: **tu vas**
third person: **il, elle, on va**

Plural
first person: **nous allons**
second person: **vous allez**
third person: **ils, elles vont**

Review **§6.1—1** and **§7.19.** Use the verb tables beginning on page 214.

personal pronoun

A personal pronoun refers to a person. The pronoun *it/il* or *elle* is in this category.

For examples, review **§6.**

pluperfect indicative tense

This tense is defined with examples in **§7.8—9.** It is also called the past perfect indicative tense.

pluperfect subjunctive tense

This tense is defined with examples in **§7.8—14.** It is also called the past perfect subjunctive tense.

plural

Plural means more than one. *See also* person (first, second, third) and singular.

possessive adjective

A possessive adjective is an adjective that is placed in front of a noun to show possession. In French their forms change in gender (masculine or feminine) and number (singular or plural) to agree with the noun they modify.

Examples:
my book / mon livre   my books / mes livres
my dress / ma robe

Review **§5.4—4** for all the forms of possessive adjectives with examples.

possessive pronoun

A possessive pronoun is a pronoun that shows possession. It takes the place of a possessive adjective with the noun. Its form agrees in gender (masculine or feminine) and number (singular or plural) with what it is replacing.

Examples in English: mine, yours, his, hers, its, ours, theirs

Examples in French:

Possessive Adjective	Possessive Pronoun
my book / **mon livre**	*mine* / **le mien**
my dress / **ma robe**	*mine* / **la mienne**
my shoes / **mes chaussures**	*mine* / **les miennes**

Review **§6.1—11** for all the forms of possessive pronouns with examples.

predicate

The predicate is that part of the sentence that tells us something about the subject. The main word of the predicate is the verb.

Example:
The tourists are waiting for the tour bus / **Les touristes attendent l'autocar.**
The subject is *the tourists / les touristes*. The predicate is *are waiting for the tour bus / attendent l'autocar*. The verb is *are waiting / attendent*. The direct object is *the tour bus / l'autocar*.

preposition

A preposition is a word that establishes a rapport between words.

Examples:
with me / *avec* **moi**   *in* the drawer / *dans* **le tiroir**
on the table / *sur* **la table**   *at* six o'clock / *à* **six heures**
between him and her / *entre* **lui et elle**

Review **§9.** for special uses of certain prepositions. Also, review **§7.5** for verbs with prepositions.

present indicative tense

This tense is defined with examples in **§7.8—1.**

present participle

A present participle is derived from a verb form. In French it is regularly formed like this: take the **nous** form of the present indicative tense of the verb you have in mind, then drop the ending **ons** and add **ant**. In English a present participle ends in *ing*.

Examples:

Infinitive	Present Indicative nous form	Present participle
chanter to sing	nous chantons we sing	chantant singing
finir to finish	nous finissons we finish	finissant finishing
vendre to sell	nous vendons we sell	vendant selling

Review **§7.4** for regular and irregular present participles and their uses.

present subjunctive tense

This tense is defined with examples in **§7.8—6.**

pronoun

A pronoun is a word that takes the place of a noun.

Examples:
l'homme/*il*   la femme/*elle*   l'arbre/*il*   la voiture/*elle*
the man/*he*   the woman/*she*   the tree/*it*   the car/*it*

Review **§6.** for the different kinds of pronouns and their uses.

reflexive pronoun and reflexive verb

In English a reflexive pronoun is a personal pronoun that contains *self* or *selves*. In French and English a reflexive pronoun is used with a verb that is called reflexive because the action of the verb falls on the reflexive pronoun.

In French there is a required set of reflexive pronouns for a reflexive verb.

Examples:
se laver   Je me lave   se blesser   Elle s'est blessée.
to wash   I wash   to hurt   She hurt herself.
oneself   myself.   oneself

In French a reflexive verb is conjugated with **être** to form the compound tenses. The French term for a reflexive verb is **un verbe pronominal** because a pronoun goes with the verb.

Review **§6.1—12** and **§7.3—1**. *See also* agreement of past participle of a reflexive verb with its reflexive pronoun.

regular verb

A regular verb is a verb that is conjugated in the various tenses according to a fixed pattern.

Review **§7.** for examples and uses, in particular **§7.8.** Use the verb tables beginning on page 214. *See also* conjugation, irregular verb.

relative pronoun

A relative pronoun is a pronoun that refers to its antecedent.

Example:
The girl who is laughing over there is my sister / **La jeune fille qui rit là-bas est ma soeur**. The antecedent is *girl/la jeune fille*. The relative pronoun *who/qui* refers to the girl.

Review **§6.1—13**. *See also* antecedent.

sentence

A sentence is a group of words that contains a subject and a predicate. The verb is contained in the predicate. A sentence expresses a complete thought.

Example:
The train leaves from the North Station at two o'clock in the afternoon / **Le train part de la Gare du Nord à deux heures de l'après-midi**.
The subject is *train/le train*. The predicate is *leaves from the North Station at two o'clock in the afternoon/part de la Gare du Nord à deux heures de l'après-midi*. The verb is *leaves/part*.

See also complex sentence, compound sentence, simple sentence.

simple sentence

A simple sentence is a sentence that contains one subject and one predicate. The verb is the core of the predicate. The verb is the most important word in a sentence because it tells us what the subject is doing.

Example:
Mary is eating an apple from her garden / Marie mange une pomme de son jardin.
The subject is *Mary*/ Marie. The predicate is *is eating an apple from her garden*/ *mange une pomme de son jardin*. The verb is *is eating*/ *mange*. The direct object is *an apple*/ *une pomme. From her garden*/ *de son jardin* is an adverbial phrase. It tells you from where the apple came.

See also complex sentence, compound sentence.

singular

Singular means one. *See also* plural.

stem of a verb

The stem of a verb is what is left after you drop the ending of its infinitive form. It is needed to add to it the required endings of a regular verb in a particular verb tense.

Examples:

Infinitive	Ending of infinitive	Stem
donner / to give	er	donn
choisir / to choose	ir	chois
vendre / to sell	re	vend

See also ending of a verb.

subject

A subject is that part of a sentence that is related to its verb. The verb says something about the subject.

Example:
Clara and Isabel are beautiful / Clara et Isabel sont belles.

subjunctive mood

The subjunctive mood is the mood of a verb that is used in specific cases, *e.g.,* after certain verbs expressing a wish, doubt, emotion, fear, joy, uncertainty, an indefinite expression, an indefinite antecedent, certain conjunctions, and others.

The subjunctive mood is used more frequently in French than in English.

Review the uses of the subjunctive mood with examples in **§7.15.**

subordinate clause

Subordinate clause is another term for dependent clause. *See* dependent clause.

superlative adjective

A superlative adjective is an adjective that expresses the highest degree when making a comparison of more than two persons or things.

Examples:

Adjective	Comparative	Superlative
bon / good	meilleur / better	le meilleur / best
mauvais / bad	plus mauvais / worse	le plus mauvais / worst

Review **§5.4—5** and **§5.4—6.** *See also* comparative adjective.

superlative adverb

A superlative adverb is an adverb that expresses the highest degree when making a comparison of more than two persons or things.

Examples:

Adverb	Comparative	Superlative
vite / quickly	plus vite / more quickly	le plus vite / most quickly
	moins vite / less quickly	le moins vite / least quickly

Review **§8.3—3.** *See also* comparative adverb.

tense of verb

In English and French grammar, tense means time. The tense of the verb indicates the time of the action or state of being. The three major segments of time are past, present, and future. In French there are fourteen verb tenses, of which seven are simple tenses and seven are compound.

For the complete conjugation of two model French verbs in all the tenses with their English translations, see **§7.6** and **§7.7**.

Review **§7.16** for the names of the fourteen tenses and **§7.19** where you can see four commonly used verbs conjugated fully in all the tenses as well as in the imperative mood.

Use the verb tables beginning on page 214.

transitive verb

A transitive verb is a verb that takes a direct object.

Example:
I am closing the window / Je ferme la fenêtre.
The subject is *I/Je*. The verb is *am closing/ferme*. The direct object is *the window/la fenêtre*.

Review **§7.3—2.**

verb

A verb is a word that expresses action or a state of being.

Examples:
Action: Les oiseaux volent / The birds are flying.
The verb is *volent/are flying.*

State of being: La jeune fille est heureuse / The girl is happy.
The verb is *est/is.*

APPENDIX

French-English Vocabulary

After you look up a verb form in this vocabulary, remember to consult also the French Verb Conjugation Tables beginning on page 214 and the Irregular Verb Tables beginning on page 241, as well as §7. in this book. A list of abbreviations is also provided on page xiii.

A

a *third pers., s., pr. ind. of* **avoir**

à *prep.* at, to, in; *see §3.1, §12.2*

à moins que *conj.* unless; *see §7.15, §10.*

accepter *v.* to accept; *see Verb Tables*

accès *n.m.* access

achètent *third pers., pl., pr. ind. of* **acheter**; *see §7.17*

acheter *v.* to buy, to purchase; *see Verb Tables*

actif, active *adj.* active

activité *n.f.* activity

aéroport *n.m.* airport

affreusement *adv.* frightfully; *see §8.1*

âge *n.m.* age; **âgé** *adj.* aged

agréable *adj.* pleasant, agreeable

ai *first pers., s., pr. ind. of* **avoir**; *see §7.19*

aider *v.* to help

aimable *adj.* amiable, likeable, pleasant, kind

aimé *past part. of* **aimer**; **je l'ai beaucoup aimé** I liked it a lot

aimer *v.* to love; **aimer bien** to like

ainsi *adv.* thus, in this way

alimentaire *adj.* food; **un régime alimentaire** food regimen (diet)

allait, allaient *third pers., s. & pl., impf. ind. of* **aller**; *see §7.19*

allant *pr. part. of* **aller**

allé *past part. of* **aller**, to go; **je suis allé(e) à la plage** I went to the beach

Allemagne *n.f.* Germany

allemand *n.m.* German (language)

Allemand, Allemande *n.m., f.* German (person)

aller *v.* to go; *see §7.19, §12.2*; **s'en aller** to go away

aller mieux to feel better

allez-vous-en! *second pers., pl., imp. of* **s'en aller**; go away!

allons *first pers., pl., pr. ind. of* **aller**, **nous allons** we are going

allons! *first pers., pl., imp. of* **aller**; let's go!

alors *adv.* so

amèrement *adv.* bitterly

Américain, Américaine *n.m.,f.* American (person)

ami, amie *n.m., f.* friend

amour *n.m.* love

amusant, amusante *adj.* amusing

amuser *v.* to amuse; **s'amuser** to amuse oneself, to have fun

an *n.m.* year

ancien, ancienne *adj.* old, ancient

anglais *n.m.* English (language)

Anglais, Anglaise *n.m., f.* English (person)

Angleterre *n.f.* England

animal, animaux *n.m.s., pl.* animal, animals; *see §4.2*

année *n.f.* year

anniversaire *n.m.* anniversary; **mon anniversaire de naissance** my birthday

appartement *n.m.* apartment

appeler *v.* to call; **s'appeler** *rv.* to call oneself, to be named; *see Verb Tables*

apporter *v.* to bring

apportez-moi bring me

apprécié *adj.* appreciated

apprendre *v.* to learn; *see Verb Tables*

apprennent *third pers., pl., pr. ind. of* **apprendre**

appris *past part. of* **apprendre**

après *prep., adv.* after; **l'après-midi** *n.m. or f.* afternoon

arbre *n.m.* tree
argent *n.m.* money
arrêt *n.m.* halt, stop
arriver *v.* to arrive; *see §7.12*
art *n.m.* **l'art moderne** modern art
artiste *n.m.f.* artist
Asie *n.f.* Asia
aspirateur *n.m.* vacuum cleaner
asseoir *v.* to seat; **s'asseoir** *rv.* to sit;
 past part. **assis**; *see Verb Tables*
asseyez-vous! *second pers., pl., imp. of*
 s'asseoir, sit down!
assez *adv.* enough, rather; **assez**
 mouvementée somewhat choppy;
 assez grand big enough
assez (de) *adv.* enough (of); **assez bien**
 quite well, well enough
assieds-toi! *second pers., s., fam., imp.*
 of ***s'asseoir***, sit down!; see Verb Tables
assis *past part. of* ***asseoir***
assister à *v.* to attend, to be present at
au (à + le) at the, to the; *see §3.1, §12.2*
aucun, aucune *adj., m.f.* not any;
 see §11.
augmenter *v.* to increase, to augment
aujourd'hui *adv.* today
auprès (de) *adv.* close to, near to, by
auront *third pers., pl., fut. of* ***avoir***; *see*
 Verb Tables
aussi *adv.* also, too; **aussi...que** *conj.*
 as...as
Australie *n.f.* Australia
auteur *n.m.* author; **une femme auteur**
 woman author
authentique *adj.* authentic
autobus *n.m.* bus
automobiliste *n.m.f.* driver
autoroute *n.f.* highway
autre *adj.* other; *pron.* another
autrefois *adv.* formerly
aux (à + les) at the, to the; *see §3.1, §12.2*
avaient, avait *third pers., pl. & s., impf.*
 ind. of ***avoir***
avance *n.f.* advance; **à l'avance** in
 advance, beforehand
avancer *v.* to advance
avant *prep.* before
avec *prep.* with; **avec moi** with me
avez, avons *second pers., pl. & first pers.*
 pl., pr. ind. of ***avoir***
avion *n.m.* airplane; **en avion** by plane
avocat *n.m.,* **avocate** *n.f.* lawyer
avoir *v.* to have; *past part.* **eu**; see *§7.12,*
 §7.19, §12.2

B

bagages *n.m.pl.* baggage
bain *n.m.* bath
baisse *third pers., s., pr. ind. of* ***baisser***,
 to lower
balai *n.m.* broom
balle *n.f.* ball
bande *n.f.* strip
banlieue *n.f.* suburbs
banque *n.f.* bank; **emprunter de l'argent**
 aux banques to borrow money from
 banks
bas *n.m.* stocking; *adv.* low; **en bas**
 down, downstairs; *adj.* **bas, basse**
 low; *see §12.2*
bateau *n.m.* boat; **en bateau** by boat
battre *v.* to beat; **se battre** to fight; **ils se**
 battent they are hitting each other
beau *adj.m.* handsome, beautiful
beaucoup (de) *adv.* much, many
bel *adj.m.* handsome, beautiful; **un bel**
 arbre a beautiful tree; *see §5.1*
belle *adj.f.* beautiful; **une belle femme** a
 beautiful woman
bénir *v.* to bless
besoin *n.m.* need; **avoir besoin (de)** to
 have need (of), to need
bête *n.f.* beast, animal
bibliothèque *n.f.* library
bicyclette *n.f.* bicycle
bien *adv.* well; **bien entendu** of course;
 see §12.2
bien que *conj.* although
bientôt *adv.* soon
bijou, bijoux *n.m., s.pl.* jewel, jewels
billet *n.m.* ticket, note
blanc, blanche *adj.* white; **une maison**
 blanche a white house; *see §5.1*
blesser *v.* to injure, to wound
bloqué *adj.* blocked
boeuf *n.m.* beef
boire *v.* to drink; *past part.* **bu**; *see Verb*
 Tables
boisson *n.f.* drink
boivent *third pers., pl., pr. ind. of* ***boire***
bon, bonne *adj.* good; **un bon livre** a
 good book; **une bonne omelette** a
 good omelet
bonbons *n.m.* candies
bouche *n.f.* mouth (of a person); **la**
 gueule (mouth of an animal)
boucherie *n.f.* butcher shop; **les**
 boucheries chevalines horsemeat
 butcher shops
bras *n.m.* arm

brioche *n.f.* sweet roll
briser *v.* to break, to smash
bruyant *adj.* noisy
bu *past part. of* **boire**
but *n.m.* goal

C

ça *pron.* that; (shortening of *cela*); *see §6.1—8, §12.2*
cacher *v.* to hide
cadeau, cadeaux *n.m., s., pl.* gift, gifts; *see §4.2*
café *n.m.* coffee, coffee shop; **du café** some coffee; *see §3.3*
cahier *n.m.* notebook
campagne *n.f.* countryside; **à la campagne** in the countryside
Canada *n.m.* Canada
canadien *adj.* Canadian
canot *n.m.* boat; dinghy
capitale *n.f.* capital
car *conj.* for, because; *see §10.*
carotte *n.f.* carrot
carrefours *n.m., pl.* crossroads
casser *v.* to break; **il s'est cassé une dent** he broke a tooth
catholique *n.m., f.* Catholic
causer *v.* to cause; to chat
ce *dem. adj.* this; **ce stylo** this pen; **ce livre** this book; *see §5.4—2*
cela *pron.* that; **aimez-vous cela?** do you like that?; *see §12.2*
célèbre *adj.* famous
celle *pron., f.s.* the one; **celles** *pron., f.pl.* the ones; *see §6.1—8*
celui *pron., m.s.* the one; *see §6.1—8*
cent one hundred
cependant *adv.* however
ces *dem. adj.* these; *pl. of* **ce, cet, cette**; *see §5.4—2*
c'est combien?; it's how much?; *see §6.1—14, §12.2*
c'est un cadeau it's a gift
cet *adj.* this; **cet été** this summer; *see §5.4—2*
cette *dem. adj.* this; *see §5.4—2*
ceux *pron., m.pl.* the ones, those; *see §6.1—8*
chaleur *n.f.* heat
changement *n.m.* change
chanson *n.f.* song
chanté *past part. of* **chanter**, to sing; **j'ai chanté** I sang
chanteur, chanteuse *n.m.f.* singer
chapeau *n.m.* hat

chaque *adj.* each
charcuterie *n.f.* delicatessen
charme *n.m.* charm
chaud, chaude *adj.* warm, hot
chaussette *n.f.* sock
chaussure *n.f.* shoe
chef *n.m.* chief, boss, chef
chemin *n.m.* route
cher, chère, chers, chères *adj.* expensive; dear
cherchant *pr. part. of* **chercher**, **en cherchant** while (by) searching
chercher *v.* to look for, to search
cheval, chevaux *n.m., s.pl.* horse, horses; **chevalin** *adj.* equine; *see* **boucherie**
cheveux *n.m., pl.* hair (on head)
chez *prep.* at the place of, at the home of, at the shop of; **chez moi** at my place
chien *n.m.* dog
choisir *v.* to choose
chose *n.f.* thing; **quelque chose** something
ciel *n.m.* sky
cinéma *n.m.* cinema, movie theater; **au cinéma** to the movies
cinq five; **il est presque cinq heures et demie** it's almost five thirty
circulation *n.f.* traffic
circuler *v.* to move in traffic
classique *adj.* classic, classical
clé, clef *n.f.* key
client *n.m.* customer, client
coin *n.m.* corner
colère *n.f.* anger
Colombie Britannique *n.f.* British Columbia
combien (de) *adv.* how much (of), how many (of)
combiner *v.* to combine
comme *adv.* as, like
commencer *v.* to begin
comment *adv.* how
compagnie *n.f.* company; **la Compagnie de la Baie d'Hudson** Hudson Bay Company
comprendre *v.* to understand; *see §7.11 and Verb Tables*
compris *past part. of* **comprendre**
compter *v.* to count; + *inf.* to intend
conduire *v.* to drive
connaître *v.* to know, to be acquainted with; *see §7.11 and Verb Tables*
consacré *adj.* devoted

conserve *n.f.* preserve; **en conserve** in tin cans
considérablement *adv.* considerably
consommation *n.f.* consumption
construire *v.* to build, to construct
content, **contente** *adj.* content, happy, pleased
contient *v. form of* **contenir** to contain; *see* **tenir** *in Verb Conjugation Tables*
contre *prep.* against; **par contre** on the other hand
copain *n.m.*, **copine** *n.f.* pal, buddy
copieuse *adj.* copious, plentiful
correspond *third pers., s., pr. ind. of* **correspondre**, to correspond
cou *n.m.* neck; **j'ai mal au cou** I have a pain in the neck
couche *n.f.* layer
cour *n.f.* yard, courtyard
courageux *adj.* courageous
courent *third pers., pl., pr. ind. of* **courir**
courir *v.* to run; *past part.* **couru**; *see Verb Tables*
cours *n.m.* course
course *n.f.* running; **faire ses courses** to do one's shopping
court, **courte**, **courts**, **courtes** *adj.* short
cousin *n.m.* cousin
coûter *v.* to cost; **il ne coûte pas cher** it doesn't cost much
couverture *n.f.* blanket
cravate *n.f.* necktie
crayon *n.m.* pencil
croire *v.* to believe; *see Verb Tables*
croit *third pers., s., pr. ind. of* **croire**
cru *past part. of* **croire**
cruel, **cruelle** *adj.* cruel
curieusement *adv.* curiously

D

d'abord *adv.* first of all; *see* §12.2
d'autre part *conj.* moreover
dame *n.f.* lady
dangereusement *adv.* dangerously
dangereux, **dangereuse** *adj.* dangerous
dans *prep.* in; *see* §9.1
dansé *past part. of* **danser**, to dance; **j'ai dansé** I danced
de *prep.* of, from; **de plus en plus** more and more; **de moins en moins** less and less
dé *n.m.* thimble
débarquer *v.* to disembark (get off) from a boat
debout *adv.* standing

décider *v.* to decide
décomposer *v.* to decompose
découvrir *v.* to discover
décrire *v.* to describe
dedans *adv.* inside
degré *n.m.* degree
dehors *adv.* outside
déjà *adv.* already; **déjà vu** already seen
demander *v.* to ask (for), to request; **se demander** to ask oneself, to wonder
demeurer *v.* to remain
demi, **demie** *adj.* half
dent *n.f.* tooth
dentiste *n.m.f.* dentist
déplacer *v.* to shift
depuis *adv.* since; **depuis longtemps** since (for) a long time; *see* §12.1
dernier, **dernière** *adj.* last
des (de + les) of the, from the; some; *see* §3.1
dès *prep.* since, from; **dès aujourd'hui** from today
désastre *n.m.* disaster
désire *first & third pers, s., pr. ind. of* **désirer**, to desire
détresse *n.f.* distress
deux two; *see* §16.
devant *prep.* in front of
devenir *v.* to become; *see Verb Tables*
devenu *past part. of* **devenir**
deviennent *third pers., pl., pr. ind. of* **devenir**
devoir *v.* must, have to; *see* §7.11; *n.m.* duty; **les devoirs** homework; duties
dimanche *n.m.* Sunday
diminuer *v.* to diminish
diminution *n.f.* diminution, reduction
dîner *v.* to dine, to have dinner
dire *v.* to say, to tell; *past part.* **dit**; **vouloir dire** to mean; *see Verb Tables*
dis *first & second pers., s., pr. ind. of* **dire**
dix-huit eighteen
donc *conj.* therefore, consequently
donnait, **donnaient** *third pers., s. & pl., impf. ind. of* **donner**, to give
donnés *adj.* given
dont *pron.* whose; **la mère dont le bébé est malade** the mother whose baby is sick
dorment *third pers., pl., pr. ind. of* **dormir**, to sleep; *see Verb Tables*
douche *n.f.* shower (bath)
doute *n.m.* doubt
douter *v.* to doubt

droit *n.m.* right; straight; **les droits** the rights; **tout droit** straight ahead

drôle *adj.* funny, droll

du (de + le) of the, from the; some; *see §3.1, §12.2*

dû *past part. of* ***devoir***; **il a dû partir** he had to leave

dur, dure *adj.* hard, difficult

durant *prep.* during

E

eau *n.f.* water

échapper *v.* to escape

école *n.f.* school; **à l'école** in (at, to) school; **une école de filles** girls' school

écouter *v.* to listen (to)

écrire *v.* to write; *past part.* **écrit**; *see Verb Tables*

écrivons *first pers., pl., pr. ind. of* ***écrire***

effet *n.m.* effect; **en effet** in fact, as a matter of fact

égal, égaux, égale, égales *adj.* equal

église *n.f.* church

élevé *adj.* increased, raised

elle *pron.* she, her, it; **elles** they (persons or things); *see §6.1—1, §6.1—2*

embouteillage *n.m.* traffic jam

émission *n.f.* telecast

émotion *n.f.* emotion

emploi *n.m.* job, employment

employés *n.m.* employees

emprunter *v.* to borrow; **emprunter de l'argent aux banques** to borrow money from banks

en *pron.* of it, of them, some of it, some of them; *prep.* in; *see **en** in Index*

encore *adv.* still, yet, again

encourager *v.* to encourage

encre *n.f.* ink

enfant *n.m.f.* child

enlever *v.* to remove

enneigé *adj.* covered with snow

ennui *n.m.* worry, concern

enregistrer *v.* to record (on tape, record)

enseigne *n.f.* sign

enseigner *v.* to teach

entendre *v.* to hear; *see §7.11, §7.12 and Verb Tables*

entendu *past part. of* ***entendre***; **bien entendu** of course

enthousiasme *n.m.* enthusiasm

entre *prep.* between; *also v. form of* ***entrer***, to enter

envers *prep.* toward; *see §9.2*

environ *adv.* nearly, about

envoyer *v.* to send; **envoyer chercher** to send for; *see §7.12 and Verb Tables*

épaule *n.f.* shoulder

épicier *n.m.* grocer

épinards *n.m., pl.* spinach

épouse *n.f.* wife

époux *n.m.* husband

équipe *n.f.* team

Espagne *n.f.* Spain

espagnol *n.m.* Spanish (language)

Espagnol, Espagnole *n.m., f.* Spanish (person)

esprit *n.m.* mind; spirit; **un état d'esprit** a state of mind

est *third pers., s., pr. ind. of* ***être***; *see §7.19*

est-ce? is it?

est-ce que...? *see §21.*; **Est-ce que vous parlez français?** Do you speak French?

estimer *v.* to estimate

estomac *n.m.* stomach

et *conj.* and; *see §10.*

établir *v.* to establish

étaient, était *third pers., pl. & s., impf. ind. of* ***être***; *see §7.19*

état *n.m.* state, condition; **un état d'esprit** a state of mind

Etats-Unis *n.m.pl.* United States

été *n.m.* summer; *also past part. of* ***être***; **l'été prochain** next summer

étoile *n.f.* star

étonnant *adj.* astonishing

étranger *n.m. & adj.* foreigner, foreign; **à l'étranger** abroad

être *v.* to be; *past part.* **été**; *see §7.12, §7.19, §12.2, and Verb Tables*

étudiant, étudiante *n.m., f.* student

étudier *v.* to study

eu *past part. of* ***avoir***, *see §7.19*

eux *disjunctive pron.* them; *pl. of* ***lui***; **chez eux** to (at) their home; *see §6.1—7*

évidente *adj.* evident

éviter *v.* to avoid

exactement *adv.* exactly

examen *n.m.* examination

exemple *n.m.* example; **par exemple** for example

exister *v.* to exist

expliquent *third pers., pl., pr. ind. of* ***expliquer***, to explain

exportent *third pers., pl., pr. ind. of* ***exporter***, to export

extrême *adj.* extreme

F

fable *n.f.* fable
fabriquer *v.* to manufacture
faim *n.f.* hunger; **avoir faim** to be hungry
faire *v.* to do, to make; *past part.* **fait**; *see §7.14, §7.19, §12.2, and Verb Tables*
fais *first & second pers., s., pr. ind. of* **faire**
fait *third pers., s., pr. ind. & past part. of* **faire**; *see Verb Tables*
falloir *v.* to be necessary; *see §7.11 and Verb Tables*
fallu *past part. of* **falloir**
famille *n.f.* family
faudra *third pers., s., fut. of* **falloir**, **il faudra** it will be necessary
faut *third pers., s., pr. ind. of* **falloir**, **il faut** it is necessary
faut-il? is it necessary?
faux, fausse *adj.* false
favori, favorite *adj.* favorite
félicitations *n.f., pl.* congratulations
femme *n.f.* woman; **ma femme** my wife
fête *n.f.* feast, holiday, party
feu *n.m.* fire; **le feu rouge** red traffic light
feuille *n.f.* leaf
février *n.m.* February
fil *n.m.* thread
fille *n.f.* daughter; **la jeune fille** girl; **la petite fille** little girl
film *n.m.* film
fils *n.m.* son
fin *n.f.* end; **les fins de semaine** weekends
financer *v.* to finance
finir *v.* to finish, to end; *see Verb Tables*
fixer *v.* to fasten
fleur *n.f.* flower
fois *n.f.* time; **une fois** one time, once; **deux fois** twice
fonctionner *v.* to function
font *third pers., pl., pr. ind. of* **faire**; **elles font du mal à...** they do harm to...
forcés *adj.* forced
forêt *n.f.* forest
fourchette *n.f.* fork
fourrure *n.f.* fur
frais, fraîche *adj., m.f.* fresh
français *n.m.* French (language)
Français, Française *n.m., f.* French (person)
franchement *adv.* frankly
frère *n.m.* brother
frites *adj.* fried; **les pommes frites** French fries

froid *n.m.* cold
fromage *n.m.* cheese
fui *past part. of* **fuir**
fuir *v.* to flee, to run away

G

garçon *n.m.* boy
gâteau *n.m.* cake
genou *n.m.* knee
genre *n.m.* type
gens *n.m.pl.* people
gentil, gentille *adj.* nice, pleasant
glace *n.f.* ice; ice cream
glacée *adj.* iced, icy
gomme *n.f.* rubber eraser
Grand Nord *n.m.* Great North
grand, grande *adj.* great, big, large; **le grand magasin** department store
Grande Bretagne *n.f.* Great Britain
grands-parents *n.m.pl.* grandparents
gratuitement *adv.* free, at no charge
grave *adj.* serious, grave
gris, grise *adj.* gray
gros, grosse *adj.* big, fat, large
groupe *n.m.* group
gueule *n.f.* mouth (of an animal)
guider *v.* to guide

H

habitant *n.m.* inhabitant
habitude *n.f.* habit
haricots verts *n.m., pl.* green string beans
heure *n.f.* hour; **à quelle heure?** at what time? *see §14.*
heureusement *adv.* fortunately, happily; *see §8.1*
heureux, heureuse *adj.* happy
hier *adv.* yesterday
histoire *n.f.* story; history
hiver *n.m.* winter
homme *n.m.* man
honneur *n.m.* honor
huître *n.f.* oyster
humeur *n.f.* mood; **de mauvaise humeur** in a bad mood

I

ici *adv.* here
il *pron.* he, it; **ils** they (persons or things); *see §6.1—1*
il faut (que)... it is necessary (that)...; *see* **falloir** *in Verb Conjugation Tables*
il y a there is (are); ago; **il y a plusieurs mois** several months ago; *see §12.1*

île *n.f.* isle, island
imaginer *v.* to imagine
imiter *v.* to imitate
immeuble *n.m.* apartment building
incendie *n.m.* fire
inquiétude *n.f.* anxiety
interdire *v.* to prohibit
intéressant *adj.* interesting
intéresser *v.* to interest; **s'intéresser à** to
  be interested in
interrompre *v.* to interrupt; *past part.*
  interrompu
inventé *past part. of* **inventer**, to invent
italien *n.m.* Italian (language)
Italien, Italienne *n.m., f.* Italian (person)

J

j'ai une réservation I have a reservation
j'aimerais... I would like...
jambe *n.f.* leg
janvier *n.m.* January
jardin *n.m.* garden
je, j' *pron.* I; *see §6.1—1*
je ne veux pas payer beaucoup I don't
  want to pay much
jeter *v.* to throw; **se jeter** *rv.* to throw
  oneself
jeu, jeux *n.m., s.pl.* game, games
jeune *adj.* young; **la jeune fille** young
  girl; **les jeunes** young people
joli, jolie *adj.* pretty
joué *past part. of* **jouer**, to play; **j'ai joué
  à la balle** I played ball
jouet *n.m.* toy
jour *n.m.* day; **par jour** a day, per day;
  toute la journée all day long
journal, journaux *n.m., s.pl.* newspaper,
  newspapers; *see §4.2*
joyeux, joyeuse *adj.* joyous, merry; *see
  §5.1*
juillet *n.m.* July; *see §13.3*
juin *n.m.* June; *see §13.3*
jus *n.m.* juice; **du jus d'orange** some
  orange juice; *see §3.3*

K

kilo *n.m.* kilo; (1 kilogram = 2.2 pounds)
kilomètre *n.m.* kilometer; (1.61 kilometers
  = 1 mile)

L

la *def.art., f.s.* the; *also dir.obj.pron.* her,
  it; *see §3.1, §6.1—2*
là *adv.* there
lac *n.m.* lake

laid, laide *adj.* ugly
laideur *n.f.* ugliness
laissées *adj.* left
laisser *v.* to leave; *see §7.11*
lait *n.m.* milk; **du lait** some milk; *see §3.3*
lampe *n.f.* lamp
large *adj.* wide
lave-linge *n.m.* clothes washing machine
lave-vaisselle *n.m.* dishwashing machine
laver *v.* to wash (something or someone);
  se laver *rv.* to wash oneself
lavez *second pers., pl., pr. ind. of* **laver**
lavons *first pers., s., pr. ind. of* **laver**
le *def.art., m.s.* the; *also dir.obj.pron.* him,
  it; *see §3.1, §6.1—2*
légèrement *adv.* lightly
légume *n.m.* vegetable
lent, lente *adj.* slow; *see §8.1*
lentement *adv.* slowly; *see §8.1*
lequel, laquelle, lesquels, lesquelles
  pron. which; *see §6.1—10, §6.1—13*
les *def.art., m.f., pl.* the; *also dir.obj.pron.*
  them; *see §3.1, §6.1—2*
leur, leurs *poss.adj.* their; *also indir.obj.
  pron.* to them; *see §5.4—4, §6.1—3*
liberté *n.f.* liberty
librairie *n.f.* bookstore; *see §20.*
libre *adj.* free
lieu *n.m.* **en premier lieu** in the first
  place; **au lieu de** instead of
limiter *v.* to limit
lire *v.* to read; *past part.* **lu**; *see Verb
  Tables*
lisse *adj.* smooth
lit *n.m.* bed; *also pr.ind., third pers., s. of*
  lire
livre *n.m.* book; **la livre** pound; *see §4.1*
Londres *n.* London
long, longue *adj.* long
longtemps *adv.* long time; **depuis
  longtemps** since (for) a long time
lorsque *conj.* when; *synonym of* **quand**
lu *past part. of* **lire**
lui *indir.obj.pron., third pers., s.* to him, to
  her, to it; *see §6.1—3*
lundi *n.m.* Monday; *see §13.2*

M

M. *abbrev. for* **Monsieur** Mr.
ma *poss.adj.f.s.* my; **ma mère** my mother;
  see §5.4—4
magasin *n.m.* store; **le grand magasin**
  department store
magazine *n.m.* magazine
main *n.f.* hand; **à la main** in one's hand

maintenant *adv.* now
mais *conj.* but
maïs *n.m.* corn
maison *n.f.* house
mal *adv.* badly; *n.m.* harm; evil; **j'ai mal à la tête** I have a headache
malade *adj.* sick
maladie *n.f.* sickness
malfaisant *adj.* harmful
malgré *prep.* in spite of
malheur *n.m.* unhappiness
malheureusement *adv.* unfortunately
malheureux, malheureuse *adj.* unhappy
mangé *past part. of **manger**,* to eat
mangent *third pers., pl., pr. ind. of **manger**,* to eat
mangeur *n.m.* eater; **grand mangeur** big eater
manque *n.m.* lack
marchand *n.m.* merchant
marchandise *n.f.* merchandise
marché *n.m.* market; **à bon marché** inexpensive, at a good price
marcher *v.* to walk, to march, to run (a machine)
mardi *n.m.* Tuesday; *see §13.2*
mari *n.m.* husband
mars *n.m.* March; *see §13.3*
matin *n.m.* morning; **le matin** in the morning
médecin *n.m.* doctor, physician
médecine *n.f.* medicine (profession)
médicament *n.m.* medicine (that you take)
meilleur, meilleure *adj.* better; **le (la) meilleur (meilleure)** the best; *see §5.4—6*
même *adj.* same
mener *v.* to lead; **l'émotion nous mène à...** emotion leads us to...
mer *n.f.* sea
mère *n.f.* mother
mes *poss.adj.m.f., pl.* my; **mes parents** my parents; *see §5.4—4*
mesure *n.f.* measure
métro *n.m.* subway
mettre *v.* to put, to place; to put on (clothing); *see §7.12 and Verb Tables*
mieux *adv.* better; *see §12.2*
mille thousand
mis *past part. of **mettre**; see **mettre** in Verb Tables*
modéré *adj.* moderate
moi *pron.* me; **avec moi** with me; *see §6.1—7*

moins *adv.* less; **de moins en moins** less and less
mois *n.m.* month
moment *n.m.* moment; **à ce moment-là** at that time
mon *poss.adj.m.s.* my; **mon père** my father; *see §5.4—4*
mon nom est... my name is...
monde *n.m.* world; **tout le monde** everybody
monnaie *n.f.* change (money); **une pièce de monnaie** coin
monsieur *n.m.* gentleman, sir, mister
montagne *n.f.* mountain
montrer *v.* to show
mort, morte *adj., m.f.* dead
morue *n.f.* cod
mourir *v.* to die; *past part.* **mort**; *see **mourir** in Verb Tables*
moyen *n.m.* means, way
musique *n.f.* music
mystérieuse *adj.* mysterious

N

n'importe quel âge any age
nagé *past part. of **nager**,* to swim; **j'ai nagé** I swam
naître *v.* to be born; *see Verb Tables*
natation *n.f.* swimming
né *past part. of **naître***
nécessaire *adj.* necessary
neige *third pers., s., pr. ind. of **neiger**; **il neige** it's snowing; **la neige** snow
nettoyer *v.* to clean
Noël *n.m.* Christmas; **le Père Noël** Santa Claus; **Joyeux Noël** Merry Christmas
noir, noire *adj.* black
nom *n.m.* name
nombre *n.m.* number
nombreux, nombreuse *adj.* numerous
non *adv.* no; *see §12.2*
Nord *n.m.* North
nos *poss.adj.m.f.pl.* our; **nos amis (amies)** our friends; *see §5.4—4*
notre *poss.adj.m.f.s.* our; **notre ami** our friend; *see §5.4—4*
nourriture *n.f.* food
nous *pron.* we, us; *see §6.1*
nouveau, nouvel, nouveaux, nouvelle *adj.* new; **de nouveau** again; **les nouvelles** news

O

objectif *n.m.* objective
objet *n.m.* object

oeil *n.m.* eye; **les yeux** eyes; *see §4.2*
oeuf *n.m.* egg
offrir *v.* to offer
oiseau *n.m.* bird
omelette *n.f.* omelet; **une omelette au fromage** cheese omelet
on *pron.* one; **on ne sait jamais** one never knows; *see §6.1—1, §6.1—9*
ont *third pers., pl., pr. ind. of* ***avoir***; *see §7.19*
ont été *pc. of* ***être***; have been; *see §7.19*
onze eleven; *see §16.*
ordre *n.m.* order
oreille *n.f.* ear
oser *v.* to dare
ou *conj.* or; **où** *adv.* where
ouvrir *v.* to open; *past part.* **ouvert**; *see* ***ouvrir*** *in Verb Tables*

P

pain *n.m.* bread
panier *n.m.* basket
papeterie *n.f.* stationery shop
papier *n.m.* paper; **les sacs en papier** paper bags
par *prep.* by; **par contre** on the other hand; **par terre** on the floor, on the ground
paralyser *v.* to paralyse
parapluie *n.m.* umbrella
parc *n.m.* park
parcouraient *third pers., pl., impf. ind. of* ***parcourir*** to travel through
parents *n.m.pl.* parents
paresse *n.f.* laziness
paresseux, paresseuse *adj.* lazy
parfois *adv.* at times
parler *v.* to speak, to talk; *see Verb Tables*; **en parlant** by (while) talking
parmi *prep.* among
particulièrement *adv.* particularly
particulières *adj.* particular
partir *v.* to leave; *past part.* **parti**; *see* ***partir*** *in §7.11 and in Verb Tables*
passer *v.* to spend (time); to go by, to pass by, to pass
passionnés *adj.* intrigued, fascinated
patinage *n.m.* skating
patiner *v.* to skate
patinoire *n.f.* skating rink
payer *v.* to pay
pays *n.m.* country
paysage *n.m.* landscape
peau *n.f.* skin
peindre *v.* to paint

pendant *prep.* during; *see §9.3*; **pendant que** *conj.* while; *see §10*
penser *v.* to think; with **à** or **de** to think of; *see §7.5*
perdre *v.* to lose; *past part.* **perdu**
père *n.m.* father
Père Noël *n.m.* Santa Claus
perle *n.f.* pearl
permet *third pers., s., pr. ind. of* ***permettre***, to permit
permis *past part. of* ***permettre***
personne *n.f.* person; with **ne**, nobody; *see §7.18*
perspicacité *n.f.* perspicacity, insight
perte *n.f.* loss
petit, petite *adj.* small
peu (de) *adv.* little (of)
peur *n.f.* fear; **avoir peur** to be afraid
peut *third pers., s., pr. ind. of* ***pouvoir***
peut-être *adv.* perhaps
pied *n.m.* foot; **à pied** on foot; **aller à pied** to walk, to go on foot
piétons *n.m.pl.* pedestrians
piscine *n.f.* swimming pool
pittoresque *adj.* picturesque, colorful
plage *n.f.* beach, seashore
plaisir *n.m.* pleasure
plan *n.m.* map; **un plan du métro** subway map
plante *n.f.* plant
plastique *n.m.* plastic
plat *n.m.* plate, dish
pleut *third pers., s., pr. ind. of* ***pleuvoir***, **il pleut** it's raining
pleuvoir *v.* to rain; *past part.* **plu**; *see* ***pleuvoir*** *in Verb Tables*
pluie *n.f.* rain
plupart *n.f.* most; **la plupart du temps** most of the time
plus *adv.* more; **plus de (que)** more than; **le plus** the most; *see §11., §12.2*
plusieurs *adj. & pron.* several
pluvieux *adj.* rainy; **en temps pluvieux** in rainy weather
poche *n.f.* pocket
pois *n.m.* pea; **les petits pois** small sweet peas
poison *n.m.* poison
poisson *n.m.* fish
policiers *adj.* detective
pomme *n.f.* apple; **la pomme de terre** potato; **les pommes frites** French fries
populaire *adj.* popular
porc *n.m.* pork
port *n.m.* port

possède *third pers., s., pr. ind. of*
  posséder, to possess, to own
poule *n.f.* hen
poulet *n.m.* chicken
poupée *n.f.* doll
pour *prep.* for; in order + *inf.*; **pour cent**
  percent
pourquoi *adv.* why
pourrait *third pers., s., cond. of* ***pouvoir***
pourtant *adv.* however
pousser *v.* to push; to bud
pouvoir *v.* to be able, can; *past part.* **pu**;
  see §7.11 and ***pouvoir*** *in Verb Tables*
pratique *adj.* practical
pratiquer *v.* to practice
précis, **précise** *adj.* precise
préfère *first & third pers., s., pr. ind. of*
  préférer, to prefer
premier, **première** *adj. & n.m., f.* first
prendre *v.* to take; *past part.* **pris**; *see*
  prendre *in Verb Tables*
préparatifs *n.m., pl.* preparations
préparé *past part. of* ***préparer***,
  to prepare
près *adv.* near; **à peu près** nearly,
  almost; **de près** closely
presque *adv.* almost, nearly
presse *n.f.* press (printing)
prévoir *v.* to foresee; to make provision for
prévu *past part. of* ***prévoir***
pris *past part. of* ***prendre***; *see*
  Verb Tables
prise *adj.* taken
prix *n.m.* price
probablement *adv.* probably
produire *v.* to produce
programme *n.m.* program
progrès *n.m.* progress
projet *n.m.* project
promenade *n.f.* walk; **faire une**
  promenade to take a walk; *see* ***faire*** *in*
  §7.19
provoquer *v.* to provoke
psychologique *adj.* psychological
pu *past part. of* ***pouvoir***
public, **publique** *adj., m.f.* public
publié *past part. of* ***publier*** to publish
puis *adv.* then; *also v. form of* ***pouvoir***; **je**
  puis or **je peux** I can
puisque *conj.* since

Q

quand *conj.* when; *synonym of* ***lorsque***
quantité *n.f.* quantity
quarante forty

quatorze fourteen
que *pron., conj.* what, that; than; *see*
  §6.1—13
Québécois *n.m.* Quebecer (person from
  Québéc)
quel, **quelle**, **quels**, **quelles** *adj.* what,
  which; *see §12.2*
quel temps fait-il? what's the weather
  like? *see §15.*
quelque *adj.* some, a few; **quelque**
  chose something; *see §12.2*
quelquefois *adv.* sometimes
qu'est-ce que...? what...? (as dir. obj.);
  see §6.1—10
qu'est-ce que c'est que cela? what's
  that?
qu'est-ce qui...? what...? (as subject);
  see §6.1—10
qui *pron.* who, whom, which;
  see §6.1—10
qui est-ce qui *subject pron.* who; *see*
  §6.1—10
quitter *v.* to leave (a person or place);
  see §7.11
quoi *pron.* what (as obj. of a prep.); **avec**
  quoi with what; *see §6.1—10, §12.2*
quoique *conj.* although

R

raison *n.f.* reason; **avoir raison** to be
  right; *see* ***avoir*** *in §12.2*
rang *n.m.* rank, row
rapidement *adv.* rapidly
rapides *n.m.* rapids
raquette *n.f.* racket; snowshoe
rassurer *v.* to reassure
ravitaillement *n.m.* supplies
réalité *n.f.* reality
récentes *adj.f.* recent
recevoir *v.* to receive; *see Verb Tables*
recherché *adj.* sought after
recouvertes *adj.* covered
reçu *past part. of* ***recevoir***
refaire *v.* to redo, to remake
regarde *third pers., s., pr. ind. of*
  regarder
regarder *v.* to watch, to look at; **j'ai**
  regardé la télé I watched TV
régime *n.m.* regimen (diet)
région *n.f.* region
religieuse *n.f.* nun
remarquer *v.* to remark, to notice
remplacer *v.* to replace
rencontrer *v.* to meet; **en rencontrant**
  des artistes by meeting artists

rendre *v.* to render; **cela peut nous rendre indifférents** that can make us indifferent
renseignements *n.m.pl.* information
réparation *n.f.* repair
repas *n.m.* meal
répondre *v.* to answer, to reply, to respond
réponse *n.f.* answer
reposer (se) *rv.* to rest; **il faut que je me repose** I must rest
réservé *adj.* reserved
ressembler *v.* to resemble, to look like
restaurant *n.m.* restaurant
reste *n.m.* rest, remainder
rester *v.* to stay, to remain
résultat *n.m.* result
retard *n.m.* delay
retour *n.m.* return; **de retour chez eux** upon returning to their home
révélé *past part.* revealed
rêver *v.* to dream
ri *past part. of* **rire**; *see Verb Tables*
rien *adv.* nothing; *see §12.2*
rire *v.* to laugh; *past part.* **ri**; *see* **rire** *in Verb Tables*
risquent-elles? do they risk?
rivière *n.f.* river
robe *n.f.* dress
robinet *n.m.* faucet
rond, ronde *adj.* round
rose *n.f.* rose; *adj.* pink
rouler *v.* to roll along; **une voiture qui roule** a car in motion
route *n.f.* road
rue *n.f.* street

S

sa *poss.adj.f.s.* his, her, its; **sa soeur** his (her) sister; *see §5.4—4*
sac *n.m.* bag; **les sacs en papier** paper bags
saison *n.f.* season
sait *third pers, s., pr. ind. of* **savoir**; *see Verb Tables*
salade *n.f.* salad; **une salade de tomates** tomato salad
samedi *n.m.* Saturday
sans *prep.* without; **sans avoir** without having
saumon *n.m.* salmon
sauvage *adj.* savage, wild
sauver *v.* to save; **se sauver** to run away
savoir *v.* to know (how); *see §7.11 and Verb Tables*

scolaire *adj.* scholastic; **l'année scolaire** academic (school) year
se *reflex. pron.* himself, herself, oneself, itself; *see §6.1—12*
sec, sèche *adj.* dry
secourir *v.* to help
seize sixteen
semaine *n.f.* week; **la fin de semaine** weekend; **par semaine** a week, per week
sembler *v.* to seem; **ils semblent** they seem
sentir *v.* to feel, to smell; *see Verb Tables*
septembre *n.m.* September
sera *third pers., s., fut. of* **être**; *see §7.19*
sérieux *adj.* serious
servir *v.* to serve; *see Verb Tables*
ses *poss. adj.* his, her, its; *pl. of* **son, sa**; *see §5.4—4*
seul, seule, seuls, seules *adj.* only
seulement *adv.* only
si *conj.* if
s'il vous plaît please
sinon *conj.* if not, otherwise
ski *n.m.* ski, skiing; **le ski de fond** cross-country skiing
soeur *n.f.* sister
soient *third pers., pl., pr. sbj. of* **être**; *see §7.19*
soin *n.m.* care
soir *n.m.* evening; **le soir** in the evening
soixante sixty; *see §16.*
sol *n.m.* soil
sole *n.f.* filet of sole
soleil *n.m.* sun; **il fait du soleil** it's sunny
solides *adj.* solid
son *poss.adj.m.s.* his, her, its; *see §5.4—4; also n.m.* sound
sont *third pers., pl., pr. ind. of* **être**; *see §7.19*
sorte *n.f.* sort
sortir *v.* to go out; *see §7.11 and Verb Tables*
SOS S.O.S.
souffrent *third pers., pl., pr. ind. of* **souffrir**
souffrir *v.* to suffer
soupe *n.f.* soup
sous *prep.* under
souvent *adv.* often
spécialiser *v.* to specialize
spectacle *n.m.* show, performance
stationnement *n.m.* parking
statistiques *n.f.pl.* statistics
stylo *n.m.* pen

succès *n.m.* success
sucette *n.f.* lollipop; **sucer** to suck
suis *first pers., s., pr. ind. of* ***être****; see §7.19*
suivra *third pers., s., fut. of* ***suivre***
suivre *v.* to follow; *see Verb Tables*
sur *prep.* on
sûr *adj.* sure
surtout *adv.* especially
système *n.m.* system

T

ta *poss.adj.f.s., fam.* your; **ta mère** your mother; *see §5.4—4*
tant *adv.* so much; *see §12.2*
tasse *n.f.* cup
tel, telle *adj.* such; **une telle quantité** such a quantity
téléspectateurs *n.m.pl.* TV viewers
télévisés *adj.* televised
télévision *n.f.* television
tellement *adv.* so
tempête *n.f.* tempest, storm
temps *n.m.* time; **beaucoup de temps** much time; weather; *see §15.*
tendues *adj.* stretched
tenir *v.* to hold; *past part.* **tenu**; *see* ***tenir*** *in Verb Tables*
terminer *v.* to end
terrasse *n.f.* terrace
terre *n.f.* earth; **la pomme de terre** potato
tes *poss.adj.m.f., pl.fam.* your; **tes parents** your parents; *see §5.4—4*
tête *n.f.* head; **j'ai mal à la tête** I have a headache; *see* ***avoir*** *in §12.2*
thé *n.m.* tea
thème *n.m.* theme
tirés *adj.* pulled, drawn
tomber *v.* to fall; **il est tombé** he fell
touriste *n.m.f.* tourist
tous *pl. of* ***tout*** all; *see §12.2*
tout *adj., m.s.* all; **tout le monde** everybody; **tout droit** straight ahead; *see §12.2*
toute *adj., f.s.* all; **toutes les semaines** every week; *see §12.2*
traîneaux *n.m., pl.* sleighs
tranche *n.f.* slice
transformer *v.* to transform
transmettront *third pers., pl., fut. of* ***transmettre****,* to transmit
transport *n.m.* transportation
transporter *v.* to transport
travail, travaux *n.m., s.pl.* work, works
travailler *v.* to work

traversée *n.f.* crossing; **une traversée mouvementée** a choppy crossing
très *adv.* very
trois three
trop (de) *adv.* too much (of), too many (of); **trop cher** too expensive
trouver *v.* to find; **se trouver** *rv.* to be located
trouveront *third pers., pl., fut. of* ***trouver***
truite *n.f.* trout
tu *pron. second pers., s.* you *(fam.)*; *see §6.1—1*
tuer *v.* to kill
typique *adj.* typical

U

un *indef. art., m.s.;* **une** *f.s.* a, an (one); *see §3.2*
universitaire *adj.* university; **du système universitaire** of the university system
université *n.f.* university

V

va *third pers., s., pr. ind. of* ***aller****; see §7.19*
vacances *n.f.pl.* vacation; **les grandes vacances** summer vacation
vache *n.f.* cow
vais *first pers., s., pr. ind. of* ***aller****; see §7.19*
valeur *n.f.* value
variété *n.f.* variety
vase *n.m.* vase
vécu *past part. of* ***vivre****; see Verb Tables*
véhicule *n.m.* vehicle
vélo *n.m.* bike
venant *pres. part. of* ***venir***
vend-on? is sold?
vendre *v.* to sell; *see Verb Tables; past part.* **vendu**; **se vend** is sold
venir *v.* to come; *past part.* **venu**; *see §7.12 and Verb Tables*
vent *n.m.* wind; **il fait du vent** it's windy
vers *prep.* around, about, toward; **vers onze heures** about eleven o'clock; *see §9.2*
vêtements *n.m., pl.* clothing
veulent *third pers., pl., pr. ind. of* ***vouloir***
veux *first pers., s., pr. ind. of* ***vouloir****,* **je ne veux pas** I don't want
veux-tu? do you want?
viande *n.f.* meat
vie *n.f.* life
vieil, vieille, vieux *adj.* old

vient, **viennent** *third pers., s. & pl., pr. ind. of* **venir**
vieux, **vieil**, **vieille** *adj.* old
ville *n.f.* city
vin *n.m.* wine
vingt twenty; *see §16.*
vingt-cinq twenty-five
vingt-quatre twenty-four
violente *adj.* violent
vite *adv.* quickly, fast; **plus vite** more quickly, faster
vivre *v.* to live; *see Verb Tables*
voici here is, here are; **voici mon passeport** here is my passport; *see §12.1*
voilier *n.m.* sailboat
voir *v.* to see; *past part.* **vu**; *see Verb Tables*
voit *third pers., s., pr. ind. of* **voir**
voiture *n.f.* car, automobile; **en voiture** by car
voler *v.* to steal; **a été volée** was stolen; to fly
voleur *n.m.* thief
vont *third pers., pl., pr. ind. of* **aller**; *see §7.19*
vos *poss.adj.m.f.pl.* your; **vos amis (amies)** your friends; *see §5.4—4*
votre *poss.adj.m.f.s.* your; **votre ami (amie)** your friend; *see §5.4—4*
vouloir *v.* to want; *see §7.11 and Verb Tables*
voulu *past part. of* **vouloir**
vous *pron., s. & pl.* you; *see §6.1*
voyage *n.m.* trip; **faire un voyage** to take a trip; **bon voyage!** have a good trip!
voyageur *n.m.* voyager, traveler
voyez *second pers., pl., pr. ind. of* **voir**
vrai *adj.* real, true
vraiment *adv.* really
vu *past part. of* **voir**; **j'ai vu un bon film français** I saw a good French film

Y

y *adverbial pron.* there, in it, on it; **il y a** there is, there are; *see §12.2*
yeux *n.m.pl.* eyes; **l'oeil** *n.m.* eye; *see §4.2*

Z

zèbre *n.m.* zebra
zéro *n.m.* zero

English-French Vocabulary

Regarding verb forms, remember to consult the French Verb Conjugation Tables beginning on page 214 and the Irregular Verb Tables beginning on page 241 as well as §7. in this book. A list of abbreviations is also provided on page xiii.

References to **§** numbers in this vocabulary list will help you master points in French grammar and vocabulary if you refer to them for study.

If you do not find the desired English-French word in the following vocabulary list, consult a standard English-French dictionary.

A

a, an *indef. art.* **un**, **une**; *see §3.2*
accept *v.* **accepter**; *see Verb Tables*
after *prep.* **après**; afternoon **l'après-midi** *n.m. or f.*
again *adv.* **encore, de nouveau**
age *n.* **l'âge** *n.m.*
agreeable *adj.* **agréable**
airport *n.* **un aéroport**
already *adv.* **déjà**; already seen **déjà vu**; *see §8.*
also *adv.* **aussi**
although *conj.* **quoique**
always *adv.* **toujours**
American (person) **un Américain, une Américaine**
amiable *adj.* **aimable**
amuse oneself *v.* **s'amuser**
amusing *adj.* **amusant, amusante**
ancient *adj.* **ancien, ancienne**
animal, animals *n.* **un animal, des animaux**; *see §4.2*
another *pron.* **un autre, une autre**
apartment *n.* **un appartement**
apartment building *n.* **un immeuble**
arrive *v.* **arriver**
art *n.* **l'art** *n.m.*; modern art **l'art moderne**
artist *n.* **un artiste, une artiste**
as ... as *conj.* **aussi...que**; as tall as **aussi grand que**
at *prep.* **à**; *see §3.1; see à in idioms, §12.2*
at the, to the **à la, à l', au, aux**; *see §3.1*
at the place (home, shop) of **chez**; at my place **chez moi**; at our place **chez nous**

Australia *n.* **l'Australie** *nf.*
author *n.* **un auteur**; woman author **une femme auteur**

B

ball *n.* **la balle**
bath *n.* **le bain**
be *v.* **être**; *see §7.19 and Verb Tables*
beast *n.* **la bête**
beautiful *adj.* **beau, bel, belle, beaux, belles**; *see §5.1*
bed *n.* **le lit**
been *past part.* **été**; *see être in §7.19*
believe *v.* **croire**
better *adj.* **meilleur, meilleure**; *adv.* **mieux**; *see §5.4—6*
between *prep.* **entre**
big *adj.* **grand, grande**; **gros, grosse**
bird *n.* **un oiseau**
birthday *n.* **l'anniversaire** *n.m.* **de naissance** *n.f.*
bitterly *adv.* **amèrement**
black *adj.* **noir, noire**
blanket *n.* **la couverture**
book *n.* **le livre**
born, to be *v.* **naître**; *past part.* born **né**
boss *n.* **le chef**
boy *n.* **le garçon**
bring *v.* **apporter**; bring me a cup of coffee **apportez-moi un café**
broom *n.* **le balai**
brother *n.* **le frère**
buddy *n.* **le copain**
but *conj.* **mais**
buy *v.* **acheter**; *see Verb Tables*

C

cake *n.* **le gâteau**
call *v.* **appeler**; to be named **s'appeler**;
    my name is... **je m'appelle...**
can, to be able *v.* **pouvoir**; I can
    je peux
Canada *n.* **le Canada**
Canadian *adj.* **canadien, canadienne**
candies *n.* **les bonbons**
Catholic *adj.* **catholique**
change (money) *n.* **la monnaie**
cheese *n.* **le fromage**
chief *n.* **le chef**
child *n.* **un enfant, une enfant**
choose *v.* **choisir**
church *n.* **une église**
coffee, coffee shop *n.* **le café**
coin *n.* **une pièce de monnaie**
consequently *conj.* **donc**
corn *n.* **le maïs**
corner *n.* **le coin**
country *n.* **le pays**
countryside *n.* **la campagne**
cousin *n.* **le cousin, la cousine**

D

dare *v.* **oser**
daughter *n.* **la fille**
day *n.* **le jour**; **la journée**
department store *n.* **le grand magasin**
die *v.* **mourir**
do *v.* **faire**; *see §7.19*
doctor *n.* **le médecin**
door *n.* **la porte**
doubt *v.* **douter**; *n.* **le doute**
down, downstairs *adv.* **en bas**; *see **bas**
    and **en** in idioms, §12.2*
drink *v.* **boire**; *n.* **la boisson**
droll *adj.* **drôle**
duty *n.* **le devoir**

E

each *adj.* **chaque**
eat *v.* **manger**
egg *n.* **un oeuf**
end *v.* **finir**
England n. **l'Angleterre** *n.f.*
English (language) *n.* **l'anglais** *n.m.*
English (person) *n.* **un Anglais, une
    Anglaise**
enough (of) *adv.* **assez (de)**; quite well,
    well enough **assez bien**
enter *v.* **entrer**
equal *adj.* **égal, égaux, égale, égales**
eraser (rubber) *n.* **la gomme**

especially *adv.* **surtout**
eye *n.* **l'oeil**; eyes **les yeux**

F

fable *n.* **la fable**
false *adj.* **faux, fausse**
fat *adj.* **gros, grosse**
feast *n.* **la fête**
February *n.* **le février**; *see §13*
feel better *v.* **aller mieux**; *see **aller** in
    idioms, §12.2*
finish *v.* **finir**; *see Verb Tables*
fire *n.* **le feu**
fish *n.* **le poisson**
flee *v.* **fuir**
foot *n.* **le pied**
fork *n.* **la fourchette**
formerly *adv.* **autrefois**
fortunately *adv.* **heureusement**
frankly *adv.* **franchement**
French (language) *n.* **le français**
French (person) *n.* **un Français, une
    Française**
friend *n.* **un ami, une amie**
frightfully *adv.* **affreusement**
from *prep.* **de**; from the **des, du, de la,
    de l'**; *see §3.1*
funny *adj.* **amusant, amusante, drôle**

G

gentleman *n.* **le monsieur**
German (language) *n.* **l'allemand** *n.m.*
German (person) *n.* **un Allemand, une
    Allemande**
Germany *n.* **l'Allemagne** *n.f.*
gift *n.* **le cadeau, les cadeaux**; *see §4.2*
girl *n.f.* **la jeune fille**; little girl **la petite
    fille**
give *v.* **donner**
give back *v.* **rendre**
go *v.* **aller**; *see §7.19*; *see **aller** in idioms,
    §12.2*; to go away **s'en aller**
go away! *v.* **allez-vous-en!**
goal *n.* **le but**
good *adj.* **bon, bonne**; a good film **un
    bon film**; a good omelet **une bonne
    omelette**
gray *adj.* **gris, grise**
great *adj.* **grand, grande**
Great Britain *n.* **la Grande Bretagne**

H

had *past part.* **eu**; *see §7.19*
hair (on head) *n.* **les cheveux** *n.m., pl.*
hand *n.* **la main**

handsome *adj.* **beau, bel, belle, beaux,
    belles**; *see §5.1*
happily *adv.* **heureusement**
happy *adj.* **heureux, heureuse**
hat *n.* **le chapeau**
have *v.* **avoir**; *see §7.19; see* ***avoir*** *in
    idioms, §12.2*
have fun *v.* **s'amuser**
head *n.* **la tête**
hear *v.* **entendre**
help *v.* **aider**
here *adv.* **ici**; here is..., here are... **voici**;
    see §12.1
his, her *poss.adj.* **sa, son, ses**; *see
    §5.4—4*
holiday *n.* **le jour de fête**
homework *n.* **les devoirs** *n.m., pl.*
honor *n.* **l'honneur** *n.m.*
horse *n.* **le cheval, les chevaux**;
    see §4.2
hot *adj.* **chaud, chaude**
house *n.* **la maison**
how much (of), how many (of) *adv.*
    combien (de)
however *adv.* **pourtant**
hunger *n.* **la faim**; to be hungry **avoir
    faim**; *see* ***avoir*** *in §12.2*
husband *n.* **le mari, l'époux**

I

I *pron.* **je**; *see §6.1—1*
I am **je suis**; to be **être**; *see §7.19*
I am doing **je fais**; to do **faire**; *see* ***faire*** *in
    §7.19*
I am making **je fais**; to make **faire**; *see*
    faire *in §7.19*
I am saying **je dis**; to say, to tell **dire**
if not *conj.* **sinon**
in *prep.* **dans, en**
injure *v.* **blesser**
ink *n.* **l'encre** *n.f.*
inside *adv.* **dedans**
invitation *n.* **une invitation**
island *n.* **une île**
it's sunny **il fait du soleil**
Italian (language) *n.* **l'italien** *n.m.*
Italian (person) *n.* **un Italien, une
    Italienne**

J

January *n.* **le janvier**; *see §13.*

K

key *n.* **la clé, la clef**
kilo *n.* **le kilo** (1 kilogram = 2.2 pounds)

kilometer *n.* **le kilomètre** (1.61 kilometers
    = 1 mile)
(he) knows **il sait**; to know (how) **savoir**

L

lady *n.* **la dame**
large *adj.* **grand, grande; gros, grosse**;
    see §5.1
last *adj.* **dernier, dernière**
lawyer *n.* **un avocat, une avocate**
learn *v.* **apprendre**
leg *n.* **la jambe**
let's go! *v.* **allons!**; *see* ***aller*** *in §7.19*
library *n.* **la bibliothèque**
like *v.* **aimer bien**
likeable *adj.* **aimable**
listen (to) *v.* **écouter**
London *n.* **Londres**
look (at) *v.* **regarder**
look for *v.* **chercher**
love *n.* **l'amour** *n.m.*; to love **aimer**
low *adj.* **bas, basse**
lower *v.* **baisser**

M

make *v.* **faire**; *see §7.19*
man *n.* **un homme**
March *n.* **le mars**; *see §13.*
march *v.* **marcher**
me *pron.* **me, moi**; *see §6.1—2, §6.1—3,
    §6.1—7*
mean *v.* **vouloir dire**; what do you mean?
    que voulez-vous dire?
medicine (profession) *n.* **la médecine**;
    (that you take) **le médicament**
mister *n.* **le monsieur**
modern *adj.* **moderne**
Monday *n.* **le lundi**; *see §13.*
money *n.* **l'argent** *n.m.*
month *n.* **le mois**
more *adv.* **plus**
morning *n.* **le matin**; in the morning **le
    matin**
most *adv.* **le plus**
mother *n.* **la mère**
mouth *n.* **la bouche** (of a person); **la
    gueule** (of an animal)
movies (theater) *n.* **le cinéma**; movie
    (film) **le film**
music *n.* **la musique**
must, have to *v.* **devoir**
my name is... **mon nom est...**
my *poss. adj.* **ma, mon, mes**;
    see §5.4—4

N

name *n.* **le nom**; my name is... **mon nom est...**

necessary, to be **falloir**; it is necessary **il faut**

neck *n.* **le cou**

necktie *n.* **la cravate**

need *n.* **le besoin**; to have need (of), to need **avoir besoin (de)**; *see avoir in §12.2*

new *adj.* **nouveau, nouvel, nouveaux, nouvelle**; *see §5.1*

newspaper, newspapers *n.* **le journal, les journaux**; *see §4.2*

nice *adj.* **gentil, gentille**

nobody *pron.* **personne**; *see §11.*

notebook *n.* **le cahier**

now *adv.* **maintenant**

O

of *prep.* **de**; of the **des, du, de la, de l'**; *see §3.1*

of it, of them **en**; *see en in §6.1—5 and in Index*

of which *pron.* **dont**; *see §6.1—13*

old *adj.* **ancien, ancienne**

omelet *n.* **une omelette**

other *adj.* **autre**; *pron.* another **un (une) autre**

outside *adv.* **dehors**

oyster *n.* **une huître**

P

pal *n.* **le copain, la copine**

party *n.* **la fête**

pen *n.* **le stylo**

pencil *n.* **le crayon**

person *pron.* **la personne**

physician *n.* **le médecin**

place *v.* **mettre**

play *v.* **jouer**

pleasant *adj.* **gentil, gentille; agréable**

please **s'il vous plaît**

poison *n.* **le poison**

port *n.* **le port**

pound *n.* **la livre**

present *n.* **le cadeau, les cadeaux**; *see §4.2*

pretty *adj.* **joli, jolie**

purchase *v.* **acheter**

put *v.* **mettre**

Q

quite *adv.* **assez**; quite well **assez bien**

R

read *v.* **lire**

reason *n.* **la raison**

record (on a tape, record) *v.* **enregistrer**

red traffic light *n.* **le feu rouge**

reveal *v.* **révéler**

run *v.* **courir**; to run (a machine) **faire marcher**; *see faire in §7.19, §12.2*

run away *v.* **fuir, se sauver**

S

save *v.* **sauver**; to run away **se sauver**

say *v.* **dire**; *see Verb Tables*

school *n.* **une école**; in (at, to) school **à l'école**

sea *n.* **la mer**

send *v.* **envoyer**; to send for **envoyer chercher**

shoe *n.* **la chaussure**

shoulders *n.* **les épaules** *n.f., pl.*

shower (bath) *n.* **la douche**

since *adv.* **depuis, dès**; since (for) a long time **depuis longtemps**; *see §12.1*

sing *v.* **chanter**

singer *n.* **le chanteur, la chanteuse**

sir *n.* **le monsieur**

sit down *v.* **s'asseoir**; sit down! **asseyez-vous!** *second pers., pl.*; **assieds-toi!** *(fam.)*

sleep *v.* **dormir**

slow *adj.* **lent, lente**

slowly *adv.* **lentement**

sock (hosiery) *n.* **la chaussette**

some *adj.* **quelque(s); de, des, du, de la, de l'**; *see §3.1*

some of it, some of them **en**; *see §6.1—5 and en in Index*

something *pron.* **quelque chose**

son *n.* **le fils**

soon *adv.* **bientôt**

soup *n.* **la soupe**

Spain *n.* **l'Espagne** *n.f.*

Spanish (language) *n.* **l'espagnol** *n.m.*

Spanish (person) *n.* **un Espagnol, une Espagnole**

standing *adv.* **debout**

statistics *n.* **les statistiques** *n.f., pl.*

still, yet *adv.* **encore**

stocking *n.* **le bas**

student *n.* **un étudiant, une étudiante**

study *v.* **étudier**

summer *n.* **l'été** *n.m.*; *see §13.*

Sunday *n.* **le dimanche**; *see §13.*

sure *adj.* **sûr**

swim *v.* **nager**

swimming *n.* **la natation**
swimming pool *n.* **la piscine**

T

take *v.* **prendre**; to take a trip **faire un voyage**; to take a walk **faire une promenade**
tall *adj.* **grand, grande**
teach *v.* **enseigner**
telecast *n.* **l'émission** *n.f.*
television *n.* **la télévision**
tell *v.* **dire**; see Verb Tables
that *conj.* **que**; *see §10.; pron.* **cela**; do you like that? **aimez-vous cela?** *see §6.1—8*
the *def. art.* **le, la, l', les**; *see §3.1*
the one *pron.* **celui, celle**; the ones *pron.* **ceux, celles**; *see §6.1—8*
their *poss.adj.* **leur, leurs**; *see §5.4—4*
there *adv.* **là**
there is, there are **il y a**; *see y in §6.1—6, §12.2*
therefore *conj.* **donc**
these *dem. adj.* **ces**; *see §5.4—2*
thimble *n.* **le dé**
thing *n.* **la chose**
this *dem. adj.* **ce, cet, cette**; *see §5.4—2*
thousand **mille**; *see §16*
thread *n.* **le fil**
throw *v.* **jeter**
ticket *n.* **le billet**
to *prep.* **à**; to the **à la, à l', au, aux**; *see §3.1*
today *adv.* **aujourd'hui**
too (also) *adv.* **aussi**; **moi aussi** me too; too much **trop (de)**
tooth *n.* **la dent**
toward *prep.* **envers**; *see §9.2*
toy *n.* **le jouet**
traffic lights *n.* **les feux**
tree *n.* **l'arbre** *n.m.*
Tuesday *n.* **le mardi**; *see §13.*
TV *n.* **la télé**
two **deux**; *see §16.*

U

ugliness *n.* **la laideur**
ugly *adj.* **laid, laide**
understand *v.* **comprendre**
unfortunately *adv.* **malheureusement**
unhappiness *n.* **le malheur**
United States *n.* **les Etats-Unis** *n.m., pl.*; to the United States **aux Etats-Unis**
unless *conj.* **à moins que**

V

vacuum cleaner *n.* **un aspirateur**
very *adv.* **très**

W

walk *v.* **marcher**; to take a walk **faire une promenade**; *see faire in §12.2*
warm *adj.* **chaud, chaude**
wash (something or someone) *v.* **laver**; to wash oneself *rv.* **se laver**
watch *v.* **regarder**; to watch TV **regarder la télé**
water *n.* **l'eau** *n.f.*
we wash **nous lavons**; to wash **laver**; to wash oneself **se laver**
well *adv.* **bien**; well enough **assez bien**
what *adj.* **quel, quelle, quels, quelles**; *see §5.4—3*
what's that? **qu'est-ce que c'est que cela?**
where *adv.* **où**
which *adj.* **quel, quelle, quels, quelles**; *see §5.4—3*
white *adj.* **blanc, blanche**; a white house **une maison blanche**
who, whom *pron.* **qui**; *see §6.1—10*
whose *pron.* **dont**; *see §6.1—13*
why *adv.* **pourquoi**
wide *adj.* **large**
wife *n.* **la femme, l'épouse**
with *prep.* **avec**
within *adv.* **dedans**
woman *n.* **la femme**
wound *v.* **blesser**
write *v.* **écrire**

Y

yard *n.* **la cour**
year *n.* **un an, une année**
yet, still *adv.* **encore**
you wash **vous lavez, tu laves**; to wash **laver**; to wash oneself **se laver**
young *adj.* **jeune**
your *poss.adj.* **ta, ton, tes, votre, vos**; *see §5.4—4*

Index

References are to **§** numbers in this book. Some references are to page numbers. As for verb tense forms, consult not only the **§** numbers given but also the Tables of French Verb Conjugations beginning on page 214 and the Tables of Irregular Verbs beginning on page 241.

3 Foreign Language Series From Barron's!

The **VERB SERIES** offers more than 300 of the most frequently used verbs. The **GRAMMAR SERIES** provides complete coverage of the elements of grammar. The **VOCABULARY SERIES** offers more than 3500 words and phrases with their foreign language translations. Paperback, $5.95, Can. $7.95

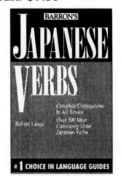

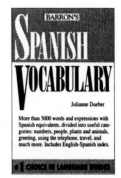

FRENCH GRAMMAR ISBN: 4292-1	FRENCH VERBS ISBN: 4294-8	FRENCH VOCABULARY ISBN: 4496-7
GERMAN GRAMMAR ISBN: 4296-4	GERMAN VERBS ISBN: 4310-3	GERMAN VOCABULARY ISBN: 4497-5
ITALIAN GRAMMAR ISBN: 4311-1	ITALIAN VERBS ISBN: 4313-8	ITALIAN VOCABULARY ISBN: 4471-1
JAPANESE GRAMMAR ISBN: 4643-9	JAPANESE VERBS ISBN: 4252-4	JAPANESE VOCABULARY ISBN: 4743-5
RUSSIAN GRAMMAR ISBN: 4902-0	RUSSIAN VERBS ISBN: 4754-0	
SPANISH GRAMMAR ISBN: 4295-6	SPANISH VERBS ISBN: 4283-2	SPANISH VOCABULARY ISBN: 4498-3

Barron's Educational Series, Inc.
250 Wireless Blvd., Hauppauge, NY 11788
Call toll-free: 1-800-645-3476
In Canada: Georgetown Book Warehouse
34 Arnstrong Ave., Georgetown, Ont. L7G 4R9
Call toll-free: 1-800-247-7160

Books may be purchased at your bookstore or by mail from Barrons. Enclose check or money order for total amount plus sales tax where applicable and 10% for postage and handling (minimum charge $3.75, Canada $4.00). Prices subject to change without notice.   ISBN PREFIX: 0 8120   R 6/94

BARRON'S

THE "INSTANT" FOREIGN LANGUAGE PROGRAM FOR TRAVELERS.

If you're planning a trip abroad, these concise little guides will teach you enough of the language to "get by." You'll pick up the most useful expressions for everyday situations like ordering a meal and asking directions. Tips on pronunciation and grammar are included.

For that extra touch of finesse, try the set of two cassettes available with each booklet. They feature real-life conversations and include timed pauses for your responses.

Each book: $3.95–$4.95.
Book-cassette pack: $17.95–$18.95.
In Canada: Chinese $6.95. Book-cassette pack $23.95.
*= No Canadian Rights

FOREIGN PHRASE BOOKS Series

Barron's new series gives travelers instant access to the most common idiomatic expressions used during a trip—the kind one needs to know instantly, like "Where can I find a taxi?" and "How much does this cost?"

Organized by situation (arrival, customs, hotel, health, etc.) and containing additional information about pronunciation, grammar, shopping plus special facts about the country, these convenient, pocket-size reference books will be the tourist's most helpful guides.

Special features include a bilingual dictionary section with over 2000 key words, maps of each country and major cities, and helpful phonetic spellings throughout.

Each book paperback, 256 pp., 3 3/4" x 6"

ARABIC AT A GLANCE, Wise (2979-8) $5.95, Can. $7.95
CHINESE AT A GLANCE, Seligman, Chen (2851-1) $6.95, Can. $9.95
FRENCH AT A GLANCE, 2nd, Stein & Wald (1394-8) $5.95, Can. $7.95
GERMAN AT A GLANCE, 2nd, Strutz (1395-6) $5.95, Can. $7.95
ITALIAN AT A GLANCE, 2nd, Costantino (1396-4) $5.95, Can. $7.95
JAPANESE AT A GLANCE, 2nd, Akiyama (1397-2) $6.95, Can. $8.95
KOREAN AT A GLANCE, Holt (3998-X) $8.95, Can. $10.95
RUSSIAN AT A GLANCE, Beyer (4299-9) $5.95, Can. $7.95
SPANISH AT A GLANCE, 2nd, Wald (1398-0) $5.95, Can. $7.95

Barron's Educational Series, Inc.
250 Wireless Blvd., Hauppauge, NY 11788
Call toll-free: 1-800-645-3476
In Canada: Georgetown Book Warehouse, 34 Armstrong Ave.
Georgetown, Ont. L7G 4R9, Call toll-free: 1-800-247-7160

Books may be purchased at your bookstore, or by mail from Barron's. Enclose check or money order for total amount plus sales tax where applicable and 10% for postage and handling (minimum charge $3.75, Canada $4.00). Prices subject to change without notice.
ISBN PREFIX: 0-8120